D0198301

LUKE

J. Vernon McGee

THOMAS NELSON PUBLISHERS

Nashville • Atlanta • London • Vancouver

Published in Nashville, Tennessee, by Thomas Nelson, Inc.

Scripture quotations are from the KING JAMES VERSION of the Bible.

Library of Congress Cataloging-in-Publication Data

McGee, J. Vernon (John Vernon), 1904–1988
   [Thru the Bible with J. Vernon McGee]
   Thru the Bible commentary series / J. Vernon McGee.
     p.   cm.
   Reprint. Originally published: Thru the Bible with J. Vernon McGee. 1975.
   Includes bibliographical references.
   ISBN 0-7852-1040-7 (TR)
   ISBN 0-7852-1100-4 (NRM)
   1. Bible—Commentaries. I. Title.
BS491.2.M37 1991
220.7′7—dc20
                          90–41340
                            CIP

PRINTED IN MEXICO

20 21 22 23 – 06 05 04

CONTENTS

LUKE

PREFACE

The radio broadcasts of the Thru the Bible Radio five-year program were transcribed, edited, and published first in single-volume paperbacks to accommodate the radio audience.

There has been a minimal amount of further editing for this publication. Therefore, these messages are not the word-for-word recording of the taped messages which went out over the air. The changes were necessary to accommodate a reading audience rather than a listening audience.

These are popular messages, prepared originally for a radio audience. They should not be considered a commentary on the entire Bible in any sense of that term. These messages are devoid of any attempt to present a theological or technical commentary on the Bible. Behind these messages is a great deal of research and study in order to interpret the Bible from a popular rather than from a scholarly (and too-often boring) viewpoint.

We have definitely and deliberately attempted "to put the cookies on the bottom shelf so that the kiddies could get them."

The fact that these messages have been translated into many languages for radio broadcasting and have been received with enthusiasm reveals the need for a simple teaching of the whole Bible for the masses of the world.

I am indebted to many people and to many sources for bringing this volume into existence. I should express my especial thanks to my secretary, Gertrude Cutler, who supervised the editorial work; to Dr. Elliott R. Cole, my associate, who handled all the detailed work with the publishers; and finally, to my wife Ruth for tenaciously encouraging me from the beginning to put my notes and messages into printed form.

Solomon wrote, ". . . of making many books there is no end; and much study is a weariness of the flesh" (Eccl. 12:12). On a sea of books that flood the marketplace, we launch this series of THRU THE BIBLE with the hope that it might draw many to the one Book, *The Bible.*

J. Vernon McGee

The Gospel According to

LUKE

INTRODUCTION

Luke was the beloved physician of Colossians 4:14, "Luke, the beloved physician, and Demas, greet you." He used more medical terms than Hippocrates, the father of medicine. The choice of Luke by the Holy Spirit to write the third gospel reveals that there are no accidental writers of Scripture. There was a supernatural selection of Luke. There were "not many wise" called, but Luke belongs to that category. He and Paul were evidently on a very high intellectual level as well as a high spiritual level. This explains partially why they traveled together and obviously became fast friends in the Lord. Dr. Luke would rank as a scientist of his day. Also he wrote the best Greek of any of the New Testament writers, including Paul. He was an accurate historian, as we shall see. Luke was a poet; he alone records the lovely songs of Christmas. Luke was an artist; he sketches for us Christ's marvelous, matchless parables.

A great deal of tradition surrounds the life of Dr. Luke. He writes his Gospel from Mary's viewpoint, which confirms the tradition that he received his information for his Gospel from her. Surely he conferred with her. Also, there is every reason to believe that he was a Gentile. Most scholars concur in this position. Paul, in the fourth chapter of Colossians, distinguishes between those "who are of the circumcision" and the others who are obviously Gentiles, in which group he mentions Luke. Sir William Ramsay and J. M. Stifler affirm without reservation that Luke was a Gentile. This makes it quite interesting to those of us who are Gentiles, doesn't it?

Remember that Luke wrote the Book of Acts where we learn that he was a companion of the apostle Paul. In Acts 16:10 he says, "And after he had seen the vision, immediately we endeavoured to go into Macedonia. . . ." He was with Paul on the second and, I think, the third missionary journeys. From this verse on he writes in the first person—it is the "we" section of the Book of Acts. Prior to this verse he writes in the third person. So we can conclude from Acts 16 that Luke was with Paul on that historical crossing over into Europe. He probably was a convert of Paul, then went with him on this second missionary journey, and stayed with him to the end. When Paul was writing his "swan song" to Timothy, he says, "Only Luke is with me . . ." (2 Tim. 4:11). All this explains why Paul calls him the *beloved* physician.

Jesus is the *second* man, but the *last* Adam. "And so it is written, The first man Adam was made a living soul; the last Adam was made a quickening spirit. . . . The first man is of the earth, earthy: the second man is the Lord from heaven" (1 Cor. 15:45, 47). God is making men like Jesus: "Beloved, now are we the sons of God, and it doth not yet appear what we shall be: but we know that, when he shall appear, we shall be like him; for we shall see him as he is" (1 John 3:2). Therefore, Jesus is the *second* man—for there will be the third and the fourth—and the millionth. However, He is the *last* Adam. There will *not* be another head of the human family. Jesus was ". . . made like unto his brethren . . ." (Heb. 2:17) that His brethren might be made like unto Him.

At the close of the nineteenth century there was a wave of skepticism that swept over Europe and the British Isles. There was delusion and disappointment with the optimism which the Victorian era had produced. There was, on the lighter side, a rebellion against it which produced the Gay Nineties. Also it caused many scholars to begin a more serious investigation of the Bible, which had been the handbook of the Victorian era. They were skeptical before they began. Among them was a very brilliant young scholar at Cambridge by the name of William Ramsay. He was an agnostic, who wanted to disprove the accuracy of the Bible. He knew that Luke had written an historical record of Jesus in his Gospel and that he had written of the missionary journeys of Paul in the Book of Acts. He also knew that all historians make mistakes and that many of them are liars.

Contemporary authors Will and Ariel Durant, who spent forty years studying twenty civilizations covering a four thousand year period, made the following statement in their book, *The Lessons of History:* "Our knowledge of the past is always incomplete, probably inaccurate, beclouded by ambivalent evidence and biased historians, and perhaps distorted by our own patriotic or religious partisanship. Most history is guessing; the rest is prejudice."

It is safe to say that this was also the attitude of Sir William Ramsay when he went as an archaeologist into Asia Minor to disprove Dr. Luke as an historian. He carefully followed the journeys of Paul and made a thorough study of Asia Minor. He came to the conclusion that Dr. Luke had not made one historical inaccuracy. This discovery caused William Ramsay to become a believer, and he has written some outstanding books on the journeys of Paul and on the churches of Asia Minor.

Dr. Luke wrote his Gospel with a twofold purpose. First, his purpose was literary and historical. Of the four Gospels, Luke's Gospel is the most complete historical narrative. There are more wide-reaching references to institutions, customs, geography, and history of that period than are found in any of the other Gospels. Secondly, his purpose was spiritual. He presented the person of Jesus Christ as the perfect, divine Man and Savior of the world. Jesus was God manifest in the flesh.

Matthew emphasizes that Jesus was born the Messiah.

Mark emphasizes that Jesus was the Servant of Jehovah.

Luke stresses the fact that Jesus was the perfect Man.

John presents the fact that God became a Man.

However, it is interesting to note that John did not use the scientific approach. Dr. Luke states that he examined Jesus of Nazareth, and his findings are that Jesus is God. He came to the same conclusion as John did, but his procedure and technique were different.

Matthew presents the Lord Jesus as the Messiah, King, and Redeemer.

Mark presents Christ as the mighty Conqueror and Ruler of the world.

John presents Christ as the Son of God.

Luke presents the perfect, divine Son of God as our great High Priest, touched with the feeling of our infirmities, able to extend help, mercy, and love to us.

Luke wrote to his countrymen, just as Matthew wrote to his. Luke wrote to the Greek mind and to the intellectual community.

In the fourth century B.C. the Greeks placed on the horizon of history the most brilliant and scintillating display of human genius the world has ever seen. It was called the Periclean Age, pertaining to Pericles and the period of the intellectual and material preeminence of Athens. The Greeks attempted to perfect humanity and to develop the perfect man. This attempted perfection of man is found in the physical realm in such work as the statues of Phidias, as well as in the mental realm. They were striving for the beautiful as well as a thinking man. The literary works of Plato, Aristotle, Homer, Aeschylus, Sophocles, Euripides, Aristophanes, and Thucydides all move toward the picture of perfect man and strive to obtain the universal man.

The Greeks made their gods in the likeness of men. In fact, their gods were but projections of man. The magnificent statues of Apollo, Venus, Athena, and Diana were not the ugly representations that have come out of the paganism of the Orient. They deified man with his noble qualities and base passions. Other Greek gods include Pan, Cupid, Bacchus (the god of wine and revelry), and Aphrodite. Not all of their gods were graces; some of them were the avenging Furies because they were making a projection of mankind.

Alexander the Great scattered this gripping culture, language, and philosophy throughout the lands which he conquered. Greek became the universal language. In Alexandria, Egypt, the Old Testament was translated into Greek. We call that translation the Septuagint. It is one of the finest translations of the Old Testament that we have. The New Testament was written in Greek. The Greek language provided the vehicle for the expression and communication of the gospel to all of mankind. It has been the finest language to express a fact or communicate a thought.

Even though Greek culture, language, and philosophy were the finest ever developed, the Greeks fell short of perfecting humanity.

The Greeks did not find Utopia. They never came upon the Elysian fields, and they lost sight of the spiritual realm. This world became their home, playground, schoolroom, workshop, and grave.

Dr. F. W. Robertson said this of the Greeks: "The more the Greek attached himself to this world, the more the unseen became a dim world." This is the reason the Greeks made an image to the UNKNOWN GOD, and when the apostle Paul preached the gospel to them, this is where he began. The cultivated Athenians were skeptics, and they called Paul a "babbler" and mocked him as he endeavored to give them the truth.

Paul declared that the gospel is foolishness to the Greeks, but he also wrote to the Greek mind. He told them that in times past they were Gentiles, having no hope and without God in the world. That is the picture of the Greek, friend. But Paul also told them that when the right time had come, God sent forth His Son, made of a woman, made under the Law, and that this Son of God died for them. Paul walked the Roman roads with a universal language, preaching a global gospel about the perfect Man who had died for the men of the world. The religion of Israel could produce only a Pharisee, the power of Rome could produce only a Caesar, and the philosophy of Greece could produce only a global giant like Alexander the Great who was merely an infant at heart. It was to this Greek mind that Luke wrote. He presented Jesus Christ as the perfect Man, the universal Man, the very person the Greeks were looking for.

Note these special features of Luke's Gospel:

1. Although the Gospel of Luke is one of the synoptic Gospels, it contains many features omitted by Matthew and Mark.

2. Dr. Luke gives us the songs of Christmas.

3. Dr. Luke has the longest account of the virgin birth of Jesus of any of the Gospels. In the first two chapters, he gives us an unabashed record of obstetrics. A clear and candid statement of the Virgin Birth is given by Dr. Luke. All the way from Dr. Luke to Dr. Howard Kelly, a gynecologist at Johns Hopkins, there is a mighty affirmation of the Virgin Birth, which makes the statements of pseudo-theologians seem rather puerile when they unblushingly state that the Virgin Birth is a biological impossibility.

4. Dr. Luke gives us twenty miracles of which six are recorded in no other Gospel.

5. He likewise gives us twenty-three parables, and eighteen of them are found nowhere else. The parables of the Prodigal Son and the Good Samaritan are peculiar to this third Gospel.

6. He also gives us the very human account of the walk to Emmaus of our resurrected Lord. This proves that Jesus was still human after His resurrection. Dr. Luke demonstrates that the Resurrection was not of the spirit, but of the body. Jesus was ". . . sown a natural body . . . raised a spiritual body . . ." (1 Cor. 15:44).

7. A definite human sympathy pervades this Gospel, which reveals the truly human nature of Jesus, as well as the big-hearted sympathy of this physician of the first century who knew firsthand a great deal about the suffering of humanity.

8. Dr. Luke uses more medical terms than Hippocrates, the father of medicine.

OUTLINE

THEME: The purpose of the gospel; Gabriel appears to Zacharias and announces the birth of John; Gabriel appears to Mary and announces the virgin birth of Jesus; Mary visits Elisabeth; birth of John

Historically Dr. Luke begins his Gospel before the other synoptic Gospels. Heaven had been silent for over four hundred years when the angel Gabriel broke through the blue at the golden altar of prayer to announce the birth of John the Baptist. Luke gives us the background as well as the births of John and Jesus.

Three songs are in this chapter: (1) Elisabeth's greeting of Mary—verses 42–45; (2) Mary's magnificat—verses 46–55; and (3) Zacharias' prophecy—verses 68–79.

THE PURPOSE OF THE GOSPEL

Forasmuch as many have taken in hand to set forth in order a declaration of those things which are most surely believed among us,

Even as they delivered them unto us, which from the beginning were eyewitnesses, and ministers of the word;

It seemed good to me also, having had perfect understanding of all things from the very first, to write unto thee in order, most excellent Theophilus,

That thou mightest know the certainty of those things, wherein thou hast been instructed [Luke 1:1–4].

Two words are important in this passage and should not be passed over. "Eyewitness" is the Greek word *autoptai*—*auto* meaning "that which is of itself," and *opsomai* meaning "to see." "To see for your-

self" would be an eyewitness. It is a medical term which means to make an autopsy. In fact, what Dr. Luke is trying to say is, "We are eyewitnesses who made an autopsy, and I am writing to you about what we found."

The second important word Dr. Luke uses is *ministers,* which is the Greek *huperatai,* meaning "an under-rower on a boat." In a hospital the "under-rower" is the intern. Dr. Luke is saying that all of them were just interns under the Great Physician. What Dr. Luke is telling us is that as a physician and a scholar, he made an autopsy of the records of those who had been eyewitnesses.

The first four verses of this chapter form a tremendous beginning. Luke wrote his Gospel to give people certainty and assurance about the Lord Jesus Christ.

My friend, how much assurance do you have? Do you *know* that you are a child of God through faith in Jesus Christ? Do you *know* that the Bible is the Word of God? I feel sorry for the person who is not sure about these things. Do you wobble back and forth and say, "I am not sure about my salvation or the Bible. I guess I do not have enough faith." Not having enough faith may not be your problem. Your problem may be that you do not *know* enough. You see, ". . . faith cometh by hearing, and hearing by the word of God" (Rom. 10:17). If you really knew the Word of God, you would believe it. Those who are ignorant of the Bible have the problems. The problem is not with the Bible or with the Lord Jesus Christ; the problem lies with us.

GABRIEL APPEARS TO ZACHARIAS AND ANNOUNCES THE BIRTH OF JOHN

There was in the days of Herod, the king of Judaea, a certain priest named Zacharias, of the course of Abia: and his wife was of the daughters of Aaron, and her name was Elisabeth [Luke 1:5].

God breaks through after 400 years of silence. Chronologically Dr. Luke begins the New Testament. He goes back to the birth of John the Baptist, to where the angel Gabriel appeared to John's father as he served in the temple. John's parents were Zacharias and Elisabeth. *Zacharias* means "God remembers," and *Elisabeth* means "His oath." Together their names mean, "God remembers His oath." When did God take an oath? Psalm 89:34–37 records God's oath: "My covenant will I not break, nor alter the thing that is gone out of my lips. Once have I sworn by my holiness that I will not lie unto David. His seed shall endure for ever, and his throne as the sun before me. It shall be established for ever as the moon, and as a faithful witness in heaven. Selah." God swore an oath to David that one of his descendants would have an eternal reign. Christ is that descendant. "God remembers His oath!" God is ready to break through into human history after 400 years of silence.

Notice that the Scripture tells us both Zacharias and Elisabeth were righteous. That is, they were right. How were they right? They recognized they were sinners and brought the necessary sacrifices.

And they were both righteous before God, walking in all the commandments and ordinances of the Lord blameless [Luke 1:6].

Their walk commended their salvation. When they committed a sin or made a mistake, they brought the proper sacrifice.

However, there was tragedy in their lives because they had no child.

And they had no child, because that Elisabeth was barren, and they both were now well stricken in years [Luke 1:7].

Here was an old couple who did not have a child. To be childless was practically a disgrace for a Hebrew woman, and Elisabeth had no children.

Zacharias, belonging to the tribe of Levi, served in the temple.

And it came to pass, that while he executed the priest's office before God in the order of his course,

According to the custom of the priest's office, his lot was
to burn incense when he went into the temple of the
Lord.

And the whole multitude of the people were praying
without at the time of incense.

And there appeared unto him an angel of the Lord
standing on the right side of the altar of incense.

And when Zacharias saw him, he was troubled, and
fear fell upon him [Luke 1:8–12].

Zacharias was serving at the golden altar, the place of prayer. It was the
time of the evening sacrifice, and in this particular part of the service
he placed incense upon the altar. Suddenly an angel appeared. If you
saw an angel, what would you do? Your reaction would be the same as
this man's. You would be troubled and fearful.

But the angel said unto him, Fear not, Zacharias: for thy
prayer is heard; and thy wife Elisabeth shall bear thee a
son, and thou shalt call his name John [Luke 1:13].

Zacharias was praying for a son. Elisabeth was praying for a son. I
think that many people were praying that they would have a son. How
do I know he is praying for a son? Because the angel said, "Your prayer
is heard."

And thou shalt have joy and gladness; and many shall
rejoice at his birth.

For he shall be great in the sight of the Lord, and shall
drink neither wine nor strong drink; and he shall be
filled with the Holy Ghost, even from his mother's womb
[Luke 1:14—15].

The son of Elisabeth and Zacharias was to be a Nazarite. One of the
things the Nazarite vowed was that he would not drink strong drink or

wine. He was to find his joy in the Holy Spirit and in God. That is the reason Paul, in Ephesians 5:18, says, "And be not drunk with wine, wherein is excess; but be filled with the Spirit." Get your joy from God, not from a bottle. There are a lot of bottle-babies today. I am not speaking of crib babies but of adult babies hanging over a bar. And there are some Christians today who have to be pepped up and hepped up in order to face life. We need to recognize that the Holy Spirit of God can give us the strength to face life.

> **And many of the children of Israel shall he turn to the Lord their God.**
>
> **And he shall go before him in the spirit and power of Elias, to turn the hearts of the fathers to the children, and the disobedient to the wisdom of the just; to make ready a people prepared for the Lord [Luke 1:16–17].**

Let us understand clearly that although John the Baptist went forth in the spirit and power of Elijah, he was not Elijah. John would turn the hearts of the fathers to the children. He was to bridge the generation gap. Our problem today is not so much that there is a gap between the adults and youth but that there is a gap between adults and God. If adults had a proper relationship with God, they would not have the problem with young people that exists.

> **And Zacharias said unto the angel, Whereby shall I know this? for I am an old man, and my wife well stricken in years [Luke 1:18].**

I cannot help but laugh at a verse like this. A great many people do not find humor in the Bible, but there is—and this verse gives us a taste of it. Here is a man, a priest, who has gone to God in prayer. At the altar of incense he says, "Oh, God, give me a son." Now when God says through the angel Gabriel, "I am going to give you a son," Zacharias replies, "How do I know?" He says, "My wife is old and I am old, and I do not think we can have a child." Yet he was praying for a son!

Have you ever prayed like that? You ask God for something, but you really do not believe He is going to give it to you. This is one reason we do not receive answers to our prayers. We have no faith at all. This man Zacharias is quite human, and I cannot help but laugh at him because that's the way I pray sometimes.

> **And the angel answering said unto him, I am Gabriel, that stand in the presence of God; and am sent to speak unto thee, and to shew thee these glad tidings [Luke 1:19].**

The Word of God has the seal of God upon it. The Word of God carries authority. What Vernon McGee says is not important, but what the Word of God says is important. God speaks to us through His Word.

> **And, behold, thou shalt be dumb, and not able to speak, until the day that these things shall be performed, because thou believest not my words, which shall be fulfilled in their season [Luke 1:20].**

Zacharias, who has been so vocal, will be dumb for a period of time. Unbelief is always dumb. That is, it never has a message. I agree with Elizabeth Barrett Browning who said that one without faith should be silent. There are many babblers around who are everlastingly spouting off about their unbelief. If they haven't anything to say, they should keep quiet. Let the man speak who believes in God and has something to say.

> **And the people waited for Zacharias, and marvelled that he tarried so long in the temple.**
>
> **And when he came out, he could not speak unto them: and they perceived that he had seen a vision in the temple: for he beckoned unto them, and remained speechless [Luke 1:21–22].**

This passage also strikes me as being funny. God, after 400 years of silence, once again breaks through to the human race, but the very man that He communicates with does not believe Him. And now he is made dumb. Can you imagine his trying to explain to the people that he is dumb? How would you make known to people that you had seen an angel and could not talk? It would not be easy. Think about the gyrations Zacharias must have used trying to make known his predicament. It must have been comical.

And it came to pass, that, as soon as the days of his ministration were accomplished, he departed to his own house [Luke 1:23].

Long ago King David had arranged that the priests in the temple would serve a certain period of time, then have a vacation. One priest would serve, then have some time off, and another priest would serve. This is what happened with Zacharias, but he had to finish his term of office without speaking. When his vacation time came, he still had to keep quiet; so I imagine he went home and listened to Elisabeth.

And after those days his wife Elisabeth conceived, and hid herself five months, saying,

Thus hath the Lord dealt with me in the days wherein he looked on me, to take away my reproach among men [Luke 1:24–25].

This is an interesting situation. Zacharias cannot talk. Elisabeth, because of her condition, remains in seclusion for several months. I imagine she talked his arm off for that period of time and constantly reminded him, "Zacharias, we are going to have a son!"

GABRIEL APPEARS TO MARY AND ANNOUNCES THE VIRGIN BIRTH OF JESUS

And in the sixth month the angel Gabriel was sent from God unto a city of Galilee, named Nazareth,

To a virgin espoused to a man whose name was Joseph, of the house of David; and the virgin's name was Mary [Luke 1:26–27].

We move now from Jerusalem to Nazareth. Six months after the angel Gabriel appeared to Zacharias, he appears to Mary.

Two times in one verse she is called a virgin. Do you know what a virgin is? I ask this because many folk do not seem to know. A virgin is a woman who could never have a child in a natural way because she has never had a relationship with a man that would make the birth of a child possible. Someone needs to talk rather plainly today because there are men saying that the virgin birth is biologically impossible. When I hear a man make that statement, I always feel like calling him up and saying, "I would like to have lunch with you and tell you about the birds and the bees because you do not seem to know much about them." The Scripture makes it clear that the Lord Jesus Christ was virgin born.

I do not object to an unbeliever saying that he does not believe in the virgin birth, but when he makes the statement that the *Bible* does not teach it, I object. I say very plainly that one who makes this statement must have something wrong with his intellect or is ignorant of the birds and the bees. It should be remembered that Luke was a doctor, and he gives the most extended account of the virgin birth.

And the angel came in unto her, and said, Hail, thou that art highly favoured, the Lord is with thee: blessed art thou among women [Luke 1:28].

There is a tendency among Protestants to play down the role of Mary, but this verse tells us that she was highly favored. In the same breath, however, let me say that she was blessed *among* women, not *above* women. She is not lifted above women; she lifted up womanhood. This is the role she played. It is so easy to say that a woman brought sin into the world, but remember, it was a woman, and not a man, who brought the Savior into the world.

And when she saw him, she was troubled at his saying, and cast in her mind what manner of salutation this should be [Luke 1:29].

Mary was troubled at the sayings of the angel. When the supernatural touches the natural, it always creates fear. Mary also "cast in her mind what manner of salutation this should be." I cannot resist saying this, but Mary's reaction was similar to a black friend of mine in Memphis, Tennessee. Years ago he said to me, "You know, I never believed in ghosts either, until I saw one!" Believe me, friends, when you have seen an angel, you have a right to be afraid. I think I would be afraid if I saw one.

And the angel said unto her, Fear not, Mary: for thou hast found favour with God.

And, behold, thou shalt conceive in thy womb, and bring forth a son, and shalt call his name JESUS.

He shall be great, and shall be called the Son of the Highest: and the Lord God shall give unto him the throne of his father David:

And he shall reign over the house of Jacob for ever; and of his kingdom there shall be no end [Luke 1:30–33].

This is plain language. There is no way of misinterpreting it. This passage is quite literal. Those folk who deny the virgin birth also do not believe that the Lord is going to sit on the throne of His father David. Apparently it was understood that what Luke is writing about is literal. The virgin's womb is literal, and the throne of David is literal. He shall literally reign over the house of Jacob, and of His Kingdom there shall be no end. That Kingdom is also a reality.

Then said Mary unto the angel, How shall this be, seeing I know not a man? [Luke 1:34].

Mary was the first one to question the virgin birth. She said, "How can it be?" This is still a good question. Dr. Luke quotes the angel Gabriel and gives us the answer.

> **And the angel answered and said unto her, The Holy Ghost shall come upon thee, and the power of the Highest shall overshadow thee: therefore also that holy thing which shall be born of thee shall be called the Son of God [Luke 1:35].**

No man had anything to do with the birth of Jesus Christ. We are told in the Book of Leviticus that the birth of a child caused a woman to be unclean because she brought a sinner into the world. Mary is told that she is *not* bringing a sinner into the world; He is holy. The union of man and woman can only produce a child with a sin nature. By the virgin birth is the only way God could get that "holy thing" into the human family. In Psalm 51:5 David said, "Behold, I was shapen in iniquity; and in sin did my mother conceive me." Mary's Son would be different. He would be virgin born.

You can deny the virgin birth if you want to. If you are an unbeliever, I would expect you to deny it. If, however, you write and tell me that you are not a Christian but you believe the virgin birth, I will be terribly upset. If you are not a Christian, of course you don't believe it. However, you cannot say that the Bible does not teach the virgin birth, because it does.

Do you know why this Baby is going to be called the Son of God? Because He *is* the Son of God. Remember that Dr. Luke approaches his Gospel from the scientific point of view. He states that he examined Jesus of Nazareth, and his findings are that Jesus is God. Luke came to the same conclusion that John came to in his Gospel, but his procedure and technique were different. Dr. Luke has used plain, simple language to present his findings and if we cannot understand his message, we need to go back and learn our ABCs again.

> **And, behold, thy cousin Elisabeth, she hath also conceived a son in her old age: and this is the sixth month with her, who was called barren.**

For with God nothing shall be impossible [Luke 1:36-37].

The birth of John the Baptist is also miraculous, but it is not a virgin birth. The statement of the angel, "For with God nothing shall be impossible," is a good one and something we need to hold onto during these days. I want to emphasize, however, that there are folk who have taken this statement and twisted and distorted its meaning. There is nothing impossible with God when He has determined to do it, but He will not necessarily do the impossible we ask of Him. Many people use this verse as a cliché to cover up the fact that they want their own selfish desires. Nothing is impossible with God, but there is a great deal that is impossible with you and me. When a man says, "Nothing is impossible with God" and fails at some task he claims the Lord gave him to do, it causes unbelievers to ridicule God. Anything God determines to do He can accomplish, because there is nothing impossible with God. But that does not mean He will do everything believers want Him to do, because some things are not included in His plan. Let us put everything in proper perspective before we do a lot of talking that will hurt and harm the cause of Jesus Christ rather than help it.

And Mary said, Behold the handmaid of the Lord; be it unto me according to thy word. And the angel departed from her [Luke 1:38].

This verse reveals Mary's submission to the will of God. She told the angel, "Be it unto me according to thy word." At that very moment a cloud came over her life, and that cloud was there until the Lord Jesus Christ came back from the dead. The resurrection of Christ proves His virgin birth. It was questioned until then. You cannot deny the virgin birth and believe the Resurrection, or vice versa. The virgin birth and the Resurrection go together; they stand or fall together.

MARY VISITS ELISABETH

After a time Mary decided to visit Elisabeth up in the hill country of Judea.

> And Mary arose in those days, and went into the hill
> country with haste, into a city of Juda;
>
> And entered into the house of Zacharias, and saluted
> Elisabeth.
>
> And it came to pass, that, when Elisabeth heard the sal-
> utation of Mary, the babe leaped in her womb; and Elisa-
> beth was filled with the Holy Ghost [Luke 1:39–41].

What we are dealing with here is miraculous, and there is no use trying to offer a natural explanation. You either believe what happened in
these verses or you do not. I am so weary of people today, especially
preachers, who try to appear intellectual by attempting to explain
away the miracles in the Bible. You either accept the miracles of the
Bible or you do not, and what took place in these verses was a miracle.
This woman is filled with the Holy Spirit, and the babe leaps in her
womb.

> And she spake out with a loud voice, and said, Blessed
> art thou among women, and blessed is the fruit of thy
> womb [Luke 1:42].

This begins the first song given to us in Luke's Gospel, and it is lovely.
Dr. Luke was the poet who gives us all the songs of Christmas; this is
the first one, and it comes from Elisabeth.

> And whence is this to me, that the mother of my Lord
> should come to me?
>
> For, lo, as soon as the voice of thy salutation sounded in
> mine ears, the babe leaped in my womb for joy.
>
> And blessed is she that believed: for there shall be a per-
> formance of those things which were told her from the
> Lord [Luke 1:43–45].

Little is said in Scripture about Elisabeth. She sang the first song of
the New Testament, and when you have a soloist like this, you should

not ignore her. She is a remarkable person. She had faith while her husband Zacharias did not. He was struck dumb because of his unbelief, but Elisabeth was not. She believed God. Now she encourages Mary. Mary is a young woman and Elisabeth is an old woman. Elisabeth had walked with God for many years, and she assures her that there would be a performance of those things which had been revealed to her. I would like to give Elisabeth a little credit along with the others. She should not be deified, of course. She was only a woman, just as Mary was only a woman. And Mary needed the encouragement that Elisabeth could give.

And Mary said, My soul doth magnify the Lord,

And my spirit hath rejoiced in God my Saviour.

For he hath regarded the low estate of his handmaiden: for, behold, from henceforth all generations shall call me blessed [Luke 1:46–48].

Now Mary sings a song. This is known as the *Magnificat*. This song teaches us several interesting things. Mary tells us in her song that she needed a Savior and that she rejoiced in Him. Protestant friend, let us call her blessed. We don't make her a goddess and kneel before her, but we do need to call her blessed. It was her glorious privilege to be the mother of the Son of God, to bring Him into the world. We should not play it down, but we should not play it up either. She was a wonderful person, and it was no accident that she was chosen by God. It was His definite decision, and God makes no mistakes.

Listen as Mary continues to sing her song:

For he that is mighty hath done to me great things; and holy is his name.

And his mercy is on them that fear him from generation to generation.

He hath shewed strength with his arm; he hath scattered the proud in the imagination of their hearts.

> He hath put down the mighty from their seats, and ex-
> alted them of low degree.
>
> He hath filled the hungry with good things; and the rich
> he hath sent empty away.
>
> He hath holpen his servant Israel, in remembrance of
> his mercy;
>
> As he spake to our fathers, to Abraham, and to his seed
> for ever [Luke 1:49–55].

Mary sings, "He hath shewed strength with his arm." In Isaiah 53:1
the prophet Isaiah said, ". . . to whom is the arm of the LORD revealed?"
Then Isaiah begins immediately to reveal the Lamb of God that takes
away the sin of the world. God has shown the strength of His arm and
revealed His power and love in the salvation He has given to mankind.

Mary also mentions Abraham in her song. There is more reference
to Abraham than to any other person in the Old Testament. In fact,
there is more about Abraham on the human plane than about anyone
else in the Bible.

> And Mary abode with her about three months, and re-
> turned to her own house [Luke 1:56].

BIRTH OF JOHN

The remainder of this chapter records the birth of John the Baptist
and the song of Zacharias. I will lift out some of the high points.

> Now Elisabeth's full time came that she should be deliv-
> ered; and she brought forth a son.
>
> And her neighbours and her cousins heard how the
> Lord had shewed great mercy upon her; and they re-
> joiced with her.

> And it came to pass, that on the eighth day they came to circumcise the child; and they called him Zacharias, after the name of his father.
>
> And his mother answered and said, Not so; but he shall be called John [Luke 1:57–60].

They named the baby after his father at first. Elisabeth, however, set the record straight and said that he was to be called John.

> And they said unto her, There is none of thy kindred that is called by this name.
>
> And they made signs to his father, how he would have him called.
>
> And he asked for a writing table, and wrote, saying, His name is John. And they marvelled all.
>
> And his mouth was opened immediately, and his tongue loosed, and he spake, and praised God [Luke 1:61–64].

In those days a family name was usually given to a new baby. When the question of naming the baby came along, the relatives assumed he would be called Zacharias—Zacharias Jr., I guess. Elisabeth made the correction, but they appealed to Zacharias. Since he could not speak, he wrote for them, "His name *is* John." He had already been named by God. Those present marveled at the name.

After this, Zacharias was able to speak again, and he immediately began to sing praises to God. Although he did not have much faith, when the baby was born he could rejoice in God. Again, the lack of faith displayed by Zacharias is a quality many of us have. When God hears and answers prayer, we really get up and rejoice. I sometimes think that the reason God answers prayer for some of us weaker saints is so that we will have something to rejoice about. As a rule, weaker saints do not do much rejoicing. The stronger saints, with more faith, rejoice in all circumstances.

And fear came on all that dwelt round about them: and all these sayings were noised abroad throughout all the hill country of Judaea.

And all they that heard them laid them up in their hearts, saying, What manner of child shall this be! And the hand of the Lord was with him.

And his father Zacharias was filled with the Holy Ghost, and prophesied, saying,

Blessed be the Lord God of Israel; for he hath visited and redeemed his people,

And hath raised up an horn of salvation for us in the house of his servant David [Luke 1:65–69].

It was quite obvious that John was going to be an unusual child.

At John's birth, Zacharias, who has been dumb for about nine months, is not only able to speak, but he will sing a solo. Elisabeth sang the first song, Mary sang the second one, and now it is quite proper that Zacharias sing a song. His song is one of prophecy. Although Zacharias is not in the line of David, he does recognize that his son is going to be the forerunner of Jesus Christ, as foretold by Malachi and Isaiah. John is to be the one to announce the coming of the Messiah. The presence of the forerunner indicates that the Messiah is not far behind. He is coming soon.

As he spake by the mouth of his holy prophets, which have been since the world began:

That we should be saved from our enemies, and from the hand of all that hate us;

To perform the mercy promised to our fathers, and to remember his holy covenant;

The oath which he sware to our father Abraham,

> That he would grant unto us, that we being delivered out
> of the hand of our enemies might serve him without fear,
>
> In holiness and righteousness before him, all the days of
> our life [Luke 1:70–75].

God made these promises to Abraham. Mary, Elisabeth, and Zach-arias still believed that the promises made to Abraham would be ful-filled. There are some today who have given up and do not believe God will make good His promises to Abraham. Friends, if you believe God is going to make good John 3:16 to you, you have no right to discount the promises God made to Abraham.

> And thou, child, shalt be called the prophet of the High-est: for thou shalt go before the face of the Lord to pre-pare his ways;
>
> To give knowledge of salvation unto his people by the remission of their sins,
>
> Through the tender mercy of our God; whereby the day-spring from on high hath visited us,
>
> To give light to them that sit in darkness and in the shadow of death, to guide our feet into the way of peace.
>
> And the child grew, and waxed strong in spirit, and was in the deserts till the day of his shewing unto Israel [Luke 1:76–80].

John was to be called a prophet of the Highest. He was to go before the face of the Lord to prepare His ways. John knew that the Messiah was in their midst. John the Baptist was a very unusual person. He was prepared to do a special task for God.

CHAPTER 2

THEME: Birth of Jesus at Bethlehem in a stable; reception of Jesus; angels announce His birth to shepherds; shepherds visit stable; circumcision of Jesus and purification of Mary; incident in temple concerning Simeon; incident in temple concerning Anna; return to Nazareth; visit of Joseph, Mary, and Jesus to Jerusalem when Jesus was twelve

Jesus was brought to the temple when He was eight days old to be circumcised according to Mosaic Law: "But when the fulness of the time was come, God sent forth his Son, made of a woman, made under the law, To redeem them that were under the law, that we might receive the adoption of sons" (Gal. 4:4–5). As a result of this visit to Jerusalem, we have the songs of Simeon and Anna.

The one isolated incident from the boyhood of Jesus is recorded by Dr. Luke to let us know that Jesus had a normal human childhood (see v. 52). "Jesus increased in wisdom (mental) and stature (physical), and in favor with God and man (spiritual)."

Before we look at the text, it is necessary to consider some background material. As you recall, Luke's Gospel is historical and written especially for the Greek and the thinking man. It also has a great spiritual purpose which is to present the Son of God. Neander, one of the great saints of the past, made this statement: "The three great historical nations had to contribute, each in its own peculiar way, to prepare the soil for the planting of Christianity,—the Jews on the side of the religious element; the Greeks on the side of science and art; the Romans, as masters of the world, on the side of the political element." The Gospels of Matthew, Mark, and Luke were each directed to a particular segment of humanity. Matthew was written to the Jew, Mark was written to the Roman, and Luke was written to the Greek.

Dr. Gregory wrote: "The Greeks are clearly distinguished from the other great historic races by certain marked characteristics. They were the representatives of reason and humanity in the ancient world. They looked upon themselves as having the mission of perfecting men" (*Key to the Gospels,* p. 211). They were the cosmopolitans of that age. They made their gods in the likeness of men, as well as in their own likeness, and therefore joined to human culture utter worldliness and godlessness.

Paul was the right person to go to Athens to enlighten the Greeks about their altar to the "UNKNOWN GOD." Dr. Luke, a Gentile, went with Paul.

The mission of the Greeks was thus evidently a part of the preparation for the coming of the Lord Jesus Christ into the world. It forced the thinking men of that age to feel and confess the insufficiency of human reason (even in its most perfect development) for the deliverance and perfection of mankind. It left them waiting and longing for one who could accomplish this work.

The Greek language became a vehicle for getting the Word of God out. The gospel was communicated to the world in the Greek language. God used Alexander the Great to make it possible.

Of Alexander the Great it has been written: "He took up the meshes of the net of civilization, which were lying in disorder on the edges of the Asiatic shore, and spread them over all other countries which he traversed in his wonderful campaigns. The East and the West were suddenly brought together. Separated tribes were united under a common government. New cities were built, as the centres of political life. New lines of communication were opened, as the channels of commercial activity. The new culture penetrated the mountain ranges of Pisidia and Lycaonia. The Tigris and Euphrates became Greek rivers. The language of Athens was heard among the Jewish colonies of Babylonia; and a Grecian Babylon was built by the conqueror in Egypt and called by his name" (Conybeare and Howson, *Life, Times, and Travels of St. Paul,* vol. 1, p. 9). That city was Alexandria; it still bears this name.

Keep this background in mind as we look at the birth of the Lord Jesus Christ.

BIRTH OF JESUS AT BETHLEHEM IN A STABLE

And it came to pass in those days, that there went out a decree from Caesar Augustus, that all the world should be taxed.

(And this taxing was first made when Cyrenius was governor of Syria.) [Luke 2:1–2].

Someone might think when they read the phrase, "all the world should be taxed" that the Roman Empire was taxing the United States of America too. The Greek word for *world, oikoumene,* means "inhabited earth" and referred to the civilized world of that day. My uncivilized ancestors in northern Europe in those days were not even included in this taxing, although Caesar Augustus would have loved to have taxed everybody if he could have gotten to them.

Who was Caesar Augustus? He was the adopted son of Julius Caesar. Actually his name was Octavianus and he took the name Caesar—I think he had a right to it. Now the name *Augustus* was not a name at all but a title. When the senate submitted to him certain titles like king, emperor, and dictator, he was not satisfied. Instead he chose the title *Augustus.* It had a religious significance, and it was an attempt to deify himself.

It was no accident that Dr. Luke mentioned the name of Caesar Augustus. This man signed a tax bill that the whole world (of that day) be taxed. He needed money to raise an army to control his vast empire and to live in luxury himself. Notice Luke's historical reference that this taxing was first made when Cyrenius was governor of Syria.

And all went to be taxed, every one into his own city.

And Joseph also went up from Galilee, out of the city of Nazareth, into Judaea, unto the city of David, which is called Bethlehem; (because he was of the house and lineage of David:)

To be taxed with Mary his espoused wife, being great with child.

And so it was, that, while they were there, the days were accomplished that she should be delivered.

And she brought forth her firstborn son, and wrapped him in swaddling clothes, and laid him in a manger; because there was no room for them in the inn [Luke 2:3–7].

Joseph and Mary came out of Nazareth in Galilee and went into Judea to Bethlehem, the city of David. Joseph did this because he was of the house and lineage of David. Why did Mary have to go to Bethlehem? She also was of the lineage of David.

I am thrilled when I read this simple, historically accurate passage with tremendous spiritual truth behind it. Caesar Augustus attempted to make himself a god. He wanted to be worshiped. He signed a tax bill which caused a woman and man, peasants, living in Nazareth, to journey to Bethlehem to enroll. That woman was carrying in her womb the Son of God! This is tremendous! This Caesar Augustus tried to make himself God, but nobody today reverences him or pays taxes to him. But that little baby in Mary's womb—many of us worship Him today and call Him our Savior.

Caesar Augustus was merely the tool in God's hand to bring to pass the prophecy, "But thou, Beth-lehem Ephratah, though thou be little among the thousands of Judah, yet out of thee shall he come forth unto me that is to be ruler in Israel; whose goings forth have been from of old, from everlasting" (Mic. 5:2). This is a remarkable account.

Everything that happened was arranged by God. If anyone had said to Caesar, "Wait a minute; women about to give birth are going to have to be moved in order for you to get your taxes," I think he would have replied, "I do not care about babies or their mothers; I am only interested in taxes, armies, money and luxury." Well, that is all gone now, including Caesar.

Dr. Luke gets right down to the little human details in this passage. He is saying that Mary put swaddling clothes on this little child—baby clothes and diapers on the Son of God! How perfectly human He was—God manifest in the flesh!

RECEPTION OF JESUS: ANGELS ANNOUNCE HIS BIRTH TO SHEPHERDS; SHEPHERDS VISIT STABLE

And there were in the same country shepherds abiding in the field, keeping watch over their flock by night [Luke 2:8].

Many people ask the question, "When was Jesus Christ born?" It could not have been in the dead of winter or the shepherds would not have been out at night with their sheep. But the date of His birth is irrelevant, just as the day upon which He was crucified is irrelevant. The Scripture does not say *when* He was born; the important thing is that He was born. The Scripture does not say *when* He was crucified; the important thing is that He died for our sins.

And, lo, the angel of the Lord came upon them, and the glory of the Lord shone round about them: and they were sore afraid.

And the angel said unto them, Fear not: for, behold, I bring you good tidings of great joy, which shall be to all people.

For unto you is born this day in the city of David a Saviour, which is Christ the Lord [Luke 2:9–11].

It is wonderful to see a little baby come into the world, and your heart goes out to him; there is a sympathy that goes from you to him. That is the way God entered the world. He could have entered—as He will when He comes to earth the second time—in power and great glory. Instead, He came in the weakest way possible, as a baby. George Macdonald put it this way:

> They all were looking for a King
>   To slay their foes and lift them high:
> Thou cam'st, a little baby thing
>   That made a woman cry.

That is the way the Saviour came into the world. He did not lay aside His deity; He laid aside His glory. There should have been more than just a few shepherds and angels to welcome Him—all of creation should have been there. Instead of collecting taxes, that fellow Caesar should have been in Bethlehem to worship Him. Jesus Christ could have forced him to do that very thing, but He did not. He laid aside, not His deity, but His prerogatives of deity. He came a little baby thing.

And this shall be a sign unto you; Ye shall find the babe wrapped in swaddling clothes, lying in a manger [Luke 2:12].

Again Dr. Luke is emphasizing His humanity. He came into this world as a human being. He is touched with the feeling of our infirmities.

God knows about mankind. He knows you, and He knows me. He understands us because He came into this world a human being. This also means that we can know something about God, because He took upon Himself our humanity.

And suddenly there was with the angel a multitude of the heavenly host praising God, and saying,

Glory to God in the highest and on earth peace, good will toward men [Luke 2:13–14].

Our Authorized Version gives the wrong impression here. The angels did not say, "on earth peace, good will toward men." What they actually said was, "peace to men of good will," or "peace among men with whom He is pleased." The angels did not make the asinine statement that many men make today which goes, "Let's have peace, peace, peace." My friend, "There is no peace, saith the LORD, unto the wicked" (Isa. 48:22). We live in a day when we need to beat our plowshares into swords—not the other way around. We live in a wicked world. We live in a Satan-dominated world, and therefore there is no peace. There is, however, peace to men of good will. If you are one of those who has come to Christ and taken him as Savior, you can know this peace of God. Romans 5:1 states: "Therefore being justified by faith, we have peace with God through our Lord Jesus Christ." When Christ came the first time, this is the kind of peace He brought. At His second coming He will come as the Prince of Peace; at that time He will put down unrighteousness and rebellion in the world. He will establish peace on the earth. But until He comes again, there will be no peace on this earth.

> **And it came to pass, as the angels were gone away from them into heaven, the shepherds said one to another, Let us now go even unto Bethlehem, and see this thing which is come to pass, which the Lord hath made known unto us.**
>
> **And they came with haste, and found Mary, and Joseph, and the babe lying in a manger [Luke 2:15–16].**

The shepherds hurried to Bethlehem. There they found Mary, Joseph, and the baby Jesus. They were probably the first to visit the Babe since Matthew tells us that the wise men did not arrive until much later. In fact, when the wise men finally found the Lord Jesus, He was living in a house and probably many months had elapsed.

> **And when they had seen it, they made known abroad the saying which was told them concerning this child.**
>
> **And all they that heard it wondered at those things which were told them by the shepherds.**
>
> **But Mary kept all these things, and pondered them in her heart.**
>
> **And the shepherds returned, glorifying and praising God for all the things that they had heard and seen, as it was told unto them [Luke 2:17–20].**

Mary pondered many things in her heart as a mother would do. Because of danger to His life, Mary and Joseph took the young child into Egypt for a time and later returned to Nazareth.

Since He had come into the human family, and since He had been born under the Mosaic Law, He followed the Law.

CIRCUMCISION OF JESUS AND PURIFICATION OF MARY

And when eight days were accomplished for the circumcising of the child, his name was called JESUS, which was so named of the angel before he was conceived in the womb.

And when the days of her purification according to the law of Moses were accomplished, they brought him to Jerusalem, to present him to the Lord [Luke 2:21–22].

40 days if a boy baby, 80 days for a ♀

For forty days a woman was considered unclean after the birth of a child, according to the Mosaic Law. Mary as a sinner had to bring a sacrifice to the Lord. She needed a Savior as she said.

(As it is written in the law of the Lord, Every male that openeth the womb shall be called holy to the Lord;)

And to offer a sacrifice according to that which is said in the law of the Lord, A pair of turtledoves, or two young pigeons [Luke 2:23–24].

Mary and Joseph offered turtledoves as a sacrifice, which were an evidence of their poverty. The sacrifice was for Mary and not for the Child. As far as we know, Jesus never offered a sacrifice.

INCIDENT IN TEMPLE CONCERNING SIMEON

And, behold, there was a man in Jerusalem, whose name was Simeon; and the same man was just and devout, waiting for the consolation of Israel: and the Holy Ghost was upon him.

> And it was revealed unto him by the Holy Ghost, that he
> should not see death, before he had seen the Lord's
> Christ.
>
> And he came by the Spirit into the temple: and when the
> parents brought in the child Jesus, to do for him after the
> custom of the law,
>
> Then took he him up in his arms, and blessed God, and
> said [Luke 2:25–28].

There was a man by the name of Simeon who by the Holy Spirit was
in the temple when the Lord Jesus was brought in to fulfill the Mosaic
Law. God had promised Simeon that he would *see* the salvation of
God. What did he see? He saw a little Baby. Salvation is a Person, and
not something that you *do*. Salvation is a Person, and that Person is
the Lord Jesus Christ. You either have Him, or you don't have Him.
You either trust Him, or you don't trust Him. Do *you* have Him today?
   Now here is another solo, and Simeon is singing it for us.

> Lord, now lettest thou thy servant depart in peace, ac-
> cording to thy word:
>
> For mine eyes have seen thy salvation,
>
> Which thou hast prepared before the face of all people;
>
> A light to lighten the Gentiles, and the glory of thy peo-
> ple Israel [Luke 2:29–32].

This is a remarkable statement coming from a man who was limited in
his outlook upon life—that is, he was limited to a particular area geo-
graphically. Yet he saw the One who was to be the Savior of the *world*.
This is to me one of the amazing things about the Word of God, especially the New Testament. Although given to a certain people, it is
certainly directed to the world. No other religion pointed that way.
You will notice that the religions of the world are generally localized

for a peculiar people, generally a race or nation. But Christianity has been from the outset for all people everywhere.

> **And Joseph and his mother marvelled at those things which were spoken of him.**
>
> **And Simeon blessed them, and said unto Mary his mother, Behold, this child is set for the fall and rising again of many in Israel; and for a sign which shall be spoken against;**
>
> **(Yea, a sword shall pierce through thy own soul also,) that the thoughts of many hearts may be revealed [Luke 2:33–35].**

Notice that Luke calls them "Joseph and his mother," not His father and mother.

Mary paid a tremendous price to bring the Savior into the world. She paid an awful price to stand beneath the cross of the Lord Jesus and watch Him die.

The cross of Christ has moved many people—artists have painted the picture, songwriters have written music about it, and authors and preachers have sketched those moments with words. There is a danger of dwelling on His death in a sympathetic way. Christ did not die to elicit anyone's sympathy. He does not want your sympathy, He wants your faith. Later in the Gospel of Luke, when the Lord is on the way to the cross, some women began to weep. Jesus turned to them and said, "Daughters of Jerusalem, weep not for me, but weep for yourselves, and for your children" (Luke 23:28). If you have tears for Jesus, save them for yourself and your family. Do not weep for Him, because He does not want your sympathy. Jesus Christ wants your faith.

However, when Mary stood beneath that cross and watched Jesus die, it was with a broken heart. Of course her suffering had nothing to do with your salvation; her suffering had nothing to do with her salvation. Her suffering was due to a human relationship. She was His human mother. She had brought Him into the world and raised Him. He was her son. You see, when our Lord looked down from the cross and said, ". . . Woman, behold thy son!" (John 19:26), a human relationship was there that no one else had. She was suffering as His mother. And at that time the prophecy of Simeon was fulfilled—the sword pierced through her soul also.

INCIDENT IN TEMPLE CONCERNING ANNA

There are many solos in this Gospel and now here is another one.

> **And there was one Anna, a prophetess, the daughter of Phanuel, of the tribe of Aser: she was of a great age, and had lived with an husband seven years from her virginity;**
>
> **And she was a widow of about fourscore and four years, which departed not from the temple, but served God with fastings and prayers night and day.**
>
> **And she coming in that instant gave thanks likewise unto the Lord, and spake of him to all them that looked for redemption in Jerusalem [Luke 2:36–38].**

Anna, like Simeon, was living very close to God; and He granted to her also the gracious insight of recognizing His Son, her Messiah. She gave thanks. Although her song is not recorded, it is a song of praise.

I cannot refrain from saying that there are those who say there are ten lost tribes of Israel (that is, that the ten tribes which went into Assyrian captivity in the eighth century B.C. migrated north rather than returning to the land of Israel). If you search through the Bible from the time Israel returned to the land after the captivity, you can pick up practically all of the tribes. Here Anna is mentioned as a member of the tribe of Asher. Evidently Anna did not get lost!

The account of Matthew tells us that the next event in the life of Jesus was a trip to Egypt. Luke omits this account entirely. It is well to remember again the purpose for writing each Gospel is different. Matthew presents the Lord Jesus Christ as King, and Luke presents Him as the perfect Man. The coming of the wise men does not fit into Luke's purpose for writing. The wise men came looking for a king, not for the ideal of the Greek race. Luke presents Him as the perfect Man, and notice how he carries out his purpose even at this point.

RETURN TO NAZARETH

And when they had performed all things according to the law of the Lord, they returned into Galilee, to their own city Nazareth.

And the child grew, and waxed strong in spirit, filled with wisdom: and the grace of God was upon him [Luke 2:39–40].

Luke is presenting the perfect Man. Dr. Luke looks at the Boy not only through the eyes of an obstetrician but through the watchful eye of a pediatrician. The Lord Jesus grew (physically), waxed strong in spirit (spiritually), and was filled with wisdom (mentally). The grace of God was upon this Boy and He grew physically, spiritually, and mentally.

VISIT OF JOSEPH, MARY, AND JESUS TO JERUSALEM WHEN JESUS WAS TWELVE

Next is recorded an incident that only Dr. Luke relates. Luke does this because he is a pediatrician and is interested in the Lord as a boy as well as a man. Luke lifts one scene out of the boyhood of Jesus when He was twelve years old. Since nothing is recorded in the Gospels about the early life of Jesus, some people call this segment of His life the "silent years." I do not consider them silent years; I believe that the Old Testament Scriptures fill in these years if you look closely. Luke's account is a detailed, isolated incident that took place when Jesus was twelve years old.

Now his parents went to Jerusalem every year at the feast of the passover.

> And when he was twelve years old, they went up to Jerusalem after the custom of the feast.
>
> And when they had fulfilled the days, as they returned, the child Jesus tarried behind in Jerusalem; and Joseph and his mother knew not of it.
>
> But they, supposing him to have been in the company, went a day's journey; and they sought him among their kinsfolk and acquaintance.
>
> And when they found him not, they turned back again to Jerusalem, seeking him [Luke 2:41–45].

Mary and Joseph were raising a normal, healthy child. He did not run around wearing a halo, friend. The artists of the Middle Ages had some strange conceptions about the Lord Jesus, both as a child and as an adult. I do not believe He looked like any of their ideas. He was just a normal boy.

In those days people traveled in companies. When the time came to leave Jerusalem, the folk going to Galilee gathered together at a little town right north of Jerusalem to begin the journey home. That is where they missed Him. Joseph probably said, "Where is Jesus?" And Mary replied, "I thought He was with you." They looked for Him among all the people they knew, and when they discovered that He was missing, they returned to Jerusalem. They looked for Jesus for three days, and where do you suppose they found Him? He was in the temple.

> And it came to pass, that after three days they found him in the temple, sitting in the midst of the doctors, both hearing them, and asking them questions.
>
> And all that heard him were astonished at his understanding and answers.
>
> And when they saw him, they were amazed: and his mother said unto him, Son, why hast thou thus dealt

with us? behold, thy father and I have sought thee sorrowing.

And he said unto them, How is it that ye sought me? wist ye not that I must be about my Father's business?

And they understood not the saying which he spake unto them [Luke 2:46–50].

When Mary and Joseph finally found Jesus in the temple, He was standing in the midst of the learned doctors of that day, both hearing them and asking them questions. Apparently He was asking them questions they could not answer. And they were astonished at His answers—remember, He was only twelve! I think it is clear that Mary and Joseph were a little provoked with Him.

The answer of Jesus revealed His surprise that they did not realize He should be about His Father's business. Now, if Joseph were the father, he could have stepped up and said, "Well, what are you trying to do—get some carpenter work here in Jerusalem?" No—His Father was not Joseph. He was speaking of the business of His heavenly Father. Mary, at this point, did not exactly appreciate who He was and what His work entailed, but she pondered these things in her heart.

And he went down with them, and came to Nazareth, and was subject unto them: but his mother kept all these sayings in her heart.

And Jesus increased in wisdom and stature, and in favour with God and man [Luke 2:51–52].

Jesus was subject unto His parents. This is interesting in the light of the fact that young people today are rebelling and are demanding to be heard. They say we ought to listen to them. I have listened to them, and I have not heard them say anything yet, regardless of all the publicity they are given on the television and radio. I personally do not think a college student has much to say. He is still green behind his ears, regardless of his I.Q. The information he has been given is limited and biased, and he does not have the experience to evaluate it. It is remarkable to see that this Boy, Jesus, the Son of God, obeyed His parents and was subject unto them!

Dr. Luke gives us a report about those silent years when Jesus was growing to adulthood. He grew in wisdom (mentally), in stature (physically), in favor with God (spiritually) and man (socially). In every area the Lord Jesus Christ was growing into perfect manhood.

CHAPTER 3

THEME: *Ministry of John the Baptist; baptism of Jesus; genealogy of Mary*

L uke, with a true historian's approach, dates the ministry of John the Baptist with secular history. He places the emphasis upon John's message of repentance as the condition for the coming of the Messiah. From the Mosaic system of washing in water, which was a common custom of immersion in that day, John baptized those who came to him as merely a preparation (a moral reformation) for the coming of Christ. Christ would baptize by the Holy Spirit—a real transformation.

The genealogy in this chapter is Mary's, which reveals two facts. First, it goes back to Adam, the father of the human family. Jesus was truly human. Matthew, in presenting Jesus as king, traces the genealogy back only as far as Abraham. Luke, in presenting Jesus as man, goes back to Adam. In the second place, Mary was descended from David through another than Solomon—David's son Nathan (cf. v. 31; 1 Chron. 3:5).

MINISTRY OF JOHN THE BAPTIST

This chapter contains a great deal of detail; Luke is a stickler for accuracy.

> **Now in the fifteenth year of the reign of Tiberius Caesar, Pontius Pilate being governor of Judaea, and Herod being tetrarch of Galilee, and his brother Philip tetrarch of Ituraea and of the region of Trachonitis, and Lysanias the tetrarch of Abilene [Luke 3:1].**

Six characters are identified in this verse which allow us to date the time. Caesar Augustus was emperor when the Lord Jesus Christ was born, but when John began his ministry Tiberius Caesar was emperor. Secular history, which must supply us with the details, tells us that Tiberius was brilliant but brutal. He was clever but cunning. He was inhuman and profane. He attempted to master the world.

Next the names of the puppet rulers are given.

Annas and Caiaphas being the high priests, the word of God came unto John the son of Zacharias in the wilderness [Luke 3:2].

Annas and Caiaphas were the high priests. Why were there two high priests? Two high priests reveals the power of Rome over the religion of Jerusalem in that day. Annas was the power behind the throne, but Caiaphas was the one Rome put out in front.

The normal experience for John would have been to serve in the temple as his father had. He should have been a leader in the temple, but he despised it. Instead he went into the wilderness and renounced his priesthood. He did not wish to serve in a corrupt system, and so he became a prophet. That is the picture: John was a priest and he became a prophet.

John the Baptist is one of those striking characters who appear from time to time. He reminded the people of Elijah because of certain similarities in their methods. He also reminded the people of One who was one day going to appear—the Messiah. John the Baptist was a paradoxical person. He was truly an unusual man. Luke has told us of his miraculous birth. It was attended by a visitation from the angel Gabriel. His entire boyhood was passed over, and the next event in his life was the beginning of his ministry. He was a priest, a prophet, and a preacher. He was a priest by birth because he was the son of Zacharias, but he was called by God to be a prophet.

And he came into all the country about Jordan, preaching the baptism of repentance for the remission of sins [Luke 3:3].

John preaches the baptism of repentance. He is the last of the prophets. He is actually an Old Testament character who walks out onto the pages of the New Testament. He is picturesque, unshaven, and shaggy, wearing camel's hair clothes. He is different in his dress, his diet, and his looks. He will receive the same reception that many prophets received—he will be put to death.

The most unwelcome message, even today, is the voice of the prophet. The world will not receive a man who contradicts its philosophy of life. If you want to be popular, and this is also true of preachers, you have to sing in unison with the crowd. God have mercy on the pulpit that is nothing in the world but a sounding board for what the congregation is saying. The world does not want to hear the voice of God, especially when that voice speaks of judgment. John's message was very strong.

> **As it is written in the book of the words of Esaias the prophet, saying, The voice of one crying in the wilderness, Prepare ye the way of the Lord, make his paths straight.**

> **Every valley shall be filled, and every mountain and hill shall be brought low; and the crooked shall be made straight, and the rough ways shall be made smooth;**

> **And all flesh shall see the salvation of God.**

> **Then said he to the multitude that came forth to be baptized of him, O generation of vipers, who hath warned you to flee from the wrath to come? [Luke 3:4–7].**

I wonder how long a preacher would last in any church if he began his Sunday sermon by saying, "O generation of vipers"? I do not think he would be in the pulpit the following Sunday. The people would soon get rid of him. I do not recommend using John's unusual introduction for a sermon, but I do think it would be appropriate in many churches.

Bring forth therefore fruits worthy of repentance, and begin not to say within yourselves, We have Abraham to our father: for I say unto you, That God is able of these stones to raise up children unto Abraham [Luke 3:8].

John's message was one of repentance. That is not exactly our message today, although repentance is included in faith. Paul said to the Thessalonian believers that they had ". . . turned to God from idols to serve the living and true God" (1 Thess. 1:9). You can't turn *to* God without turning *from* something. (When you turn *to* anything, you turn *from* something else.) When you turn to God, you turn from sin—and that is repentance. When you accept Christ as your Savior, you are going to turn from the things of the world. Perhaps you have heard about the love of God, but you have not been moved by it and you have wondered why. You need to hear that voice crying in the wilderness, "Repent." Repentance is not the message of the hour; we preach the grace of God, but if you have been a recipient of God's grace and have turned *to* Him, you are going to have to turn *from* your sins. If you do not turn from your sins, you have not really turned to God. Repentance is involved in salvation, but today God's message is, ". . . Believe on the Lord Jesus Christ, and thou shalt be saved . . ." (Acts 16:31).

And now also the axe is laid unto the root of the trees: every tree therefore which bringeth not forth good fruit is hewn down, and cast into the fire [Luke 3:9].

In John's day, trees that did not produce were useless. They were cut down and used for firewood. John's message is strong. John never brought the message of the redeeming love of God. He wasn't called to give that message. His was a message of impending judgment. We need to recognize that this is one of the facets of the message from God for our day also. The nation of Israel had not been productive, as God had expected, and judgment was going to be their portion. John was telling Israel that if they did not bring forth fruit, the axe would come down on the root of the tree. The Lord Jesus Christ is saying the same thing to the church today.

> And the people asked him, saying, What shall we do
> then?
>
> He answereth and saith unto them, He that hath two
> coats, let him impart to him that hath none; and he that
> hath meat, let him do likewise [Luke 3:10–11].

John was telling Israel in plain, understandable language that they
were living for "self" and not attempting to share what they had with
others.

> Then came also publicans to be baptized, and said unto
> him, Master, what shall we do?
>
> And he said unto them, Exact no more than that which
> is appointed you [Luke 3:12–13].

The publicans were tax collectors and were well known for their
greediness. They turned, however, to John and asked, "What shall we
do?" They also turned to the Lord.

> And the soldiers likewise demanded of him, saying,
> And what shall we do? And he said unto them, Do vio-
> lence to no man, neither accuse any falsely; and be con-
> tent with your wages [Luke 3:14].

This is a practical message that John gave to these people who came
from different classes and conditions. My friend, if you are a printer,
you reveal that you are a Christian by the way you print. If you are a
soldier, you reveal your Christianity by the way you soldier. If you are
a housewife, you reveal your Christianity by the way you are a housewife. You reveal what you are. "Wherefore by their fruits ye shall
know them" (Matt. 7:20).

> And as the people were in expectation, and all men
> mused in their hearts of John, whether he were the
> Christ, or not;

> John answered, saying unto them all, I indeed baptize
> you with water; but one mightier than I cometh, the
> latchet of whose shoes I am not worthy to unloose: he
> shall baptize you with the Holy Ghost and with fire:
>
> Whose fan is in his hand, and he will throughly purge
> his floor, and will gather the wheat into his garner; but
> the chaff he will burn with fire unquenchable [Luke
> 3:15–17].

John makes it clear that his message is not the final one. He is preparing the way for the One to come.

John baptized with water. Jesus has been baptizing with the Holy Spirit for over nineteen hundred years now. He shall also baptize with fire at His second coming. Fire speaks of judgment.

Some folk think that this is a reference to the Day of Pentecost when the Holy Spirit came, and there was the appearance of fire on the heads of those assembled. However, it is important to notice that in Acts 2:3 it was ". . . *like as of* fire . . ." (italics mine)—it was not fire. The coming of the Holy Spirit was not the fulfillment of the baptism of fire. That will take place at the second coming of our Lord.

> But Herod the tetrarch, being reproved by him for Herodias his brother Philip's wife, and for all the evils which Herod had done,
>
> Added yet this above all, that he shut up John in prison [Luke 3:19–20].

John had reproved Herod publicly because he had married Herodias, the wife of his brother Philip. Herodias had been furious over this and demanded that John be put in prison. Herod fulfilled her desire and had John arrested and imprisoned.

THE BAPTISM OF JESUS

Now when all the people were baptized, it came to pass, that Jesus also being baptized, and praying, the heaven was opened,

And the Holy Ghost descended in a bodily shape like a dove upon him, and a voice came from heaven, which said, Thou art my beloved Son; in thee I am well pleased [Luke 3:21–22].

Luke is not attempting to give a chronological order of events. If he were, he would have recorded the baptism of Jesus before the arrest of John the Baptist.

At the baptism of Jesus, the Trinity is revealed. The Holy Spirit descends upon Jesus, who is also a member of the Trinity, and the heavenly Father speaks from heaven.

GENEALOGY OF MARY

The rest of this chapter deals with the genealogy of Mary, not Joseph. The genealogy of Joseph is found in Matthew's Gospel. Matthew's genealogy begins with Abraham and comes down to the Lord Jesus Christ through David and through Solomon. The *legal* title to the throne came through Joseph.

Luke's genealogy is different. It is given in reverse order from Matthew's. Luke goes back to David and then back to Adam. Luke gives Mary's story, and this is clearly her genealogy. The royal blood of David flowed through her veins also, and Jesus' *blood* title to the throne of David came through her.

Two things about this genealogy should be noted. First, Dr. Luke makes it clear that Joseph was *not* the father of the Lord Jesus Christ.

And Jesus himself began to be about thirty years of age, being (as was supposed) the son of Joseph, which was the son of Heli [Luke 3:23].

The word *son* as it is used in this genealogy is not in the better manuscripts. Joseph was not the son of Heli. The word *son* is added to indicate the lineage through the father (the man) who was the head of the house. In other words, the genealogy is listed according to the man's name. In Matthew, where it is giving the genealogy through Joseph, it states that Jacob *begat* Joseph.

The second important thing to notice is verse 31 which reads:

Which was the son of Melea, which was the son of Menan, which was the son of Mattatha, which was the son of Nathan, which was the son of David [Luke 3:31].

Matthew traces the line of Christ through David's son, Solomon. That is the royal line. Luke traces the line of Christ through David's son, Nathan. Mary had the blood of David in her veins. Jesus Christ is the Son of David.

Luke reveals Jesus Christ as the Son of Man and the Savior of the *world*. His line does not stop with Abraham, but goes all the way back to Adam who was the first "son" of God—the created son of God. But he fell from that lofty position when he sinned. Jesus Christ, the last Adam and the Son of God, is come to bring mankind back into that relationship with God which Adam formerly had and lost. This relationship is accomplished through faith in the Lord Jesus Christ.

CHAPTER 4

THEME: *The temptation of Jesus; Jesus returns to Galilee and Nazareth—rejected by His hometown; Jesus moves His headquarters to Capernaum and continues His ministry*

J esus is tempted as a man by Satan. They were human temptations such as come to all of us. They cover the entire spectrum of human temptations and are threefold:

1. Satan asks Jesus to make stones into bread to satisfy needs of the body. There is nothing wrong with bread. Bread is the staff of life. The body has need of bread, and Jesus was starving. What is wrong? To use His great powers to minister to Himself would be selfish. He must demonstrate the truth of the great principle, ". . . Man shall not live by bread alone . . ." (Matt. 4:4). This is contrary to the thinking of this crass materialistic age that lives only to satisfy the whims of the body. Modern man in our secular society says, "Eat, drink, and be merry, for tomorrow we die." And as far as man is concerned, that ends it all. Selfishness is the curse of a creedless, secular society. Our Lord, in meeting this temptation, refuted the popular philosophy of the world.

2. Satan offers Jesus the nations of the world. Nations derive their power through brute force and political intrigue. War is a way of life. Hate and fear are the whips to motivate the mob. This is satanic, and Satan offers the kingdoms of the world on these terms. Men must be changed in order to enter God's Kingdom: "Jesus answered and said unto him, Verily, verily, I say unto thee, Except a man be born again, he cannot see the kingdom of God" (John 3:3). The answer of Jesus has a note of finality, ". . . Thou shalt worship the Lord thy God, and him only shalt thou serve" (Matt. 4:10). Then the apostle Paul tells us, "For though we walk in the flesh, we do not war after the flesh: (For the weapons of our warfare are not carnal, but mighty through God to the pulling down of strong holds;) Casting down imaginations, and

every high thing that exalteth itself against the knowledge of God, and bringing into captivity every thought to the obedience of Christ" (2 Cor. 10:3–5).

3. Satan tempts Jesus to cast Himself down from the temple. It would seem a logical procedure for Jesus to impress the crowd as to His person and mission. But Jesus will follow no easy way to the throne. He must wear the crown of thorns before He wears the crown of glory. Stifler states succinctly, "There are two ways of despising God, one is to ignore His power, the other is to presume upon it." Both are sin. It is easy to do nothing and then mouth pious platitudes about God providing for the sparrows and that He will take care of us. But God says, "In the sweat of thy face shalt thou eat bread . . ." (Gen. 3:19).

For example, the missionary to a foreign land will have to study to learn the language, and then God will help him. We are partners of God, not puppets. Dr. Edward Judson, after considering what his father, Adoniram Judson, suffered in Burma said, "If we succeed without suffering, it is because others have suffered before us. If we suffer without success, it is that others may succeed after us." Jesus rejected a false and phony spiritual stance. His answer was devastating: "Ye shall not tempt the LORD your God, as ye tempted him in Massah" (Deut. 6:16).

Actually, Jesus began His public ministry in His hometown of Nazareth where He was rejected and ejected. It was in the synagogue where He announced the fulfillment of Isaiah 61:1–2 in a remarkable way.

THE TEMPTATION OF JESUS

And Jesus being full of the Holy Ghost returned from Jordan, and was led by the Spirit into the wilderness,

Being forty days tempted of the devil. And in those days he did eat nothing: and when they were ended, he afterward hungered [Luke 4:1–2].

We have before us the testing of the Lord Jesus Christ. The synoptic Gospels—Matthew, Mark, and Luke—all record this testing. John does not record this incident because he is presenting the Lord Jesus as the Son of God with the emphasis upon His deity. The synoptic Gospels place the emphasis upon the humanity of the Lord Jesus. He was tempted as a man. In the Gospel of Luke He is presented as the Son of Man. Luke 3:38 says, "Which was the son of Enos, which was the son of Seth, which was the son of Adam, which was the son of God." This is the genealogy of Mary which traces the line of Christ back to Adam. Being a son of Adam takes Him right back to the beginning of the race of which we are members. It was as a human being that He was tempted in all *points* like we are; yet He was without sin.

There is a frightful and fearful darkness about the temptation of our Lord that is an appalling enigma. I must confess that I cannot explain it, but I will take you to the very edge, and at the fringe I hope we can learn something. There were unseen and hidden forces of evil all about Him. He was surrounded by powers of darkness and destruction. He grappled with the basic problems of mankind, that which is earthy, and He won a victory for you and me.

There are several preliminary considerations we need to have in mind as we look at the testing of our Lord. We are told that He was filled with the Holy Spirit. As man, the Son of God needed to be filled with the Spirit in order to meet the temptation. And, friend, I cannot face the temptations of this world in my own strength. In Romans 7:21 Paul tells us, "I find then a law, that, when I would do good, evil is present with me." Haven't you found that to be true? In Romans 8:3–4 Paul continues, "For what the law could not do, in that it was weak through the flesh, God sending his own Son in the likeness of sinful flesh, and for sin, condemned sin in the flesh: That the righteousness of the law might be fulfilled in us, who walk not after the flesh, but after the Spirit." So in Galatians 5:16 Paul concludes, "This I say then, Walk in the Spirit, and ye shall not fulfil the lust of the flesh." We *need* the Holy Spirit.

In Deuteronomy 8:2 God told the Israelites, "And thou shalt remember all the way which the LORD thy God led thee these forty years in the wilderness, to humble thee, and to prove thee, to know what was in thine heart, whether thou wouldest keep his commandments, or no." In other words, God was *testing* the Israelites. God never tests anyone with evil.

We are told that before the Lord was tested, He was led (Mark says *driven*) by the Holy Spirit into the wilderness. In other words, the Lord did not seek the temptation. Even at the Garden of Gethsemane He prayed, "Let this cup pass from me" (see Luke 22:24).

The Lord's temptation did not begin at the end of the forty days; rather, Luke is telling us that after the temptation He was hungry. He was tempted of the Devil all during those forty days. Satan did not stop tempting the Lord after the wilderness temptation either. At the Garden of Gethsemane was another onslaught of Satan. In verse 13 of this chapter Luke tells us, "And when the devil had ended all the temptation, he departed from him for a *season*."

Something else we need to understand is that Satan is a person. I understand that from thirty percent to ninety percent of the ministers say that he is not a person. The Scripture, however, makes it quite clear that the Devil is a person. When he tempted the Lord Jesus, did he come in bodily form? Did he come as a spirit or did he come as an angel of light? The Bible tells us that the Lord met him face-to-face. We need to realize that Satan is subtle—one time he is a roaring lion seeking whom he may devour, and the next time he is an angel of light deceiving even the elect if he could do so (see 1 Pet. 5:8; 2 Cor. 11:14).

What is the meaning of the Lord's temptation? The word *tempt* has a twofold meaning. To tempt means "to incite and entice to evil," and it means "to seduce." If a person can be seduced to do evil, that means there is something in the individual that causes him to yield. It would not be a temptation unless something in a person could yield to it. However, this was not true of the Lord Jesus Christ. He could say, "Hereafter I will not talk much with you: for the prince of this world cometh, and hath nothing in me" (John 14:30). I do not know about you, friend, but every time Satan comes to me he always finds some place to take hold of. Our Lord was holy, harmless, undefiled and separate from sinners (see Heb. 7:26). The temptation of Christ was not a temptation to do evil.

Then the word *tempt* is used in another way. Genesis 22:1 tells us that ". . . God did tempt Abraham . . ." in that God *tested* Abraham.

Also He proved, or tested, Israel for forty years in the wilderness. This raises a question. Could the Lord Jesus Christ have fallen? No, Christ could not have fallen. Then was it a legitimate temptation? It was a *test*. All new articles are tested. For example, tires and automobiles are tested. On television commercials the manufacturers show you the new model car and drive it through purgatory to show you the amount of punishment it can take. Everything is tested, and for anything to break down would be pretty embarrassing for the manufacturer. The Lord Jesus Christ could not have fallen; so was this a legitimate test? It was, and let me illustrate this fact with a simple story.

When I was a boy in west Texas, we lived on the west fork of the Brazos River. In the summertime there was not enough water in the stream to rust a shingle nail. It was dry. In the wintertime, however, you could have kept a battleship afloat in it. One year we had a flood, and it washed out a railroad bridge over the river. Santa Fe railroad workers came immediately to build a new bridge. When the bridge was completed, they put two engines on the bridge and tied down the whistles. In our little town we had never heard two engine whistles blow at the same time; so everyone raced to the bridge, all twenty-seven of us. One brave fellow in the crowd asked, "What are you doing?" The engineer replied, "We are testing the bridge." "Do you think it will break?" the young man queried. "Of course it won't break," the engineer said with almost a sneer. "If you know it won't break, why are you putting the engines on the bridge?" the young man wondered. "Just to prove that it won't break," said the engineer.

That is what the Lord's temptation was. It showed us that we have a Savior who is holy, harmless, undefiled, separate from sinners, and able to save to the uttermost those who come unto God through Him (see Heb. 7:25–26).

The Lord was tested in a way that we could never have been tested. When we are tested, there is always a breaking point. When we reach the breaking point, we break and then the pressure is removed. The pressure was never removed from our Lord.

His was a threefold temptation: physical, psychological, and spiritual.

The Lord was tested in the physical realm.

And the devil said unto him, If thou be the Son of God, command this stone that it be made bread [Luke 4:3]

The devil did not ask the Lord to commit a crime. Bread is the staff of life and is a necessity. On one occasion the Lord fed a multitude of five thousand persons, and four thousand persons at another time. Eve looked at the tree in the midst of the Garden of Eden and saw that it was good for food and ate of it. John calls this test the lust or the desire of the flesh (see 1 John 2:16). A man must live, you know, and in order to live he must eat. That is the philosophy of most people today. The clamor of the crowd, the medley of the mob is, "What shall we eat and drink, and wherewithal shall we be clothed?" That is just about all that life is for most people. Men will become dishonest, steal, gamble, sell liquor, and resort to almost anything to obtain something for their bodies. Women will sell their virtue for a mink coat or a diamond ring. Satan revealed his low estimate of mankind when he told the Lord, ". . . Skin for skin, yea, all that a man hath will he give for his life" (Job 2:4). That is not true because Job did not yield. And our Lord used the sword of the Spirit, which is the Word of God, to defeat Satan.

> **And Jesus answered him, saying, It is written, That man shall not live by bread alone, but by every word of God [Luke 4:4].**

Next Satan tested the Lord in the psychological realm.

> **And the devil, taking him up into an high mountain, shewed unto him all the kingdoms of the world in a moment of time.**

> **And the devil said unto him, All this power will I give thee, and the glory of them: for that is delivered unto me; and to whomsoever I will I give it.**

> **If thou therefore wilt worship me, all shall be thine.**

And Jesus answered and said unto him, Get thee behind me, Satan: for it is written, Thou shalt worship the Lord thy God, and him only shalt thou serve [Luke 4:5–8].

This test had to do with what John calls the lust of the eyes. In the Garden of Eden, Eve looked at the fruit on the tree in the midst of the garden and saw that it was pleasant to the eyes. Satan took Christ high on a mountain and showed Him the kingdoms of the world and offered them to Him. The "kingdoms of the world" encompassed the great Roman Empire. But Christ was on His way to the throne by way of the cross. Satan was saying, "Let's miss the cross." Paul tells us, "For the preaching of the cross is to them that perish foolishness . . ." (1 Cor. 1:18)—how foolish to take that route of suffering when Satan offered an easy way to the throne! Now let me say something that may shock you. It is satanic to try and build a kingdom here on earth without Jesus Christ! There are only two rulers: the Lord Jesus and Satan. If you are not taking the Lord into account, you must take the other. Paul said, "For I determined not to know any thing among you, save Jesus Christ, and him crucified" (1 Cor. 2:2).

Finally the Lord was tested in the spiritual realm.

And he brought him to Jerusalem, and set him on a pinnacle of the temple, and said unto him, If thou be the Son of God, cast thyself down from hence:

For it is written, He shall give his angels charge over thee, to keep thee:

And in their hands they shall bear thee up, lest at any time thou dash thy foot against a stone.

And Jesus answering said unto him, It is said, Thou shalt not tempt the Lord thy God.

And when the devil had ended all the temptation, he departed from him for a season [Luke 4:9–13].

Eve desired the fruit of the tree in the midst of the garden because it could make one wise. John calls this testing ". . . the pride of life . . ." (1 John 2:16). This deals with the realm of the spirit and faith. Satan wanted the Lord to demonstrate that He was the Son of God—"Show them, prove it, then they will accept you." It was not faith; it was presumption. It was daring God. Faith is quietly waiting upon God, doing His will. It is interesting to note that when Satan quoted from Psalm 91:11–12, he misquoted Scripture, just as he misquoted God's word in the garden to Eve.

Why was Jesus Christ tempted? To demonstrate that you and I have a sinless Savior. He is sinless, impeccable, and able to save. He proved that all power had been given to Him. There is a Man in glory today, friend, who understands us and is able to sympathize with us. It is wonderful to have a Savior like that! John writes, "My little children, these things write I unto you, that ye sin not. And if any man sin, we have an advocate with the Father, Jesus Christ the righteous: and he is the propitiation for our sins: and not for ours only, but also for the sins of the whole world" (1 John 2:1–2). The Lord Jesus can be depended upon in every circumstance of life.

JESUS RETURNS TO GALILEE AND NAZARETH—
REJECTED BY HIS HOMETOWN

After Satan tested the Lord Jesus Christ, He was strengthened.

And Jesus returned in the power of the Spirit into Galilee: and there went out a fame of him through all the region round about [Luke 4:14].

After the temptation the Lord comes forth in the power of the Holy Spirit. Temptation will do one of two things for an individual; it will either strengthen or weaken him. It is like the army, which will make you or break you. Whether this is actually true of the army, I do not know. This I do know, however, that suffering and testing will either sweeten or sour you, soften or harden you. There is an old familiar illustration which says that the same sun will melt the wax but harden the clay. It is the character of, or the condition of, the element and not the sun that melts the wax and hardens the clay. God is not going to harden you. He did not harden Pharaoh's heart. Pharaoh already possessed a hard heart, and God only brought that fact out into the open. Our Lord identified Himself with mankind. Scripture confirms this fact: "Wherefore in all things it behooved him to be made like unto his breathren, that he might be a merciful and faithful priest in things pertaining to God, to make reconciliation for the sins of the people" (Heb. 2:17). The Lord Jesus Christ became a man and so after His ordeal He needed the strengthening of the Holy Spirit. And if our Lord needed the strengthening of the Holy Spirit after His testing, how much more do we need Him!

And he taught in their synagogues, being glorified of all [Luke 4:15].

After the temptation the Lord returned to Galilee and taught in the synagogues. He was glorified by the people; He was praised and complimented. This verse sounds like a doxology. You know, it is possible to praise Him and still reject Him. It is possible to sing the doxology and turn down His claims. The same crowd that sang "Hosanna" and wanted to crown Him, the next day joined the mob to crucify Him. I think of a picture of the Crucifixion with the empty cross in the foreground and in the background is the donkey feeding on withered palm branches. That is the way it was. One day the Lord was praised, and the next day He was crucified.

Now we come to one of the most beautiful incidents recorded in God's Word. It is a scintillating story that flashes with light. It is fragrant with meaning. It is lovely to look at, and this is the way Dr. Luke tells it:

And he came to Nazareth, where he had been brought up: and, as his custom was, he went into the synagogue on the sabbath day, and stood up for to read.

> And there was delivered unto him the book of the prophet Esaias. And when he had opened the book, he found the place where it was written,
>
> The Spirit of the Lord is upon me, because he hath anointed me to preach the gospel to the poor; he hath sent me to heal the broken hearted, to preach deliverance to the captives, and recovering of sight to the blind, to set at liberty them that are bruised,
>
> To preach the acceptable year of the Lord.
>
> And he closed the book, and he gave it again to the minister, and sat down. And the eyes of all them that were in the synagogue were fastened on him.
>
> And he began to say unto them. This day is this scripture fulfilled in your ears [Luke 4:16–21].

This incident is recorded only by Dr. Luke and is so remarkable that we cannot pass it by. We are told that after the temptation, the Lord returned to His hometown. Generally the hometown is proud of the local boy who has become famous. As was His custom on the Sabbath, He went to the synagogue in Nazareth.

Notice that He never entertained the false notion that you can worship God in nature as well as in the appointed place. Although I enjoy playing golf, I get a little weary of hearing some men say very piously that they can worship God just as easily on the golf course on Sunday as they can in church. What they say is true, but the question I always ask them is, "When you take your golf bag out on the course on Sunday morning, do you go out to worship God or to play golf?" The fact of the matter is, they have no intention of worshiping God on the golf course. You go to church on Sunday morning to worship God, and you go out on the golf course to play golf. It was the custom of our Lord to go to the synagogue on the Sabbath day.

The synagogue was one of the most important religious institutions of the Jews in the time of our Lord. It must have come into existence during the time of the Babylonian captivity. The Jews were far from their native land, from the temple and the altar. They no doubt felt drawn to gather round those who were especially pious and God-fearing in order to listen to the Word of God and engage in some kind of worship. In Ezekiel 14:1 and 20:1 it is mentioned that the elders gathered around Ezekiel, and it may have been in such a setting as the synagogue.

After the exile, the synagogue remained. At first it was meant only for the exposition of the Mosaic Law. Later, a time of prayer and preaching was added. However, primarily, the synagogue was for instruction in the Law for all classes of people. At the time of our Lord there were synagogues in all the larger towns.

I can now fill in one day of the silent years of Christ's earthly life. I do not know much about the other six days of each week, other than He was a carpenter and worked on those days. But I know that every seventh day He went to the synagogue. He went to the appointed place to worship because He could witness there.

Now He has come home for awhile and is in the synagogue. He is handed the Book, and He begins to read it. He reads from Isaiah. In those days the Bible was not divided into chapters and verses, but had it been, He would have read Isaiah 61:1–2. The important thing to notice is where He broke off reading. He did not read, ". . . and the day of vengeance of our God. . . ." He closed the Book and gave it back to the minister. The amazing thing is that He did not stop reading at the end of a sentence but stopped before finishing it. In our translation, He stopped reading at the comma, but there was no comma in the text He was reading. He made absolutely no mention of the phrase, "the day of vengeance of our God." He made no mention of any of the text that followed this phrase. Do you know why? He looked at that crowd and said, "This day is this scripture fulfilled in your ears."

Here is a passage of Scripture that was going to be fulfilled down to a comma, and the rest of the passage would not be fulfilled until He came back the second time. The day of vengeance had not yet come. What is the day of vengeance? It is that time of which God said, "Ask of me, and I shall give thee the heathen for thine inheritance, and the uttermost parts of the earth for thy possession" (Ps. 2:8). How is the Lord going to get the heathen for His inheritance? "Thou shalt break them with a rod of iron; thou shalt dash them in pieces like a potter's vessel" (Ps. 2:9). That is the way the Lord will come to power. That will be the day of vengeance. That is the great Day of the Lord, and it will take place when Christ comes the second time. He came the first time to preach the gospel to the poor that they might be saved. He came anointed by the Holy Spirit to bring the glorious message of salvation. We are still living in that wonderful day, the day of the gospel. When He comes the second time, it will be the day of vengeance.

> **And all bare him witness, and wondered at the gracious words which proceeded out of his mouth. And they said, Is not this Joseph's son? [Luke 4:22].**

The people looked at Him and remembered Him as Joseph's son, a carpenter. That seemed to spoil it all. How could He be the Messiah? Luke is making it very clear that He took upon Himself our frail humanity.

> **And he said unto them, Ye will surely say unto me this proverb, Physician, heal thyself: whatsoever we have heard done in Capernaum, do also here in thy country.**
>
> **And he said, Verily I say unto you, No prophet is accepted in his own country.**
>
> **But I tell you of a truth, many widows were in Israel in the days of Elias, when the heaven was shut up three years and six months, when great famine was throughout all the land;**
>
> **But unto none of them was Elias sent, save unto Sarepta, a city of Sidon, unto a woman that was a widow.**
>
> **And many lepers were in Israel in the time of Eliseus the prophet; and none of them was cleansed, saving Naaman the Syrian [Luke 4:23–27].**

The Lord is illustrating this in a marvelous way. He cited two Gentiles who lived outside of the land of Israel—the widow of Sarepta and

Naaman of Syria—in whose lives God worked miraculously. He is trying to show them that they, His own people, were apt to miss a great blessing because they would not accept who He was. They would be like the many widows and the many lepers of Israel who were not healed during the time of Elijah.

> **And all they in the synagogue, when they heard these things, were filled with wrath,**
>
> **And rose up, and thrust him out of the city, and led him unto the brow of the hill whereon their city was built, that they might cast him down headlong.**
>
> **But he passing through the midst of them went his way [Luke 4:28–30].**

The people of Jesus' hometown rejected Him. The country around Nazareth is rough country, and they led Him to the brow of a hill, intending to push Him off to His death. His escape from this mob was a miracle.

JESUS MOVES HIS HEADQUARTERS TO CAPERNAUM AND CONTINUES HIS MINISTRY

> **And came down to Capernaum, a city of Galilee, and taught them on the sabbath days [Luke 4:31].**

From this verse through the rest of the chapter we have one day with the Lord Jesus. Many of us would have loved to have spent a day with Him when He was on earth. Luke makes this possible for us.

Both Matthew and Mark record the fact that the Lord Jesus moved His headquarters from His hometown of Nazareth to Capernaum on the Sea of Galilee. He did this because the people from His own town would not receive Him. There came a day when He told the people of Capernaum, "And thou, Capernaum, which art exalted to heaven, shalt be thrust down to hell" (Luke 10:15). Because His headquarters were there, what an opportunity they had. Light creates responsibility.

> And they were astonished at his doctrine: for his word
> was with power [Luke 4:32]

As the Lord taught in the synagogue on the Sabbath, He did not speak as a scribe or a Pharisee but as one who had authority.

> And in the synagogue there was a man, which had a
> spirit of an unclean devil, and cried out with a loud
> voice,
>
> Saying, Let us alone; what have we to do with thee, thou
> Jesus of Nazareth? art thou come to destroy us? I know
> thee who thou art; the Holy One of God.
>
> And Jesus rebuked him, saying, Hold thy peace, and
> come out of him. And when the devil had thrown him in
> the midst, he came out of him, and hurt him not.
>
> And they were all amazed, and spake among them-
> selves, saying, What a word is this! for with authority
> and power he commandeth the unclean spirits, and they
> come out.
>
> And the fame of him went out into every place of the
> country round about [Luke 4:33–37].

We are living in a day when demonism has lifted its ugly head again, and Satan worship is a reality. Demons were working in the days of our Lord, and they are working now. Our Lord cast a demon out of an individual. Even considering the use of drugs, it is difficult to explain some of the actions and awful crimes being committed unless the perpetrator is under the power and control of Satan.

> And he arose out of the synagogue, and entered into Si-
> mon's house. And Simon's wife's mother was taken with
> a great fever; and they besought him for her.
>
> And he stood over her, and rebuked the fever; and it left
> her: and immediately she arose and ministered unto
> them [Luke 4:38–39].

After leaving the synagogue, it seems that the Lord went to Simon Peter's house, probably for the noonday meal. While He was in Peter's house, He healed "Simon's wife's mother," Peter's mother-in-law, who had a great fever. The severity of diseases was indicated by saying one had a small or a great fever. This evidently was a serious illness. Our Lord rebuked the fever, using Luke's medical terminology, "be muzzled." The fever was like a wild dog that had broken the leash. Our Lord also dealt with sin like that. Immediately she arose and ministered unto them. When the Lord Jesus Christ healed someone, healing did not come gradually but took place immediately. It was an amazing thing.

I have heard about a meeting conducted by a "faith healer" not long ago. It was reported that a cripple was led up to the platform where he was declared healed then led away, still limping. Then someone came to the platform who said he had internal cancer, and the faith healer declared that he was immediately healed of cancer. It is amazing how people will accept that type of testimony. Why wasn't the crippled man healed immediately? If our Lord had done it, the cure would have been immediate. I can hear someone asking, "Don't you believe in divine healing?" My answer is, "What other kind of healing is there?" All healing is divine. This is what Dr. Luke is telling us. Doctors do not always recognize this fact.

A wonderful doctor who was a member of my church in Texas once said to me, "I send the bill, but God does the healing. I take out that part that is offending the body, but God will have to be the Healer." What a great testimony. God, and not an individual, does the healing.

Now when the sun was setting, all they that had any sick with divers diseases brought them unto him; and he laid his hands on every one of them, and healed them.

And devils also came out of many, crying out, and saying, Thou art Christ the Son of God. And he rebuking them suffered them not to speak: for they knew that he was Christ.

> **And when it was day, he departed and went into a desert place: and the people sought him, and came unto him, and stayed him, that he should not depart from them.**
>
> **And he said unto them, I must preach the kingdom of God to other cities also: for therefore am I sent.**
>
> **And he preached in the synagogues of Galilee [Luke 4:40–44].**

His day had started in the morning, teaching in the synagogue. Now it is late in the evening. The Lord goes outside to the multitude that had gathered, and He moves from one to another, touching and healing them. Matthew in recording this incident quotes from the prophet Isaiah: "That it might be fulfilled which was spoken by Esaias the prophet, saying, Himself took our infirmities, and bare our sicknesses" (Matt. 8:17). The Lord healed in a wonderful way. "Surely he hath borne our griefs, and carried our sorrows: yet we did esteem him stricken, smitten of God, and afflicted" (Isa. 53:4). The Lord bore the sicknesses and diseases of the people sympathetically, in spite of the fact that the nation Israel in that day esteemed Him stricken. That is the way we also esteem Him. You see, He did not heal these people on the basis of their faith as far as we know, but His great heart of sympathy caused Him to move in their behalf.

We are told to have such a heart of sympathy today. "Bear ye one another's burdens, and so fulfil the law of Christ" (Gal. 6:2).

CHAPTER 5

THEME: Jesus calls the disciples for the second time; Jesus cleanses the lepers; Jesus heals man with palsy; Jesus calls Matthew; Jesus gives parables on new garment and wine skins

JESUS CALLS THE DISCIPLES
FOR THE SECOND TIME

And it came to pass, that, as the people pressed upon him to hear the word of God, he stood by the lake of Gennesaret,

And saw two ships standing by the lake: but the fishermen were gone out of them, and were washing their nets.

And he entered into one of the ships, which was Simon's, and prayed him that he would thrust out a little from the land. And he sat down, and taught the people out of the ship [Luke 5:1–3].

The Lake of Gennesaret is the Sea of Galilee. The fishermen there had left their boats and were washing their nets. The Lord climbed into Simon Peter's boat and asked him to push the boat out a little from the land. What a pulpit! I believe this illustration is both figurative and suggestive. Every pulpit is a "fishing boat," a place to give out the Word of God and attempt to catch fish. He had told these men that He would make them fishers of men. This does not mean that you and I will catch fish every time we give out the Word—the disciples didn't—but it does mean that the one on board must not forget the supreme business of life which is to fish for the souls of men.

Now when he had left speaking, he said unto Simon, Launch out into the deep, and let down your nets for a draught [Luke 5:4].

After the Lord had finished speaking to the people, He said, "Now we'll leave off fishing for men, and we're going to fish for fish." Matthew and Mark tell us that the first time the Lord called these men He was walking by the Sea of Galilee and saw Simon Peter and his brother Andrew casting a net into the sea—they were fishermen—and the Lord said to them, ". . . Follow me, and I will make you fishers of men" (cf. Matt. 4:19; Mark 1:17). Now these men have returned to their occupation of fishing. The Lord evidently made three calls to His disciples. He met most of them in Jerusalem. John tells us about it in John chapter 1. When John the Baptist marked Him out, several of his disciples wanted to know where Jesus dwelt. Among those who followed John were Philip, Nathanael, Simon Peter, and Andrew. The Lord did not call these men to be disciples at this time; He just met them. Later on, the Lord passed by the Sea of Galilee, saw them fishing, and called them to follow Him. They left their nets and followed Him. Now they had returned to the fishing business. Later on, Dr. Luke will tell us that once again the Lord called them to go fishing for men and at that time made them apostles.

As our Lord had been speaking to the crowd from his boat, Simon Peter had been sitting in the boat listening. When He finished speaking, He told Simon, "Launch out into the deep, and let your net down. You quit fishing with Me; now I am going to fish with you."

And Simon answering said unto him, Master, we have toiled all the night, and have taken nothing: nevertheless at thy word I will let down the net [Luke 5:5].

"Nevertheless at thy word I will let down the net," indicates that Simon Peter had put up an argument. These men were expert fishermen, and thought they knew all about fishing in the Sea of Galilee—and they did. Peter makes it very clear that they had fished all night without catching anything.

The story is told that when Wellington once gave a command to one of his generals, he answered that it was impossible to execute the command. Wellington told him, "You go ahead and do it, because I don't give impossible commands." When the Lord Jesus Christ gives a command, you do not need to argue with him and say, "We've tried it before and it cannot be done." He does not give impossible commands.

> **And when they had this done, they enclosed a great multitude of fishes: and their net brake [Luke 5:6].**

Fishing must be done according to His directions. There are many lessons for us here. Fishing is an art. You must go where the fish are; you must use the right kind of bait; you must be patient; but the important lesson He is teaching us is that we must fish according to His instructions. If we are ever going to win men for Him, we must fish according to His instructions.

In this instance the net broke. Later on, in the Gospel of John, a net overloaded with fish does *not* break. The fisherman's net illustrates a truth. At this point there is no net that can hold the fish for the simple reason that He has not yet died and risen from the dead—that is the gospel. The "net" which will hold fish must be one that rests upon the death and resurrection of Christ—at this time there had been no death and resurrection. The net broke. After His death and resurrection, He told them how to fish and the net did not break (see John 21:1–11). Here He tells them to go out and preach the gospel to the very ends of the earth.

> **And they beckoned unto their partners, which were in the other ship, that they should come and help them. And they came, and filled both the ships, so that they began to sink.**
>
> **When Simon Peter saw it, he fell down at Jesus' knees, saying, Depart from me; for I am a sinful man, O Lord [Luke 5:7–8].**

Notice that this is a tremendous catch of fish!

Peter confesses his failure; he is not even a good fisherman of fish due to his lack of faith. When Simon said, "Depart from me; for I am a sinful man, O Lord," he was saying, "Lord you called me to be a fisher of men and I failed. I went back to fishing for fish—I thought I knew that kind of fishing better, but I find that I don't! Depart from me. Let me alone. I am a sinful man. You should find someone upon whom you can depend." The Lord, however, did not intend to get rid of Simon Peter. He was going to use him, and this applies to us also. All we have to do is recognize that we are not very good fishermen—recognize our failures and faithlessness. When we are willing to depend on Him, He will not put us out of the fishing business, and He will not throw us overboard. He will use us. This is an encouraging truth!

> **For he was astonished, and all that were with him, at the draught of the fishes which they had taken:**
>
> **And so was also James, and John, the sons of Zebedee, which were partners with Simon. And Jesus said unto Simon, Fear not; from henceforth thou shalt catch men [Luke 5:9–10].**

Simon Peter did catch men. Remember how well he did on the Day of Pentecost—the Lord's answer to Peter is certainly significant. Three thousand souls came to Christ after his first sermon! Peter was fishing according to God's instructions.

There is another lesson here. Do you know there is another fisherman? Do you know that Satan also is a fisherman? Paul tells us that in 2 Timothy 2:26, which says, "And that they may recover themselves out of the snare of the devil, who are taken captive by him at his will." Satan has his hook out in the water too. God is fishing for your soul, and Satan also is fishing for your soul with a hook baited with the things of the world. You might say God's hook is a cross. The son of God died upon that cross for you. This is God's message for you. By the way, whose hook are you on today? You are either on God's hook or Satan's hook. Either the Devil has you or God has you. There is no third fisherman.

JESUS CLEANSES THE LEPERS

And it came to pass, when he was in a certain city, behold a man full of leprosy: who seeing Jesus fell on his face, and besought him, saying Lord, if thou wilt, thou canst make me clean.

And he put forth his hand, and touched him, saying, I will: be thou clean. And immediately the leprosy departed from him [Luke 5:12–13].

In verses 12–15 we have the story of the healing of a leper. Luke was a good doctor. He recognized a psychological implication in the healing of this leper that was not much understood in that day.

We are not told how the man discovered that he had leprosy, but it could have happened in the following manner. One day he came in from plowing and said to his wife, "I have a little sore on the palm of my hand. It bothers me when I am plowing. Could you put a poultice on it and wrap it for me?" His wife bandaged his hand, but the next day the sore was worse. In a few days they both became alarmed. His wife said, "You should go to the priest." He went to the priest who put him in isolation for fourteen days. When he was brought out the priest looked him over and found the leprosy had spread. The priest told him he was a leper. The heartbroken man said to the priest, "Let me go to my wife and children and tell them good-bye." The priest replied, "You cannot tell them good-bye. You will never be able to take your lovely wife in your arms again. You will never be able to put your arms around those precious children of yours." The man went off, alone. His family brought his food to a certain place and then withdrew when he came to get it. In the distance he could see his wife and observe his children growing day by day.

Then one day the Lord Jesus Christ came by. The leper declared, "If You will, You can heal me." The King of kings replied, "I will, be thou clean." But notice *how* the Lord healed him. He put forth His hand and touched this man afflicted with leprosy. This poor man had not felt anyone's touch for years. Can you imagine what it must have meant to him to have the touch of Christ's hand upon him?

Has the Lord Jesus touched your life? There are so many lives that need to be touched. If you are His, and you are fishing at His command, I am confident that you can reach someone for the Lord. You need to reach out your hand and touch some soul whom only you can touch for Him today.

JESUS HEALS MAN WITH PALSY

And it came to pass on a certain day, as he was teaching, that there were Pharisees and doctors of the law sitting by, which were come out of every town of Galilee, and Judaea, and Jerusalem: and the power of the Lord was present to heal them.

And, behold, men brought in a bed a man which was taken with a palsy: and they sought means to bring him in, and to lay him before him.

And when they could not find by what way they might bring him in because of the multitude, they went upon the housetop, and let him down through the tiling with his couch into the midst before Jesus.

And when he saw their faith, he said unto him, Man, thy sins are forgiven thee [Luke 5:17–20].

This is the account of the paralytic in Capernaum who was healed. Some friends of this man let him down through the roof of a house in order for the Lord Jesus Christ to see him. Both Matthew and Mark record this incident. Mark gives the longest account, though his is the shortest Gospel. The Lord healed this man because these four men brought him into His presence where the poor fellow could hear, "Man, thy sins are forgiven thee." It was a wonderful word that came to this man.

There are many people who are not going to receive the message of salvation unless you lift a corner of their stretcher and carry them to the place where they can hear the Word of the Lord. They are paralyzed—immobilized by sin and by many other things the world holds for them. Some are paralyzed by prejudice and others by indifference. They are never going to hear Jesus say to them, "Thy sins are forgiven thee," unless you take the corner of their stretcher and bring them to Him.

All of these incidents reveal the fact that the Lord Jesus Christ wants us to spread the message of salvation to others. This is why I preach the Word of God—and remember that one man cannot carry a stretcher alone. It took four men to carry the stretcher of the paralyzed man. More men and women are needed today to help get the Word of God out to those who need Him.

JESUS CALLS MATTHEW

And after these things he went forth, and saw a publican, named Levi, sitting at the receipt of custom: and he said unto him, Follow me.

And he left all, rose up, and followed him [Luke 5:27–28].

Matthew gives us this much information in his Gospel, and Mark gives a little more detail; but Luke shares even more.

And Levi made him a great feast in his own house: and there was a great company of publicans and of others that sat down with them [Luke 5:29].

This dinner was given by Levi as a way of trying to win people to the Lord Jesus Christ. Levi had not been trained in a theological seminary. He was a tax gatherer and a rascal. When he came to the Lord Jesus, he did what he could. He was a rich publican—so he gave a dinner and invited all his rascal friends to it so that they could meet Jesus Christ.

The scribes and Pharisees who were there had a difficult time keeping their mouths shut, and finally they came to Him.

But their scribes and Pharisees murmured against his disciples, saying, Why do ye eat and drink with publicans and sinners? [Luke 5:30].

The scribes and Pharisees criticize with a question, and the Lord Jesus has a good answer for it. Our Lord protects His own men.

And Jesus answering said unto them, They that are whole need not a physician; but they that are sick.

I came not to call the righteous, but sinners to repentance [Luke 5:31–32].

The scribes and Pharisees asked the disciples why they ate with publicans and sinners. The Lord's answer was simple and wonderful. He was the Great Physician, and He did not go around healing people that were well! He came to minister to those who were sick with sin. The gospel is really for those who recognize their need. There are some people who think they are too good to be saved. They are not aware of their need. If you recognize that you have a need, then the gospel is for you. Christ can and will save you. If you are self-sufficient, recognize no personal need, and go in your self-chosen pathway, it will lead you to destruction. I am sorry. The Great Physician can do nothing for those who think they are not sick.

And they said unto him, Why do the disciples of John fast often, and make prayers, and likewise the disciples of the Pharisees; but thine eat and drink? [Luke 5:33].

The scribes and Pharisees then ask why John's disciples and the disciples of the Pharisees fast while the disciples of Jesus are having a good time.

> And he said unto them, Can ye make the children of the bridechamber fast, while the bridegroom is with them?
>
> But the days will come, when the bridegroom shall be taken away from them, and then shall they fast in those days [Luke 5:34–35].

We today are to have a good time, but fasting is also beneficial, recognizing that our Lord is in heaven, and we are in a world that has rejected Him. The point is that, whether we feast or fast, our business is to get the Word out to people who need Him.

JESUS GIVES PARABLES ON NEW GARMENT AND WINE SKINS

This is the first parable in the Gospel of Luke.

> And he spake also a parable unto them; No man putteth a piece of a new garment upon an old; if otherwise, then both the new maketh a rent, and the piece that was taken out of the new agreeth not with the old.
>
> And no man putteth new wine into old bottles; else the new wine will burst the bottles, and be spilled, and the bottles shall perish.
>
> But new wine must be put into new bottles; and both are preserved.
>
> No man also having drunk old wine straightway desireth new: for he saith, The old is better [Luke 5:36–39].

The natural man likes his old ways. He likes his old wine—that is, his old religion. The important thing is to recognize that our Lord brought something new to mankind—the gospel. He did not come into the world to do any patching of the old garment. He did not come to patch up the Law. He came to pay the penalty of sin by dying on the cross. But He did more than that. He arose from the dead so that He could place upon us His robe of righteousness. He gives us the new wine of the gospel. The new wine of the gospel must be placed in the new wineskin of grace, not into the old one of law. "And be not drunk with wine, wherein is excess; but be filled with the Spirit" (Eph. 5:18). This is the message that the Lord gives out today. He came to give us something new. He came to save us by faith in Him.

This entire chapter points in one direction, and that is to present the glorious gospel of the Lord Jesus Christ in as many ways as possible so that men might hear and have an opportunity to choose whether they will accept Him or reject Him.

All of us must make this decision for ourselves.

CHAPTER 6

THEME: Jesus defends disciples for plucking grain on Sabbath; Jesus chooses the Twelve; Jesus gives sermon on the plain

JESUS DEFENDS DISCIPLES
FOR PLUCKING GRAIN ON SABBATH

The first part of this chapter is almost a repetition of the other synoptic Gospels. It begins with the action of Christ on the Sabbath day. The first incident is in the fields on the Sabbath day.

> And it came to pass on the second sabbath after the first, that he went through the corn fields; and his disciples plucked the ears of corn, and did eat, rubbing them in their hands.
>
> And certain of the Pharisees said unto them, Why do ye that which is not lawful to do on the sabbath days?
>
> And Jesus answering them said, Have ye not read so much as this, what David did, when himself was an hungered, and they which were with him;
>
> How he went into the house of God, and did take and eat the shewbread, and gave also to them that were with him; which it is not lawful to eat but for the priests alone?
>
> And he said unto them, That the Son of man is Lord also of the sabbath [Luke 6:1–5].

As the disciples plucked the grain and rubbed it in their hands, the Pharisees accused them of threshing the grain on the Sabbath day. Of course they were not breaking the Mosaic Law, as it permitted people to pull the grain (see Deut. 23:24–25). If they had been cutting it with

a sickle, they would have been harvesting. But the Pharisees had their
own interpretation, and therefore they interpret the action as breaking
the Law.

Our Lord did not insist that they had not broken the Sabbath; He
refused to argue the issue with them. He cited an incident in the life of
David where he had definitely broken the Mosaic Law and was justified. His point was that the letter of the Law was not to be imposed
when it wrought hardship upon one of God's servants. Obviously the
disciples were hungry. It cost them something to follow Jesus.

Then we have the incident of the Sabbath day in the synagogue.

**And it came to pass also on another sabbath, that he
entered into the synagogue and taught: and there was a
man whose right hand was withered.**

**And the scribes and Pharisees watched him, whether he
would heal on the sabbath day; that they might find an
accusation against him.**

**But he knew their thoughts, and said to the man which
had the withered hand, Rise up, and stand forth in the
midst. And he arose and stood forth.**

**Then said Jesus unto them, I will ask you one thing; Is it
lawful on the sabbath days to do good, or to do evil? to
save life, or to destroy it?**

**And looking round about upon them all, he said unto
the man, Stretch forth thy hand. And he did so: and his
hand was restored whole as the other.**

**And they were filled with madness; and communed one
with another what they might do to Jesus [Luke 6:6–11].**

The man with the withered hand was planted there, you may be sure.
In doing this they really paid our Lord a wonderful compliment. They
believed He could heal him, and they believed He would heal him.
They knew He was both powerful and compassionate. They were ex-

actly correct in their estimation of Him. Our Lord healed the man. Then His enemies used the occasion to accuse Him of breaking the Sabbath day. Matthew tells us that they plotted His death from that moment on.

JESUS CHOOSES THE TWELVE

As I mentioned previously, some of the disciples were introduced to our Lord when He went to Jerusalem. Later, walking by the Sea of Galilee, He called those men to follow Him. Then they went back to fishing. And He went by and called them again, at which time, the record tells us, "they forsook all, and followed him" (Luke 5:11). Now we have come to the third stage. Out of an unspecified number of disciples, He chose twelve men to be His apostles.

> **And it came to pass in those days, that he went out into a mountain to pray, and continued all night in prayer to God.**
>
> **And when it was day, he called unto him his disciples: and of them he chose twelve, whom also he named apostles;**
>
> **Simon (whom he also named Peter,) and Andrew his brother, James and John, Philip and Bartholomew,**
>
> **Matthew and Thomas, James the son of Alphaeus, and Simon called Zelotes,**
>
> **And Judas the brother of James, and Judas Iscariot, which also was the traitor [Luke 6:12–16].**

Notice that Jesus prayed all night to God. Why? He was going to choose twelve men to be His apostles. He spent the entire night in prayer before making His choice. One of the apostles turned out to be a traitor. Another apostle denied Him but later repented. Notice, however, that God's men were always *chosen*. There are many candidates, to be sure, but consider what John 15:16 says: "Ye have not chosen me, but I have chosen you." This has been a great comfort to me. I was a clerk in a bank when the Lord called me to be a preacher. I never dreamed of becoming a preacher; in fact, I actually looked down on preachers. I did not call Him, but He called me. I've always felt good about it, because since He called me, He is responsible. That is wonderful. It gives me comfort. The Lord found it essential and practical to spend the entire night in prayer before selecting the twelve apostles. Men chosen for God's work should be selected on the basis of much prayer. The robe of Elijah did not fall by accident upon Elisha; it fell providentially. The present-day procedure of the church for choosing men to fill an office is far from God's standard. We follow our feelings and consult our own selfish desires. We use human measuring rods rather than God's measuring stick. We should spend time with God before making our decisions.

JESUS GIVES SERMON ON THE PLAIN

And he came down with them, and stood in the plain, and the company of his disciples, and a great multitude of people out of all Judaea and Jerusalem, and from the sea coast of Tyre and Sidon, which came to hear him, and to be healed of their diseases;

And they that were vexed with unclean spirits: and they were healed.

And the whole multitude sought to touch him: for there went virtue out of him, and healed them all [Luke 6:17–19].

As I have said many times before, multitudes were healed on this occasion. In our Lord's day literally thousands of people were healed. There were no healing lines, no slapping of this one and patting of that one, no having people fall backwards and forwards. The people whom the Lord healed did not have to do anything. Our Lord would even heal them at a distance. The healings performed by the Lord were genuine, and we have Dr. Luke's statement to prove it. I do not believe in faith *healers* but I do believe in faith *healing*. Take your problem to the Great Physician. He is the best doctor you can consult, and He does not send you a bill; nor do you have to be on Medicare to get Him to take your case.

Now we come to the so-called "Sermon on the Mount," which is not a sermon on the *mount* as it was delivered on a *plain*. Of course the Sermon on the Mount was delivered on a mountain, as recorded in Matthew. The similarity in content indicates that the Lord gave His teachings again and again. We do not need a harmony of the Gospels as much as we need a contrast of the Gospels. The remarkable thing about this sermon in Luke is its dissimilarity to the sermon in Matthew. There are omissions, certain inclusions, blessings and woes, attitudes and judgments.

> **And he lifted up his eyes on his disciples, and said, Blessed be ye poor; for yours is the kingdom of God.**
>
> **Blessed are ye that hunger now: for ye shall be filled. Blessed are ye that weep now: for ye shall laugh.**
>
> **Blessed are ye, when men shall hate you, and when they shall separate you from their company, and shall reproach you, and cast out your name as evil, for the Son of man's sake [Luke 6:20–22].**

Up to this point the content of the Sermon on the Plain is similar to Matthew's Sermon on the Mount. The Lord gave the same teaching in many places but in a different form. Beginning with verse 23, a new thought is introduced.

> **Rejoice ye in that day, and leap for joy: for, behold, your reward is great in heaven: for in the like manner did their fathers unto the prophets [Luke 6:23].**

This verse speaks about the reception of, and attitude toward, God's prophets by mankind. The true prophet speaks for God and is persecuted. The false prophet misrepresents God and is patronized by men.

The true prophet must have faith in God and maintain a quiet confidence which looks beyond the things which are seen to the things which are eternal. This is what keeps a man true to God.

Verses 20–22 speak about the poor, hungry and weak, who are hated, reproached, considered outcasts, and called evil. All you have to do is look back into the Old Testament to see that this is true. It is true today. The man who preaches the Word of God is going to have a rough time. If he does not have a rough time, something is wrong. The false prophets were (and *are*) rich and had plenty to eat. They could laugh and were considered good fellows. God has something to say to them.

> **But woe unto you that are rich! for ye have received your consolation.**
>
> **Woe unto you that are full! for ye shall hunger. Woe unto you that laugh now! for ye shall mourn and weep.**
>
> **Woe unto you, when all men shall speak well of you! for so did their fathers to the false prophets.**
>
> **But I say unto you which hear, Love your enemies, do good to them which hate you,**
>
> **Bless them that curse you, and pray for them which despitefully use you [Luke 6:24–28].**

We find that the false prophet is patronized by the world, and if he will say the right thing, the world will pay him well. The Lord Jesus Christ makes it clear, however, that he needn't expect God to pay him. The false prophet may become popular with the world, but he will be notorious with God. He may have a lot of fun on earth, but he will cause heaven to weep. He may be well fed, but he has a starved soul.

Very little is said today about the godless rich. The Lord had a great deal to say about the godless rich in Scripture: "Woe unto you that are rich! for ye have received your consolation." Everyone seems to be after the poor criminal who stole $25.00, or a suit of clothes, or a

$50.00 ring. The godless poor, however, are not nearly as dangerous as the godless rich. The godless rich give glamour to godlessness. There is probably more hypocrisy among the rich than any other group. They will pay a false prophet to preach in their church—they own the church and the property. No rich church has the reputation of being an evangelical church; the gospel will not be preached there. There may be a few exceptions to this, but if there are, I do not know about them.

In New York City there is a church that bears the name of a rich man. The church will not have a gospel minister preach there because a gospel preacher would condemn this rich man just as James did when he said: "Go to now, ye rich men, weep and howl for your miseries that shall come upon you. Your riches are corrupted, and your garments are moth-eaten. Your gold and silver is cankered; and the rust of them shall be a witness against you, and shall eat your flesh as it were fire. Ye have heaped treasure together for the last days" (James 5:1–3).

I wonder when Christians in this country are going to wake up to the fact that these rich politicians are throwing crumbs from their tables down to the poor. They are not interested in the poor or in the rights of an individual. They want to be able to keep their riches and enjoy them in selfishness, and they are willing to give a few crumbs to the poor in order to do it. As far as civil rights go, I am not concerned about the color of a man's skin but about the color of his heart. Has his heart been washed in the blood of the Lord Jesus Christ? If it has, then he is my brother. I am going to be living with him for eternity and I had better start learning to live with him now—and I am. A man's heart may be as black as ink and his skin white as snow, yet he is not my brother. I am sorry to have to say that, but it is true.

What I am saying may sound revolutionary, and it is, but it is what Jesus Christ said, friend. There are those who tell me that they are following Jesus. They do not dare to follow Him. Read what He says in this chapter and, believe me, it will remove the cloak of hypocrisy and peel off the skin of any man. Try on the Sermon on the Plain for size and find out if you are keeping it.

And as ye would that men should do to you, do ye also to them likewise.

For if ye love them which love you, what thank have ye? for sinners also love those that love them.

And if ye do good to them which do good to you, what thank have ye? for sinners also do even the same.

And if ye lend to them of whom ye hope to receive, what thank have ye? for sinners also lend to sinners, to receive as much again.

But love ye your enemies, and do good, and lend, hoping for nothing again; and your reward shall be great, and ye shall be the children of the Highest: for he is kind unto the unthankful and to the evil.

Be ye therefore merciful, as your Father also is merciful.

Judge not, and ye shall not be judged: condemn not, and ye shall not be condemned: forgive, and ye shall be forgiven:

Give, and it shall be given unto you; good measure, pressed down, and shaken together, and running over, shall men give into your bosom. For with the same measure that ye mete withal it shall be measured to you again.

And he spake a parable unto them, Can the blind lead the blind? Shall they not both fall into the ditch?

The disciple is not above his master: but every one that is perfect shall be as his master.

And why beholdest thou the mote that is in thy brother's eye, but perceivest not the beam that is in thine own eye?

Either how canst thou say to thy brother, Brother, let me pull out the mote that is in thine eye, when thou thyself

> beholdest not the beam that is in thine own eye? Thou
> hypocrite, cast out first the beam out of thine own eye,
> and then shalt thou see clearly to pull out the mote that
> is in thy brother's eye.
>
> For a good tree bringeth not forth corrupt fruit; neither
> doth a corrupt tree bring forth good fruit.
>
> For every tree is known by his own fruit. For of thorns
> men do not gather figs, nor of a bramble bush gather
> they grapes.
>
> A good man out of the good treasure of his heart
> bringeth forth that which is good; and an evil man out
> of the evil treasure of his heart bringeth forth that which
> is evil: for of the abundance of the heart his mouth
> speaketh.
>
> And why call ye me, Lord, Lord, and do not the things
> which I say? [Luke 6:31–46].

The minister of a church who is seeking popularity does not dare mention sin. Some use the gyration of psychoanalysis to explain away the exceeding sinfulness of sin. It is called a relic of a theological jungle. Sin is not a crime against God, according to many modern preachers. They are afraid to say that God hates sin and that Jehovah is a Man of War.

To be right in God's sight you cannot compliment the ego, pat the pride, smile upon sin, and put cold cream on the cancer of sin. You cannot write a prescription on philosophy and have it filled in the pleasures of the world. The only place you can go is to the foot of the cross. There God performs an operation, major surgery, and makes you a new creature in Christ Jesus. That is the message we have in the Sermon on the Plain. It complements the Sermon on the Mount. It is a message the Lord gave many times to many different groups of people.

The Lord concludes this with a parable.

> Whosoever cometh to me, and heareth my sayings, and doeth them, I will shew you to whom he is like:
>
> He is like a man which built an house, and digged deep, and laid the foundation on a rock: and when the flood arose, the stream beat vehemently upon that house, and could not shake it: for it was founded upon a rock.
>
> But he that heareth, and doeth not, is like a man that without a foundation built an house upon the earth; against which the stream did beat vehemently, and immediately it fell; and the ruin of that house was great [Luke 6:47–49].

The house that was built on the rock—stood. The house that was built on the sand was absolutely washed away.

This chapter reveals to me that I am a sinner before God, and it almost takes my skin off! There is a Rock, though, upon which I can build a foundation that will stand. That Rock is Christ Jesus. Paul said, "For other foundation can no man lay than that is laid, which is Jesus Christ" (1 Cor. 3:11). My friend, where are you building your foundation? Where is your house? Is it built on the Rock which is Christ Jesus, or is it built on sand?

If you can read the Sermon on the Plain and not see that you are a lost and hell-doomed sinner, I feel sorry for you. I feel sorry for the poor rich man who has not heard the gospel. Whoever will may get on the Solid Rock which is Christ. He will save without money and without price. Come to Him in simple faith, and trust Him.

CHAPTER 7

*THEME: Jesus heals the centurion's servant; Jesus re-
stores to life the son of the widow of Nain; Jesus commends John the Baptist; Jesus goes to dinner at a
Pharisee's house; Jesus gives parable of two debtors*

This chapter opens with another meticulous record of healing. In
this case it is the centurion's servant. Although Jesus had no personal contact with the servant, he was made well.

Dr. Luke alone records the raising from the dead of the son of the
widow of Nain. He is the only Gospel writer who records Jesus raising
from the dead two persons (the other was Jairus' daughter, Luke
8:54–55).

Also in this chapter is the first of eighteen parables that Luke alone
records. It grew out of Jesus' visit to the home of a Pharisee where a
woman anointed His feet with ointment. The simple parable of the
two debtors revealed that this woman of the street was better than Simon, the Pharisee.

JESUS HEALS THE CENTURION'S SERVANT

**Now when he had ended all his sayings in the audience
of the people, he entered into Capernaum.**

**And a certain centurion's servant, who was dear unto
him, was sick, and ready to die.**

**And when he heard of Jesus, he sent unto him the elders
of the Jews, beseeching him that he would come and
heal his servant.**

**And when they came to Jesus, they besought him in-
stantly, saying, That he was worthy for whom he should
do this:**

For he loveth our nation, and he hath built us a synagogue.

Then Jesus went with them. And when he was now not far from the house, the centurion sent friends to him, saying unto him, Lord, trouble not thyself: for I am not worthy that thou shouldest enter under my roof:

Wherefore neither thought I myself worthy to come unto thee: but say in a word, and my servant shall be healed.

For I also am a man set under authority, having under me soldiers, and I say unto one, Go, and he goeth; and to another, Come, and he cometh; and to my servant, Do this, and he doeth it.

When Jesus heard these things, he marvelled at him, and turned him about, and said unto the people that followed him, I say unto you, I have not found so great faith, no, not in Israel.

And they that were sent, returning to the house, found the servant whole that had been sick [Luke 7:1–10].

There were many Roman soldiers in this city. A centurion was a Roman officer who commanded one hundred men. Apparently this officer was a man of faith. His love for the Jewish nation was evidenced by his building a synagogue for them at Capernaum. In his position he was an officer with authority. He could say to a soldier, "Do this," or "Go there," and the soldier would obey. He recognized that Jesus had that kind of power and that He had only to speak the word in order that his servant might be healed. Jesus marveled at the faith of this man. It is recorded that only on two occasions Jesus marveled. He marveled at the faith of the centurion and at the unbelief of Israel.

JESUS RESTORES TO LIFE THE SON OF THE WIDOW OF NAIN

And it came to pass the day after, that he went into a city

called Nain; and many of his disciples went with him, and much people.

Now when he came nigh to the gate of the city, behold, there was a dead man carried out, the only son of his mother, and she was a widow: and much people of the city was with her.

And when the Lord saw her, he had compassion on her, and said unto her, Weep not.

And he came and touched the bier: and they that bare him stood still. And he said, Young man, I say unto thee, Arise.

And he that was dead sat up, and began to speak. And he delivered him to his mother.

And there came a fear on all: and they glorified God, saying, That a great prophet is risen up among us; and, That God hath visited his people [Luke 7:11–16].

Only Dr. Luke records this incident. It concerns a restoration to life or, as some would call it, a resurrection. The instances recorded of Jesus raising people from the dead technically are not resurrections as we think of them. All the Lord did was restore life back into old bodies. Tradition says that after the Lord raised Lazarus from the dead, Lazarus asked Him if he would have to die again. Our Lord told him he would have to die again, and Lazarus never smiled from that day on. Whether or not that tradition is accurate, I can imagine that going through the doorway of death once would be enough!

Up to this day only one Person has been raised from the dead in resurrection, and that is the Lord Jesus Christ. He is the firstfruits of them that sleep. He is the only one raised from the dead in a glorified body. One of these days, in the event we call the Rapture, the dead in Christ and the living believers will be changed into resurrected and glorified bodies, and will be caught up to be with the Lord. That resurrected body will never die.

The account of the dead son of the widow of Nain is indeed sad. He was the *only* son of a widowed mother which made his death twice as tragic. While passing through the village of Nain, the Lord met the funeral procession. Someone has said that He broke up every funeral He met. I am of the opinion that He raised from the dead more than the three people who are recorded in the Bible. These three instances are examples, probably from three age groups: a child, a young man, and an adult man.

Jesus raised this young man from the dead for the sake of this lonely mother. He had compassion for this woman and her situation. He touched the casket in which the young man lay and spoke to him. He always used the same method in raising people from the dead. He spoke directly to them. Also at the Rapture, it will be His voice. Scripture tells us, "For the Lord himself shall descend from heaven with a shout, with the voice of the archangel, and with the trump of God: and the dead in Christ shall rise first: Then we which are alive and remain shall be caught up together with them in the clouds, to meet the Lord in the air: and so shall we ever be with the Lord" (1 Thess. 4:16–17). He is coming for us with a shout. His voice will be like the voice of the archangel and the trump of God. His one solo voice will call His own back from the dead. He always used the same method in restoring life. He did not, however, use the same method in other miracles. But to raise the dead He always spoke directly to them.

JESUS COMMENDS JOHN THE BAPTIST

At this juncture John the Baptist sent some of his disciples to the Lord Jesus to ask a few questions because John was puzzled.

> **And John calling unto him two of his disciples sent them to Jesus, saying, Art thou he that should come? or look we for another?**

> **When the men were come unto him, they said, John Baptist hath sent us unto thee, saying, Art thou he that should come? or look we for another? [Luke 7:19–20].**

We have met John the Baptist before in Matthew and Mark. His dress was quite picturesque and unusual. There are those today who adopt a peculiar dress which may indicate a religious crank or a religious nut. While it is true that John the Baptist used an unusual dress, that is not what made him unusual. It was his message and ministry that set him apart. He was called of God—and we had better be sure we are called of God if we are going to wear religious garb. Many people think that by adopting the outward trappings of Christianity they will become Christians.

Not long ago a young woman was in front of our radio headquarters, taking a survey, and asked me what my occupation was. I told her that I was a minister and then asked her what a person had to do to become a Christian. She replied that to be a Christian you had to be good to your neighbors, not criticize anyone, and be friendly rather than harsh. She went on with quite a list of things that one should do to become a Christian. I told her, "You think Christianity is something you do on the outside. It is not. Christianity is a personal relationship with Jesus Christ. It is more than trying to imitate Christ, or wearing certain religious garb. You must be born again. To be a Christian means to have an experience with Christ. 'If any man be in Christ, he is a new creation'" (see 2 Cor. 5:17).

John the Baptist seems to be misplaced in the New Testament; he does not belong in the New Testament at all. He is the last of the illustrious Old Testament prophets. He is the bridge over the yawning chasm between the Old and New Testaments. He ranks with such notables as Samuel, Elijah, Isaiah, and Jeremiah. Christ told that generation to whom He preached, "Woe unto you, scribes and Pharisees, hypocrites! because ye build the tombs of the prophets, and garnish the sepulchres of the righteous, And say, If we had been in the days of our fathers, we would not have been partakers with them in the blood of the prophets. Wherefore ye be witnesses unto yourselves, that ye are the children of them which killed the prophets" (Matt. 23:29–31). They proved themselves genuine children who inherited the nature of their fathers because John the Baptist, last of the Old Testament prophets, was at that time in prison, and his voice was soon to be silenced in death.

While John was in prison, doubt had captivated his mind.

There are those who try and give a psychological explanation for the question John the Baptist asked, "Art thou he that should come?" John was looking for the Messiah and wanted to know if Christ was the one. To try and psychologically explain it away is rather amusing. They say that because he was in prison, he was depressed, discouraged, and dejected. I don't believe a word of it. John had announced the Kingdom and denounced the nation. He had pronounced the coming of the King. He was a highway builder for the King. John identified the Messiah and said, "He shall baptize you with the Holy Ghost and with fire: Whose fan is in his hand, and he will thoroughly purge his floor, and will gather the wheat into his garner; but the chaff he will burn with fire unquenchable" (Luke 3:16–17). This is strong language. John was not expecting a Sunday school picnic. John was expecting Christ to establish the Kingdom in all of its glory and power. Since this had not happened, John sent some of his disciples to ask if Christ was the One they were looking for, or were they to look for another?

Notice that the Lord Jesus received the messengers cordially, but He kept them waiting.

> **And in that same hour he cured many of their infirmities and plagues, and of evil spirits; and unto many that were blind he gave sight.**
>
> **Then Jesus answering said unto them, Go your way, and tell John what things ye have seen and heard; how that the blind see, the lame walk, the lepers are cleansed, the deaf hear, the dead are raised, to the poor the gospel is preached.**
>
> **And blessed is he, whosoever shall not be offended in me [Luke 7:21–23].**

Jesus kept John's disciples waiting while He performed many miracles so that they could go back to tell John that they had seen the fulfillment of prophecy concerning the Messiah. Isaiah 35:5–6 predicts His first coming: "Then the eyes of the blind shall be opened, and the ears of the deaf shall be unstopped. Then shall the lame man leap as an hart, and the tongue of the dumb sing. . . ." Jesus told John's disciples to tell him that they had seen the credentials of the Messiah. Actually John had fulfilled his mission. And Jesus realized that He was not moving as fast as John wanted Him to, but in the presence of intellectual difficulties, He is asking John to trust Him.

He is asking the same thing of you and me. He asks for our faith when we cannot understand. "For the preaching of the cross is to them that perish foolishness; but unto us which are saved it is the power of God" (1 Cor. 1:18). Doubts are not a sign that you are smart. On the contrary, they are a sign that you are very foolish and do not know everything. They signal the fact that you belong to a group which is perishing. Many learned professors sit in swivel chairs in dusty, musty libraries, far removed from life and human need, and write about the intellectual difficulties of accepting the Bible, the deity of Jesus Christ, and redemption by the blood of Christ. I believe the *Word of God,* friend, and I hope you do.

> **And when the messengers of John were departed, he began to speak unto the people concerning John, What went ye out into the wilderness for to see? A reed shaken with the wind?**
>
> **But what went ye out for to see? A man clothed in soft raiment? Behold, they which are gorgeously apparelled, and live delicately, are in kings' courts [Luke 7:24–25].**

Was John the Baptist a reed shaken with the wind? Indeed, he was not. John was rough and rugged. He was unshakable.

> **But what went ye out for to see? A prophet? Yea, I say unto you, and much more than a prophet.**
>
> **This is he, of whom it is written, Behold, I send my messenger before thy face, which shall prepare thy way before thee [Luke 7:26–27].**

This is a quotation from Malachi 3:1 and establishes John the Baptist as the forerunner of the Messiah.

> **For I say unto you, Among those that are born of women there is not a greater prophet than John the Baptist: but he that is least in the kingdom of God is greater than he.**
>
> **And all the people that heard him, and the publicans, justified God, being baptized with the baptism of John [Luke 7:28–29].**

This is a tremendous tribute that Jesus gives to John the Baptist.

> **But the Pharisees and lawyers rejected the counsel of God against themselves, being not baptized of him.**
>
> **And the Lord said, Whereunto then shall I liken the men of this generation? and to what are they like?**
>
> **They are like unto children sitting in the marketplace, and calling one to another, and saying, We have piped unto you, and ye have not danced; we have mourned to you, and ye have not wept [Luke 7:30–32].**

In other words, they were like a bunch of spoiled brats. A lot of folk are that way. I was a pastor for almost forty years, and a great deal of that time was spent as a wet nurse, burping spiritual babies—which is what these religious rulers were in Christ's day. The Lord said they were like children playing in a marketplace. One of the children says, "Let's play wedding." The others say, "No, that's too jolly." "Then let's play funeral." No, they don't want to play funeral because it is too sad. Our Lord said these petulant children were exactly like that religious generation. And I wonder if this is an accurate picture of the average church today.

> **For John the Baptist came neither eating bread nor drinking wine; and ye say, He hath a devil.**

> The Son of man is come eating and drinking; and ye say,
> Behold a gluttonous man, and a winebibber, a friend of
> publicans and sinners!
>
> But wisdom is justified of all her children [Luke 7:33–
> 35].

I hear people say, "I do not like that preacher because he is too intellectual, and his tone is monotonous." And the same folk say, "I do not like that preacher because he pounds the pulpit and yells at the top of his voice." The problem is not with these two types of preachers. The problem is with the spoiled baby who complains. That is what the Lord said in His day, and it is still applicable today.

JESUS GOES TO DINNER AT A PHARISEE'S HOUSE

> And one of the Pharisees desired him that he would eat
> with him. And he went into the Pharisee's house, and
> sat down to meat [Luke 7:36].

This is one of the notable occasions when the Lord Jesus Christ went out to dinner. When He went out to dinner, it was never a dull affair. Remember, He had been denouncing these Pharisees. He called them spoiled brats; so it is difficult to believe that the invitation to dinner from this Pharisee was a friendly one. The Pharisee invited Him to dinner so that he could spy on Him and find something wrong with Him.

> And, behold, a woman in the city, which was a sinner,
> when she knew that Jesus sat at meat in the Pharisee's
> house, brought an alabaster box of ointment,
>
> And stood at his feet behind him weeping, and began to
> wash his feet with tears, and did wipe them with the
> hairs of her head, and kissed his feet, and anointed
> them with the ointment.

Now when the Pharisee which had bidden him saw it, he spake within himself, saying, This man, if he were a prophet, would have known who and what manner of woman this is that toucheth him: for she is a sinner [Luke 7:37–39].

While Christ was in the home of the Pharisee, a woman came. She brought an alabaster box of ointment and entered the house of the Pharisee. When you had guests in that day, your neighbors had a perfect right to come in and stand along the wall or sit on their haunches and watch. They did not come to comment, only to watch. This woman came in and took her place behind the Lord Jesus. In those days they didn't sit on chairs at the table; they reclined on couches. So Jesus was reclining on a couch, with His feet sticking out in back, leaning on His arm, as He talked across the table to His host. As she stood by the feet of the Lord Jesus, weeping, because her sins had been forgiven, she began to wet His feet with tears and wipe His feet with the hairs of her head. Then she kissed His feet and anointed them with the costly ointment.

Now this old Pharisee would not have spoken to this type of woman on the street. He might have done business with her after dark when no one could see, but he would not have anything to do with a woman of her reputation during daylight hours. When he saw her wiping and kissing the Lord's feet, he thought, *He must not be a prophet or he would know the kind of woman she is and have nothing to do with her.*

JESUS GIVES PARABLE OF TWO DEBTORS

And Jesus answering said unto him, Simon, I have somewhat to say unto thee. And he saith, Master, say on.

There was a certain creditor which had two debtors: the one owed five hundred pence, and the other fifty.

And when they had nothing to pay, he frankly forgave them both. Tell me therefore, which of them will love him most?

> Simon answered and said, I suppose that he, to whom
> he forgave most. And he said unto him, Thou hast
> rightly judged [Luke 7:40–43].

Jesus said, "Simon, I want to talk to you." Simon said, "Go ahead."
This is one of the delightful parables Dr. Luke records. You can see
from the content of this story the direction the Lord Jesus is taking.

> And he turned to the woman, and said unto Simon,
> Seest thou this woman? I entered into thine house, thou
> gavest me no water for my feet: but she hath washed my
> feet with tears, and wiped them with the hairs of her
> head [Luke 7:44].

For the first time the Lord acknowledges this woman. He has not paid
a bit of attention to her up to this time, but now He turns and looks at
her. While He is looking at her, He says to Simon, who is on the other
side of the table, "Seest thou this woman?" Simon had already said
within himself that he did not think the Lord knew what kind of
woman she was or He would not have permitted her to touch Him.
Now our Lord says, "Simon, do you really know this woman? Look at
her. You think you see her but you do not at all." The Lord is really
rubbing this Pharisee the wrong way. This is the reason I believe that
the Lord was not invited to dinner as a friendly gesture, but so that the
Pharisee could spy upon Him. Now the Lord Jesus says:

> Thou gavest me no kiss: but this woman since the time I
> came in hath not ceased to kiss my feet.

> My head with oil thou didst not anoint: but this woman
> hath anointed my feet with ointment.

> Wherefore I say unto thee, Her sins, which are many,
> are forgiven; for she loved much: but to whom little is
> forgiven, the same loveth little.

> And he said unto her, Thy sins are forgiven [Luke
> 7:45–48].

The Lord is saying, "You did not even exercise the common courtesies of the day." The Lord declares he did not have good manners. If Simon had been the proper kind of host, he would have washed the Lord's feet. He would have anointed the Lord's head and kissed Him. That was the custom of the day, but Simon did none of these things. (Unfortunately, the same thing could be said about a lot of Christians; they may read Emily Post, but they do not have good manners.)

I wish I had been present at this dinner. Our Lord was tops as an after-dinner speaker! What he said blanched the soul of Simon. This poor woman from the streets, without hope, wanted forgiveness. The God of heaven is there and He has forgiven her. Now He tells Simon, "You have judged correctly. You said that the one who owed the most would naturally be the one who would love him most. Well, she was a great sinner and has been forgiven a whole lot. But you, because you don't think you are a sinner, have not even asked for forgiveness." And that hypocritical old Pharisee sat there—an unforgiven sinner.

And they that sat at meat with him began to say within themselves, Who is this that forgiveth sins also?

And he said to the woman, Thy faith hath saved thee; go in peace [Luke 7:49–50].

This is very pertinent for our day. If you are a church member and have never asked the Lord Jesus for forgiveness, you are lost. This woman did not have any good works to her credit, but she believed in the Lord, she trusted Christ, she asked for forgiveness.

CHAPTER 8

THEME: Jesus gives parables; parable of the sower; parable of the lighted candle; personal relationships; stills the storm; Jesus casts out demons at Gadara; Jesus heals woman with issue of blood; restores to life daughter of Jairus

JESUS GIVES PARABLES

As our Lord continued His ministry, many people were turning to Him, and some of them were officials in high places.

And it came to pass afterward, that he went throughout every city and village, preaching and shewing the glad tidings of the kingdom of God: and the twelve were with him,

And certain women, which had been healed of evil spirits and infirmities, Mary called Magdalene, out of whom went seven devils,

And Joanna the wife of Chuza Herod's steward, and Susanna, and many others, which ministered unto him of their substance [Luke 8:1–3].

PARABLE OF THE SOWER

And when much people were gathered together, and were come to him out of every city, he spake by a parable:

A sower went out to sow his seed: and as he sowed, some fell by the way side; and it was trodden down, and the fowls of the air devoured it.

And some fell upon a rock; and as soon as it sprung up, it withered away, because it lacked moisture.

And some fell among thorns; and the thorns sprang up with it, and choked it.

And other fell on good ground, and sprang up, and bare fruit an hundredfold. And when he had said these things, he cried, He that hath ears to hear, let him hear.

And his disciples asked him, saying, What might this parable be?

And he said, Unto you it is given to know the mysteries of the kingdom of God: but to others in parables; that seeing they might not see, and hearing they might not understand.

Now the parable is this: The seed is the word of God.

Those by the way side are they that hear; then cometh the devil, and taketh away the word out of their hearts, lest they should believe and be saved.

They on the rock are they, which, when they hear, receive the word with joy; and these have no root, which for a while believe, and in time of temptation fall away.

And that which fell among thorns are they, which, when they have heard, go forth, and are choked with cares and riches and pleasures of this life, and bring no fruit to perfection.

But that on the good ground are they, which in an honest and good heart, having heard the word, keep it, and bring forth fruit with patience [Luke 8:4–15].

The Sower is Jesus. The seed is His Word. The birds are a symbol of the Devil. The "rocky places" are those who receive the Word of God in the enthusiasm of the flesh. Trouble and persecution dampen the interest. For a time fleshly hearers of the Word manifest great interest and zeal, but a little trouble reveals their lack of true faith. Only some of the seeds falls on good ground and brings forth a full harvest. These are the hearers who are genuinely converted by the Word of God.

PARABLE OF THE LIGHTED CANDLE

No man, when he hath lighted a candle, covereth it with a vessel, or putteth it under a bed; but setteth it on a candlestick, that they which enter in may see the light.

For nothing is secret, that shall not be made manifest; neither any thing hid, that shall not be known and come abroad.

Take heed therefore how ye hear: for whosoever hath, to him shall be given; and whosoever hath not, from him shall be taken even that which he seemeth to have [Luke 8:16–18].

The parable of the candle is one of action. Light creates responsibility. A man who receives the truth must act. We are held responsible to the degree that light has been given us. The point is that you and I were in darkness until the light of the gospel got through to us. Sometimes we are given the impression that man is a sinner because of his weakness or because of his ignorance. But Paul says very candidly (see Rom. 1) that men, when they knew God, glorified Him not as God. Man is a willful sinner. That is the kind of sinners all of us are, and the light that comes in will create a responsibility. We come into this world lost, and if we do not accept the Light, who is Christ, we remain lost. We are held responsible for the light we have received.

PERSONAL RELATIONSHIPS

Then came to him his mother and his brethren, and could not come at him for the press.

And it was told him by certain which said, Thy mother
and thy brethren stand without, desiring to see thee.

And he answered and said unto them, My mother and
my brethren are these which hear the word of God, and
do it [Luke 8:19–21].

Christ is declaring a new relationship in this passage. He was not
denying His family relationship but was getting ready to declare one
infinitely deeper, higher, and more permanent, transcending by far
any blood relationship. This brings a believer mighty close to Him.

STILLS THE STORM

Now it came to pass on a certain day, that he went into a
ship with his disciples: and he said unto them, Let us go
over unto the other side of the lake. And they launched
forth.

But as they sailed he fell asleep: and there came down a
storm of wind on the lake; and they were filled with water, and were in jeopardy.

And they came to him, and awoke him, saying, Master,
master, we perish. Then he arose, and rebuked the wind
and the raging of the water: and they ceased, and there
was a calm.

And he said unto them, Where is your faith? And they
being afraid wondered, saying one to another, What
manner of man is this! for he commandeth even the
winds and water, and they obey him [Luke 8:22–25].

Jesus gave a command to cross the sea. An unordinary storm arose.
The intensity of the storm suggests the savagery of Satan. The Lord
went to sleep because He was weary—so weary that the violent storm
did not disturb Him. The disciples became frightened and felt that
everyone in the boat would perish. The storm did not disturb the

Lord, but the attitude of His disciples did. He rebuked the wind and the sea as one would speak to dogs on a leash. Literally His command was, "Be muzzled." The miracle lies in the fact that the wind ceased immediately, and the sea, which would have rolled for hours, instantly became as smooth as glass. How often He puts us in the storms of life in order that we might come closer to Him and learn what manner of Man He really is.

JESUS CASTS OUT DEMONS AT GADARA

Now our Lord arrives at Gadara where a maniac lived who was possessed by demons. Because of his profession Dr. Luke goes into this story more thoroughly than do the other writers.

> **And they arrived at the country of the Gadarenes, which is over against Galilee.**
>
> **And when he went forth to land, there met him out of the city a certain man, which had devils long time, and ware no clothes, neither abode in any house, but in the tombs [Luke 8:26–27].**

Apparently there were two demoniacs, and Luke selects only one for a definite purpose. Why? Luke is a doctor, and he is attempting to give an illustration. Concerning this matter of demons, there are those who think they belong to the category of ghosts, goblins, gnomes, sylvan satyrs, and stygian shades, fables and fairies. For many years the average Christian viewpoint on demons was that if they ever existed, they no longer exist today. However, I believe we are seeing a manifestation and resurgence of demon possession in our day. It is difficult to explain what is taking place in our contemporary society without believing in the existence of demons.

Dr. Luke treats demonism with remarkable insight from a doctor's viewpoint in a rather scientific way. Matthew's account of this story is matter-of-fact. Mark's account is more emotional and spectacular. Earlier in his Gospel Luke has dealt with demonism, making it clear that demonism, and diseases are different. Demon possession is just as real as cancer or leprosy. Demons disturb men physically, mentally, and spiritually. They can destroy the souls of men and be the eternal doom of men. Dr. Luke tells us in the next chapter that demons are synonymous with unclean spirits.

The case of the demon-possessed man at Gadara is one of the worst on record. There are some facts that we need to consider in connection with this account. The tribe of Gad inhabited the country of Gadara. This tribe did not cross over the river Jordan with Joshua when Israel inhabited the land. This man who was demon-possessed wore no clothes. I think there is a relationship between nudity and demon possession. He did not dwell in a house like normal people, but he dwelt among the tombs and caves. The personality of this man was degraded, debased, and destroyed. He had no will of his own; he was in the possession of demons.

> **When he saw Jesus, he cried out, and fell down before him, and with a loud voice said, What have I to do with thee, Jesus, thou Son of God most high? I beseech thee, torment me not.**

> **(For he had commanded the unclean spirit to come out of the man. For oftentimes it had caught him: and he was kept bound with chains and in fetters; and he brake the bands, and was driven of the devil into the wilderness.) [Luke 8:28–29].**

The demon recognized Jesus. James tells us, "Thou believest that there is one God; thou doest well: the devils also believe, and tremble" (James 2:19). Demons are the enemies of God, and they are going to be judged.

What is the origin of demons? We cannot be dogmatic. The physical world has something in it that cannot be seen—it is the atom. They exist and have made an impact on our day and generation. Likewise in the spiritual world there are certain things we cannot see. Angels are real, but we cannot see them. There are two classes of angels: those that are with God and serve Him and those that fell with Satan at the beginning. Homer speaks of *daimon* and *Theos* as being synonymous. Hesiod, a Greek philosopher, says that all demons are good, while another Greek philosopher, Empedocles, declares that demons are both bad and good. Behind all idolatry and ancient religions was demonism.

Demons control a man so that he cannot do what he wants to do. Demons cause people to do frightful and terrifying acts. They cause people to perform soul-destroying acts. They cause mothers to kill their children, husbands to kill their wives, and children to kill their parents. People commit senseless acts, and they do not know why they do such terrible things. These things are happening in our day, and mankind is blaming everything but demons as the cause.

> **And Jesus asked him, saying, What is thy name? And he said, Legion: because many devils were entered into him.**
>
> **And they besought him that he would not command them to go out into the deep.**
>
> **And there was there an herd of many swine feeding on the mountain: and they besought him that he would suffer them to enter into them. And he suffered them.**
>
> **Then went the devils out of the man, and entered into the swine: and the herd ran violently down a steep place into the lake, and were choked [Luke 8:30–33].**

This man was not possessed by *one* demon but by a legion of demons. There are three thousand to six thousand men in a Roman legion of soldiers. The word *legion* was used like the word *mob*. There was a *mob* of demons in this man, and they did not want to go "out into the deep." That "deep" is the bottomless pit, or the abyss, where the other fallen angels are incarcerated. Jude tells us about it in Jude 6: "And the angels which kept not their first estate, but left their own habitation, he hath reserved in everlasting chains under darkness unto the judgment of the great day." Demons want to inhabit the body of a person. When a demon is cast out of a person, he will wander around and come back to try to enter that person again; or, if he cannot gain entrance, he will go to another person. He does not want to be without a body. When the Lord cast the demons out of this man, they were willing to go into the bodies of the swine rather than go into the abyss. Notice that the pigs would rather be dead than have the demons indwell them!

> **When they that fed them saw what was done, they fled, and went and told it in the city and in the country.**
>
> **Then they went out to see what was done; and came to Jesus, and found the man, out of whom the devils were departed, sitting at the feet of Jesus, clothed, and in his right mind: and they were afraid.**
>
> **They also which saw it told them by what means he that was possessed of the devils was healed [Luke 8:34–36].**

A marvelous transformation had taken place in this man. Only Christ can deliver from the power of Satan. We are seeing a resurgence of demonism in our day. It is a frightful, ugly thing, and we need to call upon God for help.

> **Then the whole multitude of the country of the Gadarenes round about besought him to depart from them; for they were taken with great fear: and he went up into the ship, and returned back again.**
>
> **Now the man out of whom the devils were departed besought him that he might be with him: but Jesus sent him away, saying,**
>
> **Return to thine own house, and shew how great things God hath done unto thee. And he went his way and published throughout the whole city how great things Jesus had done unto him.**

> And it came to pass, that, when Jesus was returned, the
> people gladly received him: for they were all waiting for
> him [Luke 8:37–40].

It is startling to read that the people of Gadara came and asked the
Lord Jesus to leave their coasts. The reason was that they would rather
have the swine than have *Him*. That's a rather heart-searching question for the present day because there are a lot of people who would
rather have other things—which are just as bad as pigs—than to have
Christ!

JESUS HEALS WOMAN WITH ISSUE OF BLOOD; RESTORES TO LIFE DAUGHTER OF JAIRUS

When Jesus returned to the other side of the Sea of Galilee, crowds
gathered around Him. There were two desperate people in the crowd.

> And, behold, there came a man named Jairus, and he
> was a ruler of the synagogue: and he fell down at Jesus'
> feet, and besought him that he would come into his
> house:
>
> For he had one only daughter, about twelve years of age,
> and she lay a dying. But as he went the people thronged
> him.
>
> And a woman having an issue of blood twelve years,
> which had spent all her living upon physicians, neither
> could be healed of any,
>
> Came behind him, and touched the border of his gar-
> ment: and immediately her issue of blood stanched
> [Luke 8:41–44].

Jairus came to get Jesus to heal his daughter, not to raise her from the
dead. His faith was small, but his situation was desperate. He believed
that Jesus would have to touch her. As Jesus began to deal with Jairus,
He was interrupted by the woman with the issue of blood. The woman

had been suffering with the affliction for twelve years. The daughter of Jairus was twelve years old. Twelve years of darkness were ending and twelve years of light were fading.

> **And Jesus said, Who touched me? When all denied, Peter and they that were with him said, Master, the multitude throng thee and press thee, and sayest thou, Who touched me?**

> **And Jesus said, Somebody hath touched me: for I perceive that virtue is gone out of me.**

> **And when the woman saw that she was not hid, she came trembling, and falling down before him, she declared unto him before all the people for what cause she had touched him, and how she was healed immediately.**

> **And he said unto her, Daughter, be of good comfort: thy faith hath made thee whole; go in peace [Luke 8:45–48].**

Jesus did not touch the woman; she touched Him and was healed instantly. Remember that a crowd was all about Jesus. The disciples, seeing the crowd pressing in on Him, knew that He was being touched by scores of people; yet only the woman was healed.

> **While he yet spake, there cometh one from the ruler of the synagogue's house, saying to him, Thy daughter is dead; trouble not the Master.**

> **But when Jesus heard it, he answered him, saying, Fear not: believe only, and she shall be made whole.**

> **And when he came into the house, he suffered no man to go in, save Peter, and James, and John, and the father and the mother of the maiden [Luke 8:49–51].**

When they reached the home of Jairus, the paid mourners had already gone to work. They stopped weeping long enough to laugh at Jesus in their disbelief.

And all wept, and bewailed her: but he said, Weep not; she is not dead, but sleepeth.

And they laughed him to scorn, knowing that she was dead [Luke 8:52-53].

The Lord took Peter, James, John, and the father and mother of the girl inside with Him to where the little girl lay. Dr. Luke tells us that He spoke to the little girl in this lovely fashion, "Maid, arise." It could be translated, "Little lamb, wake up." The child arose. He brought her back to a world of suffering for the sake of her parents, not for her sake.

And he put them all out, and took her by the hand, and called, saying, Maid, arise.

And her spirit came again, and she arose straightway: and he commanded to give her meat.

And her parents were astonished: but he charged them that they should tell no man what was done [Luke 8:54-56].

My friend, notice again that the method Jesus uses in raising the dead is always the same. He calls them and they hear His voice! Once again our Lord demonstrated that He is indeed God.

CHAPTER 9

THEME: Jesus commissions and sends forth the Twelve; Jesus feeds the five thousand; Jesus announces His death and resurrection; transfigured; Jesus casts out demons from an only son; Jesus sets His face toward Jerusalem; Jesus puts down test for discipleship

JESUS COMMISSIONS AND SENDS FORTH THE TWELVE

Then he called his twelve disciples together, and gave them power and authority over all devils, and to cure diseases [Luke 9:1].

When our Lord was here on earth, He gave the gift of healing to His apostles. It was one of the "sign" gifts. It served as the credential of the apostles—to demonstrate that they were who they claimed to be. When the church got under way (before the New Testament was in written form), the sign of an apostle was the fact that he had the "sign" gifts. Peter could heal the sick and raise the dead. Paul could heal the sick and raise the dead. To do this was proof that they were true apostles of the Lord Jesus Christ.

Jesus sent His disciples out to preach the Kingdom of God and to heal the sick. This took place *before* He died upon the Cross. Today the important thing is not healing. If you will read the Epistles carefully, you will see that even though Paul had the gift of healing, toward the end of his ministry he apparently did not exercise it at all. He told Timothy to take a little wine for his stomach's sake (see 1 Tim. 5:23) but did not heal him. Paul himself had a ". . . thorn in the flesh . . ." (2 Cor. 12:7), and though he asked God to remove it, God did not remove it. Also he wrote to Timothy, ". . . Trophimus have I left at Miletum sick" (2 Tim. 4:20). Why did not Paul heal his friend Trophimus?

Paul, you see, had come to the end of his ministry, and the sign gifts even then were beginning to disappear from the church. Apparently when Scripture became a part of the church, the gift of healing passed from the scene. Authority moved from a *person* to the *page* of Scripture, the Word of God. Toward the end of his life John warned that correct doctrine was a man's credential. "If there come any unto you, and bring not this *doctrine*, receive him not into your house, neither bid him God speed" (2 John 10, italics mine). Paul said, "But though we, or an angel from heaven, preach any other gospel unto you than that which we have preached unto you, let him be accursed" (Gal. 1:8). The word *accursed* is the Greek word *anathema* and means "damned." That is very strong language which places absolute authority in the Scriptures.

> **And he sent them to preach the kingdom of God, and to heal the sick.**
>
> **And he said unto them, Take nothing for your journey, neither staves, nor scrip, neither bread, neither money; neither have two coats apiece [Luke 9:2–3].**

Some people use this passage as a basis for their ministry today. Watch such a preacher, and see if he takes an offering. See if he takes anything with him when he goes on a journey—scrip (which means a suitcase), food, or money. Our Lord gave these instructions to His twelve disciples, not to us.

> **And whatsoever house ye enter into, there abide, and thence depart [Luke 9:4].**

Of course today the laborer is worthy of his hire. I feel that any man who is giving out the Word of God should be supported. In the days of Christ the situation was different. The disciples had to stay in private homes because there were no Holiday Inns or Hilton Hotels. All entertaining was done in private homes.

> And whosoever will not receive you, when ye go out of
> that city, shake off the very dust from your feet for a tes-
> timony against them [Luke 9:5].

The impact of their ministry affected even Herod.

> Now Herod the tetrarch heard of all that was done by
> him: and he was perplexed, because that it was said of
> some, that John was risen from the dead;
>
> And of some, that Elias had appeared; and of others,
> that one of the old prophets was risen again.
>
> And Herod said, John have I beheaded: but who is this,
> of whom I hear such things? And he desired to see him
> [Luke 9:7–9].

Herod was the ruler who had been responsible for the imprisonment
and execution of John the Baptist. Mark tells us that Herod was afraid
Jesus was John the Baptist come back to life. The curiosity of Herod
caused him to want to see Jesus.

> And the apostles, when they were returned, told him all
> that they had done. And he took them, and went aside
> privately into a desert place belonging to the city called
> Bethsaida.
>
> And the people, when they knew it, followed him: and
> he received them, and spake unto them of the kingdom
> of God, and healed them that had need of healing [Luke
> 9:10–11].

This furnishes the setting for feeding the five thousand. He had taken
them aside to rest—but there was no opportunity for that. Certainly
the crowd was inconsiderate; yet our Lord graciously received them—
taught them and healed those who were ill.

JESUS FEEDS THE FIVE THOUSAND

They put themselves in the unlovely position of being advisors of Christ—telling Him what to do. Unfortunately, many of us are guilty of doing this today. Friend, He doesn't need our suggestions.

> **And when the day began to wear away, then came the twelve, and said unto him, Send the multitude away, that they may go into the towns and country round about, and lodge, and get victuals: for we are here in a desert place.**
>
> **But he said unto them, Give ye them to eat. And they said, We have no more but five loaves and two fishes; except we should go and buy meat for all this people [Luke 9:12–13].**

Now they become financial advisors, economic experts.

> **For they were about five thousand men. And he said to his disciples, Make them sit down by fifties in a company.**
>
> **And they did so, and made them all sit down [Luke 9:14–15].**

At last they are in their rightful place, obeying Christ.

> **Then he took the five loaves and the two fishes, and looking up to heaven, he blessed them, and brake, and gave to the disciples to set before the multitude.**
>
> **And they did eat, and were all filled: and there was taken up of fragments that remained to them twelve baskets [Luke 9:16–17].**

Matthew, Mark, and John also record the feeding of five thousand. Notice that our Lord assigns His disciples an impossible task. They must learn, as we must learn, that He always commands the impossible. The reason is obvious—He intends to do the work. The Creator, who made the fish in the beginning and causes the grain to multiply in the fields, now by His fiat word creates food for the crowd. This may have been the first time many in this crowd ever were filled. The "fragments" which were left do not refer to what we might put in the garbage can. Rather, they were pieces of food which had not been served. God always provides a surplus.

JESUS ANNOUNCES HIS DEATH
AND RESURRECTION

And it came to pass, as he was alone praying, his disciples were with him: and he asked them, saying, Whom say the people that I am?

They answering said, John the Baptist; but some say, Elias; and others say, that one of the old prophets is risen again.

He said unto them, But whom say ye that I am? Peter answering said, The Christ of God.

And he straitly charged them, and commanded them to tell no man that thing [Luke 9:18–21].

The important question here is, who is Jesus? Jesus wanted to know men's estimate of Him. I am sure His purpose in asking this question of them was to crystalize in their thinking who He actually was. There was much confusion regarding His person. Notice that all opinions were high, but all fell short of who He was and is. The finest thing Peter ever said was, ". . . Thou art the Christ, the Son of the living God" (see Matt. 16:16 for his entire statement).

> **Saying, The Son of man must suffer many things, and
> be rejected of the elders and chief priests and scribes,
> and be slain, and be raised the third day [Luke 9:22].**

Again Jesus prepares them for His approaching death. But notice that
He never mentions His death without also mentioning His resurrection.

> **And he said to them all, If any man will come after me,
> let him deny himself, and take up his cross daily, and
> follow me.**
>
> **For whosoever will save his life shall lose it: but whoso-
> ever will lose his life for my sake, the same shall save it.**
>
> **For what is a man advantaged, if he gain the whole
> world, and lose himself, or be cast away?**
>
> **For whosoever shall be ashamed of me and of my words,
> of him shall the Son of man be ashamed, when he shall
> come in his own glory, and in his Father's, and of the
> holy angels [Luke 9:23–26].**

Here He is not putting down a condition of salvation but stating the
position of those who are saved. This is what He is talking about.
"Whosoever shall be ashamed of me and of my words, of him shall the
Son of man be ashamed." What kind of Christian are you today? Are
you one who acknowledges Him and serves Him and attempts to glorify Him? My friend, this is all important in these days in which we
live.

TRANSFIGURED

In dealing with the Transfiguration, Dr. Luke adds something that the
other Gospel writers leave out.

> But I tell you of a truth, there be some standing here, which shall not taste of death, till they see the kingdom of God [Luke 9:27].

Simon Peter interprets this verse for us. He said that he saw the Kingdom. Where did he see it? Peter was with the Lord on the holy mount and was an eyewitness of it. He tells us about it in 2 Peter 1:16–18 which says, "For we have not followed cunningly devised fables, when we made known unto you the power and coming of our Lord Jesus Christ, but were eyewitnesses of his majesty. For he received from God the Father honour and glory, when there came such a voice to him from the excellent glory, This is my beloved Son, in whom I am well pleased. And this voice which came from heaven we heard, when we were with him in the holy mount." This is the explanation Simon Peter gives, and that is good enough for me. I think the man who was there ought to know more about it than some of these modern scholars who were not present.

> And it came to pass about an eight days after these sayings, he took Peter and John and James, and went up into a mountain to pray [Luke 9:28].

The Lord took Peter, James, and John up into a mountain to pray. While He prayed, the Lord's countenance was "transfigured"—this word is from the Greek *metamorphoom—metamorphosis* in English. That which took place is like the experience of the caterpillar; first you have the caterpillar, then it encases itself in the cocoon, and out comes a beautiful butterfly. The Transfiguration does not set forth the deity of Christ, but the humanity of Christ. Transfiguration is the goal of humanity. When you see the Lord Jesus Christ transfigured there on the mount, you are seeing exactly what is going to take place in that day when we are translated. The dead shall be raised, and those who are alive shall be *changed;* that is, they shall undergo metamorphosis. Then they will all be translated and brought into the presence of God.

And as he prayed, the fashion of his countenance was altered, and his raiment was white and glistering [Luke 9:29].

This verse does not mean that a light, as a spotlight, shone on Him, but that a light came from within His body and shone outwardly. Some people ask the silly question, "Are you going to wear clothes in heaven?" I think we will, but I do not believe we will need them because we will be clothed in this glory-light such as clothed our Lord.

And behold, there talked with him two men, which were Moses and Elias:

Who appeared in glory, and spake of his decease which he should accomplish at Jerusalem [Luke 9:30–31].

Two men appeared on the mount: Moses, the representative of the Law, and Elijah, the representative of the prophets, and they were bearing witness to Him. What did they talk about? They spoke about the approaching death of Christ. Paul says that the gospel he preached was one to which both the Law and prophets bore testimony. The gospel is *not* contrary to the Old Testament at all. Paul put it like this: "But now the righteousness of God without the law is manifested, being witnessed by the law and the prophets" (Rom. 3:21). The Law and the prophets reveal that the *only* way God could save us is through the righteousness that we obtain by faith. In the Old Testament this was done by bringing a sacrifice. The sacrificial system was the very heart of the Mosaic system. That little lamb that was offered on the altar is symbolic of Christ who died for our sins. And the prophets spoke of the Lamb of God that would take away the sin of the world.

But Peter and they that were with him were heavy with sleep: and when they were awake, they saw his glory, and the two men that stood with him.

> And it came to pass, as they departed from him, Peter
> said unto Jesus, Master, it is good for us to be here: and
> let us make three tabernacles; one for thee, and one for
> Moses, and one for Elias: not knowing what he said
> [Luke 9:32–33].

Good old Simon Peter just has to say something. He should have kept his mouth closed at this time, but he has to speak up, and I guess he thinks he is saying something important. But Luke adds, "not knowing what he said." Many people, like Peter, speak pious words without knowing what they say. Peter suggests they build three tabernacles, which puts Moses and Elijah on a par with Jesus Christ, although he puts the Lord at the head of the list. Many anthologies of religion list Buddha, Mohammed, Moses, and Christ as founders of religion. It may seem strange to you, but Jesus Christ is not the founder of any religion. He did not found a religion; He died on a cross for the sins of the world. He is the *Savior*, and that is why we are not saved by religion; we are saved by Christ. I remember Dr. Carrol said many times, "When I came to Christ, I lost my religion." A great many people need to lose their religion and find Christ.

> While he thus spake, there came a cloud, and overshad-
> owed them: and they feared as they entered into the
> cloud.
>
> And there came a voice out of the cloud, saying, This is
> my beloved Son: hear him.
>
> And when the voice was past, Jesus was found alone.
> And they kept it close, and told no man in those days
> any of those things which they had seen [Luke 9:34–36].

CASTS OUT DEMONS FROM AN ONLY SON

> And it came to pass, that on the next day, when they
> were come down from the hill, much people met him.

And, behold, a man of the company cried out, saying, Master, I beseech thee, look upon my son: for he is mine only child.

And, lo, a spirit taketh him, and he suddenly crieth out: and it teareth him that he foameth again, and bruising him hardly departeth from him.

And I besought thy disciples to cast him out; and they could not.

And Jesus answering said, O faithless and perverse generation, how long shall I be with you, and suffer you? Bring thy son hither.

And as he was yet a-coming, the devil threw him down, and tare him. And Jesus rebuked the unclean spirit, and healed the child, and delivered him again to his father.

And they were all amazed at the mighty power of God. But while they wondered every one at all things which Jesus did, he said unto his disciples [Luke 9:37–43].

This entire scene is a picture of today. Jesus has passed on into the glory. His disciples are with Him. We are down here in this world at the foot of the mountain where there is confusion, compromise, and impotence. The world today acts like a demon-possessed man, and the church is helpless in the presence of the world's need. When Jesus spoke to the crowd, He rebuked them for their lack of faith concerning this boy, and apparently the disciples and skeptics were included.

The condition of this boy was pitiful. Jesus turned to the father and asked him to believe. The father made a desperate plea for faith, the other Gospel writers tell us. The disciples were puzzled because they had cast out the demons previously but could not cast out this one. Our Lord confirms that this case was different because of its seriousness. The Lord rebuked the demon, healed the child, and delivered him to his father. The process of casting out the demon revealed again the seriousness of the case.

JESUS SETS HIS FACE TOWARD JERUSALEM

After delivering the demon-possessed boy, the Lord and His disciples head for Jerusalem. Once again our Lord speaks about His impending death.

> **Let these sayings sink down into your ears: for the Son of man shall be delivered into the hands of men.**
>
> **But they understood not this saying, and it was hid from them, that they perceived it not: and they feared to ask him of that saying [Luke 9:44–45].**

They didn't quite understand this matter of being raised from the dead. Here He is talking about His own death for them, and you would think that these men might have at least made some inquiry.

> **Then there arose a reasoning among them, which of them should be greatest [Luke 9:46].**

After the Transfiguration you would think they would be humbled and obedient to His will. On the contrary, they became ambitious. They were thinking of the crown and ignored the cross. They were desirous of vainglory. This has been the curse of His disciples from that day to this. It is one of the curses of the church. In Paul's letter to the Galatian Christians he wrote, "Let us not be desirous of vain glory, provoking one another, envying one another" (Gal. 5:26).

> **And Jesus, perceiving the thought of their heart, took a child, and set him by him,**
>
> **And said unto them, Whosoever shall receive this child in my name receiveth me: and whosoever shall receive me receiveth him that sent me: for he that is least among you all, the same shall be great [Luke 9:47–48].**

This is a great principle. It is my conviction that the greatest saints are the unknown folk in our churches who quietly and faithfully serve Him.

> **And John answered and said, Master, we saw one casting out devils in thy name; and we forbad him, because he followeth not with us.**

> **And Jesus said unto him, Forbid him not: for he that is not against us is for us.**

> **And it came to pass, when the time was come that he should be received up, he stedfastly set his face to go to Jerusalem,**

> **And sent messengers before his face: and they went, and entered into a village of the Samaritans, to make ready for him.**

> **And they did not receive him, because his face was as though he would go to Jerusalem [Luke 9:49–53].**

Notice the rejection by the Samaritans. We think of the "good" Samaritans because of the parable, but they were no more lovely than the Jews—both rejected Him.

> **And when his disciples James and John saw this, they said, Lord, wilt thou that we command fire to come down from heaven, and consume them, even as Elias did? [Luke 9:54].**

John is always thought of as a ladylike apostle, but notice his fiery disposition here.

> **But he turned, and rebuked them, and said, Ye know not what manner of spirit ye are of.**

> For the Son of man is not come to destroy men's lives, but
> to save them. And they went to another village [Luke
> 9:55–56].

Jesus rebukes any kind of sectarian spirit. What a stinging rebuke:
"The Son of man is not come to destroy men's lives, but to save." At
another occasion He said, "For the Son of man is come to seek and to
save that which was lost" (Luke 19:10). John entirely misunderstood
the purpose of Christ's first coming.

JESUS PUTS DOWN TEST FOR DISCIPLESHIP

In this section we see three applicants who want to become disciples
of the Lord Jesus. Notice this is not giving the way of salvation. The
question, ". . . what must I do to be saved?" (Acts 16:30), is not asked
here. Rather this is what is required to become a follower, a disciple of
Christ.

The first applicant is an impetuous and impulsive young man.

> And it came to pass, that, as they went in the way, a
> certain man said unto him, Lord, I will follow thee
> whithersoever thou goest.
>
> And Jesus said unto him, Foxes have holes, and birds of
> the air have nests; but the Son of man hath not where to
> lay his head [Luke 9:57–58].

Our Lord's answer to him revealed His own poverty when He was on
earth. When they traveled, there would be no reservations for them at
a motel. Poverty was part of the curse that He bore. Did the young man
follow Him? We are not told. I like to think that he did.

> And he said unto another, Follow me. But he said, Lord,
> suffer me first to go and bury my father.
>
> Jesus said unto him, Let the dead bury their dead: but go
> thou and preach the kingdom of God [Luke 9:59–60].

The next applicant had made a decision to follow the Lord Jesus, but he wanted to first bury his father. This verse has been greatly misunderstood. Jesus was not forbidding this boy to attend the funeral of his father. Rather, the boy is saying that he would have to take care of his father until he died. After his father was gone, he would be free to follow Jesus.

When it comes to discipleship, human affection takes second place to His will. When a conflict arises between human affections and Christ, He claims the first place. However, His will and human affection may not always conflict.

> **And another also said, Lord, I will follow thee; but let me first go bid them farewell, which are at home at my house.**
>
> **And Jesus said unto him, No man, having put his hand to the plough, and looking back, is fit for the kingdom of God [Luke 9:61–62].**

This third applicant wanted a furlough to bid loved ones good-bye. He was a halfway and halfhearted follower of Christ. He wanted to be a disciple, but he did not want to make any sacrifice. He was not impelled by the urgency, the importance of the mission. Remember that the Lord Jesus Christ was even then on His way to the Cross. He had steadfastly set His face to go to Jerusalem.

Friend, the cost of discipleship is high. It demands all we have to give. The apostle Paul wrote, "Brethren, I count not myself to have apprehended: but this one thing I do, forgetting those things which are behind, and reaching forth unto those things which are before, I press toward the mark for the prize of the high calling of God in Christ Jesus" (Phil. 3:13–14).

CHAPTER 10

THEME: Jesus sends forth the seventy; Jesus pronounces judgment on Chorazin, Bethsaida and
Capernaum; Jesus gives parable of the good Samaritan; Jesus enters the home of Mary and Martha

JESUS SENDS FORTH THE SEVENTY

**After these things the Lord appointed other seventy
also, and sent them two and two before his face into
every city and place, whither he himself would come.**

**Therefore said he unto them, The harvest truly is great,
but the labourers are few: pray ye therefore the Lord of
the harvest, that he would send forth labourers into his
harvest [Luke 10:1–2].**

The Lord sent out seventy disciples who were to prepare the way
for the ministry of Jesus. Only Luke tells us of this. The work was
for a limited time, and their office was temporary because Jesus was
journeying toward Jerusalem.

We hear a great deal today about "praying the Lord of the harvest to
send forth laborers into the harvest"—that the Lord looks out upon the
world which is ripe unto harvest, and our business today is to gather
in the harvest. This may sound strange to you, but I do not consider it
my business to harvest. My business is sowing. If you have ever been a
farmer, you know there is a vast difference between sowing seed and
harvesting the crop after the seed has matured. Someone counters,
"But the Lord said that the harvest is great and the laborers few." We
must remember *where* Jesus was when He made that statement. He
was on the other side of the cross at the time, and an age was coming
to an end. At the end of every age is judgment. The judgment that
ends an age is a harvest, and the age itself is for the sowing of seed. I
believe that we are sowing seed today, and that at the end of this age

there will be a harvest. In the parable of the tares and wheat the Lord said, "Let both grow together until the harvest: and in the time of harvest I will say to the reapers, Gather ye together first the tares, and bind them in bundles to burn them: but gather the wheat into my barn" (Matt. 13:30). My business is to sow the seed which is the Word of God. That is the business of every Christian.

> **Go your ways: behold, I send you forth as lambs among wolves.**
>
> **Carry neither purse, nor scrip, nor shoes: and salute no man by the way.**
>
> **And into whatsoever house ye enter, first say, Peace be to this house.**
>
> **And if the son of peace be there, your peace shall rest upon it: if not, it shall turn to you again.**
>
> **And in the same house remain, eating and drinking such things as they give: for the labourer is worthy of his hire. Go not from house to house.**
>
> **And into whatsoever city ye enter, and they receive you, eat such things as are set before you:**
>
> **And heal the sick that are therein, and say unto them, The kingdom of God is come nigh unto you [Luke 10:3-9].**

Jesus warns them that they can expect hardship and danger—they will be "lambs among wolves." They are to travel light and waste no time in idle conversations. They are to be men impelled by one supreme motive—to prepare hearts for the coming of Christ personally.

JESUS PRONOUNCES JUDGMENT ON CHORAZIN, BETHSAIDA, AND CAPERNAUM

> **But into whatsoever city ye enter, and they receive you not, go your ways out into the streets of the same, and say,**

Even the very dust of your city, which cleaveth on us, we do wipe off against you: notwithstanding be ye sure of this, that the kingdom of God is come nigh unto you.

But I say unto you, that it shall be more tolerable in that day for Sodom, than for that city.

Woe unto thee, Chorazin! woe unto thee, Bethsaida! for if the mighty works had been done in Tyre and Sidon, which have been done in you, they had a great while ago repented, sitting in sackcloth and ashes.

But it shall be more tolerable for Tyre and Sidon at the judgment, than for you.

And thou, Capernaum, which art exalted to heaven, shalt be thrust down to hell.

He that heareth you heareth me; and he that despiseth you despiseth me; and he that despiseth me despiseth him that sent me [Luke 10:10–16].

Our Lord solemnly speaks of the seriousness of rejecting His messengers—to reject them was to reject Him.

And the seventy returned again with joy, saying, Lord, even the devils are subject unto us through thy name.

And he said unto them, I beheld Satan as lightning fall from heaven.

Behold, I give unto you power to tread on serpents and scorpions, and over all the power of the enemy: and nothing shall by any means hurt you.

Notwithstanding in this rejoice not, that the spirits are subject unto you; but rather rejoice, because your names are written in heaven [Luke 10:17–20].

In order to complete the story of the seventy, Luke describes their return. They came back thrilled and excited. This is the same experience we have when we give out the Word of God, and someone comes to Christ. How glorious we feel! What a lesson for us to remember the words of Jesus, "rejoice not, that the spirits are subject unto you; but rather rejoice, because your names are written in heaven." When there is success in our ministry, it is His work, not ours.

> **In that hour Jesus rejoiced in spirit, and said, I thank thee, O Father, Lord of heaven and earth, that thou hast hid these things from the wise and prudent, and hast revealed them unto babes: even so, Father; for so it seemed good in thy sight.**

> **All things are delivered to me of my Father: and no man knoweth who the Son is, but the Father; and who the Father is, but the Son, and he to whom the Son will reveal him.**

> **And he turned him unto his disciples, and said privately, Blessed are the eyes which see the things that ye see:**

> **For I tell you, that many prophets and kings have desired to see those things which ye see, and have not seen them; and to hear those things which ye hear, and have not heard them [Luke 10:21-24].**

JESUS GIVES PARABLE OF THE GOOD SAMARITAN

Now we come to one of the things that characterizes the Gospel of Luke—parables. Dr. Luke majors in parables just as Mark majors in miracles. Dr. Luke records certain parables that are among some of the most familiar parts of the Bible. The parable of the Good Samaritan is probably the best-known story. Some literary critics consider it the greatest story ever told.

> **And, behold, a certain lawyer stood up, and tempted him, saying, Master, what shall I do to inherit eternal life? [Luke 10:25].**

The parable of the Good Samaritan came about as an answer to a question about eternal life. It was not an honest question, but it was a good question and a stock question. A "certain lawyer" asked the question—but he was not a lawyer in the sense we think of it.

I heard a little story about lawyers in our judicial system. Two lawyers were in court. It was a difficult case, and there was a great deal of controversy. The court opened and lawyer number one jumped up and called the other lawyer a liar. The second lawyer jumped up to retaliate and called the first lawyer a thief. The judge rapped for silence, and said, "Now that the lawyers have identified themselves, we will begin the case."

However, the lawyer in this parable was not part of a judicial system; but rather, he was an interpreter of the Mosaic Law, and in that sense he was a lawyer.

Now our Lord had a very wonderful way of dealing with questions. He answered a question by asking a question. It is known, by the way, as the Socratic method because Socrates used it: answer a question with a question. It lets a man answer his own question. So the lawyer tries to put Jesus on the witness stand, and He turns around and puts *him* on the witness stand.

> **He said unto him, What is written in the law? how readest thou? [Luke 10:26].**

Jesus knew that he was an expert in the Mosaic Law.

> **And he answering said, Thou shalt love the Lord thy God with all thy heart, and with all thy soul, and with all thy strength, and with all thy mind; and thy neighbour as thyself.**
>
> **And he said unto him, Thou hast answered right: this do, and thou shalt live [Luke 10:27–28].**

I wonder if you notice the barb that is in this.

But he, willing to justify himself, said unto Jesus, And who is my neighbour? [Luke 10:29].

Notice that our Lord said, "You have answered right." Remember that this took place before Christ died on the cross. Does it mean a man can be saved by keeping the Law? Yes, but let's follow through on this. It is not the hearers of the Law, but the doers of the Law that are justified. If you say you can keep it, I'll have to remind you that God contradicts you. He says it is impossible to be justified by the Law because no one can keep the Law—". . . by the works of the law shall no flesh be justified" (Gal. 2:16). "For what the law could not do, in that it was weak through the flesh, God sending his own Son in the likeness of sinful flesh, and for sin, condemned sin in the flesh: That the righteousness of the law might be fulfilled in us, who walk not after the flesh, but after the Spirit" (Rom. 8:3–4).

Now if the lawyer had been honest, which he was not, he would have said, "Master, I've sincerely tried to love God with all my heart, soul, strength, and mind, and my neighbor as myself. But I can't do it. I've miserably failed. So how can I inherit eternal life?" But instead of being honest, he adopted this evasive method and said, "And who is my neighbour?"

Now Christ gave him an answer to this question, and it is the parable of the Good Samaritan. It is a simple story but a marvelous one.

And Jesus answering said, A certain man went down from Jerusalem to Jericho, and fell among thieves, which stripped him of his raiment, and wounded him, and departed, leaving him half dead.

And by chance there came down a certain priest that way: and when he saw him, he passed by on the other side.

And likewise a Levite, when he was at the place, came and looked on him, and passed by on the other side [Luke 10:30–32].

It is possible that this lawyer was a Levite and that he squirmed at this point because it touched him in a personal way.

> **But a certain Samaritan, as he journeyed, came where he was: and when he saw him, he had compassion on him,**
>
> **And went to him, and bound up his wounds, pouring in oil and wine, and set him on his own beast, and brought him to an inn, and took care of him.**
>
> **And on the morrow when he departed, he took out two pence, and gave them to the host, and said unto him, Take care of him; and whatsoever thou spendest more, when I come again, I will repay thee.**
>
> **Which now of these three, thinkest thou, was neighbour unto him that fell among the thieves?**
>
> **And he said, He that shewed mercy on him. Then said Jesus unto him, Go, and do thou likewise [Luke 10:33–37].**

Dean Brown of Yale University has said that three classes of men that represent three philosophies of life are brought before us in this parable.

1. The Thief: His philosophy of life says, "What you have is mine." This is socialism or communism.

2. The Priest and Levite: His philosophy of life says, "What I have is mine." This is rugged individualism that has gone to seed. His cry is, "Let the world be damned, I will get mine." This is godless capitalism.

3. The Good Samaritan: His philosophy says, "What I have belongs to you." This is a Christian philosophy of life. "What I have is yours if I can help you." Folk who talk about "Christian socialism" don't recognize that they are two distinct philosophies.

Now our Lord intended that we bring this parable right down to where we live. We are told that a certain man went down from Jerusalem to Jericho and fell among thieves. That is a picture of humanity. That is the race that has come from Adam. Mankind came from Jerusalem, the place where they approached God, to Jericho, the accursed city. Humanity, you see, fell. Humanity found itself helpless, hopeless, and unable to save itself. Mankind was dead in trespasses and sin—this man who had fallen among thieves was half dead. The thieves are a picture of the Devil who, John 8:44 tells us, was a murderer from the beginning. Concerning this subject our Lord said, "All that ever came before me are thieves and robbers . . ." (John 10:8). When the multitude came to arrest Christ, He said to them, ". . . Are ye come out as against a thief with swords and staves for to take me? I sat daily with you teaching in the temple, and ye laid no hold on me" (Matt. 26:55). The Devil is a thief, and our Lord was crucified between two thieves—this is quite interesting, is it not?

Then we are told that a certain priest passed by on the other side. He represents ritualism and ceremonialism which cannot save a person. Someone has said that the reason the priest passed by on the other side was because he saw that the man had already been robbed! Next a Levite came by, and he too passed by on the other side. He represents legalism. Neither ritualism, ceremonialism, nor legalism can save. Then a "certain" Samaritan passed by. Whom did the "certain Samaritan" represent? He is the One who told the parable. When ritualism, ceremonialism, legalism, and religion could not do anything to help man, Christ came. He is able to bind up the brokenhearted. He is able to take the lost sinner, half-dead, lost in trespasses and sins, and help him.

This parable has a practical application for you and me today. Any person you can help is your neighbor. It does not mean that only the person living next to you is your neighbor. People need Christ, the Good Samaritan. There is a great deal of talk about getting the gospel out to the world, but not much of an effort is made to see that people know about Christ. It is like the young fellow who was courting a girl. He wrote her a letter and said to her, "I would climb the highest mountain for you, swim the deepest river for you, cross the widest sea for you, and cross the burning desert for you!" Then he added a P.S.: "If it does not rain next Wednesday, I will come to see you." That sounds like the average Christian's commitment to Christ!

The world today is like the man that fell among thieves and needs our help. The world needs Christ. Christ can not only rescue us from drowning, but He can teach us to swim. Ritualism and formalism see mankind drowning and say, "Swim, brother, swim." But man cannot swim. Legalism and liberalism push across toward man and say, "Hang on, brother, hang on." But man cannot hang on. There is a song which says, "I was sinking deep in sin far from the peaceful shore, very deeply stained within, sinking to rise no more; but the Master of the sea heard my despairing cry, from the waters lifted me, now safe am I." Christ lifted me, my friend, and He can lift you too. That is the message of the Good Samaritan.

JESUS ENTERS THE HOME OF MARY AND MARTHA

Now it came to pass, as they went, that he entered into a certain village: and a certain woman named Martha received him into her house.

And she had a sister called Mary, which also sat at Jesus' feet, and heard his word.

But Martha was cumbered about much serving, and came to him, and said, Lord, dost thou not care that my sister hath left me to serve alone? bid her therefore that she help me.

And Jesus answered and said unto her, Martha, Martha, thou art careful and troubled about many things:

But one thing is needful: and Mary hath chosen that good part, which shall not be taken away from her [Luke 10:38–42].

Without going into a lot of detail, suffice it to say that Mary had done her part; then she went to sit at the feet of Jesus. Martha, her sister, was a dear soul and if it had not been for her they would not have had that lovely dinner. She got busy, however, and became frustrated. Possibly she reached for a pan, thought is was not big enough, then reached for another, and a pan fell off the top shelf. It was too much for her, and she came walking out of the kitchen, and said something which she would not have said under normal conditions. Our Lord was very gentle with her, but said, "Mary has chosen the best part."

My frustrated, confused friend, are you at that corner of life where you do not know which way to turn? Then, for goodness sake, sit down. Sit at Jesus' feet. Look in His Word and see what He has to say. It will help you with your housework. It will make you a better dishwasher. It will help you sweep the floors cleaner. You will dig a better ditch, mow a better lawn, and study your lesson better. Your work at the office will be easier, and you will be able to drive your car better. Just take time to sit at the feet of Jesus. Mary chose the best part.

CHAPTER 11

THEME: Jesus teaches disciples to pray by using parables of the persistent friend and a good father; Jesus accused of casting out demons by Beelzebub; parable of unclean spirit leaving a man; the sign of Jonah; parable of the lighted candle; Jesus denounces the Pharisees

JESUS TEACHES DISCIPLES TO PRAY BY USING PARABLES OF THE PERSISTENT FRIEND AND A GOOD FATHER

And it came to pass, that, as he was praying in a certain place, when he ceased, one of his disciples said unto him, Lord, teach us to pray, as John also taught his disciples.

And he said unto them, When ye pray, say, Our Father which art in heaven, Hallowed be thy name. Thy kingdom come. Thy will be done, as in heaven, so in earth.

Give us day by day our daily bread.

And forgive us our sins; for we also forgive every one that is indebted to us. And lead us not into temptation; but deliver us from evil [Luke 11:1–4].

This important section deals with prayer as it is found nowhere else in the Gospels. It may sound similar to other portions in the Gospels, but it is actually different. There are those who feel that this passage is an insertion, an intrusion, in the chronological account of the ministry of Christ. It is true that it does not follow the movement, but it introduces many interesting implications.

The reason His disciple wanted to know how to pray was that he had seen and heard Christ pray. It was the custom of our Lord to retire alone to pray. A disciple evidently overheard His prayer, and a desire was born in his heart to pray like Christ prayed.

At this moment, friend, the Lord Jesus Christ is at God's right hand making intercession for us. He is our great Intercessor. And it is still a good idea to ask Him to teach us to pray. An appropriate petition is, "Lord, teach me to pray."

This disciple was not just asking *how* to pray. The Lord had given the Sermon on the Mount which outlined how one should pray. This disciple was not asking for a technique, a system, an art form, or a ritual to follow. It was not a matter of *how* to do it, but he wanted to pray like Christ prayed.

Many folk *say* their prayers. It is sort of an amen to tag on the end of the day when you put on your pajamas. I was brought up in a home where I never heard prayer nor ever saw a Bible. The first time I ever engaged in prayer was at a conference when I was a boy. I stayed in a dormitory with other boys, and at night the one in charge told us to put on our pajamas and gather together for prayer. I got the impression, at the very beginning, that in order to pray you had to put on your pajamas; you could not pray any other time. Your pajamas were sort of your prayer clothes. Of course that was a ridiculous conception, but, frankly, we need someone to teach us to pray—not just to say prayers, but to get through to God.

This disciple asked the Lord, "Teach us to pray, as John also taught his disciples." This is an unexpected glimpse into the life of John the Baptist—sort of a farewell look at him because this is the last we'll see him. In this last picture, what do we see? We see John as a man of prayer. "Teach us to pray, as John also taught his disciples." Is anyone going to say that about you or me? All great servants of God have been men of prayer. The barren lives of Christians and the deadness of the church today are the result of prayerlessness. That is our problem.

In answer to their request the Lord gives them this. I do not believe He intended it to become the prayer I hear so often in public services. It is not to be a stilted form for public services, but a spontaneous, personal prayer, like a son talks to his father. God the Father *knows* me and I do not think He wants me to put on airs, assume an unnatural voice, and use flowery language. I think He wants me to talk like

Vernon McGee. Nor does He want me to be "wordy." I get so weary of "wordy" prayers—and I think God does also.

Let us look at some of the elements of prayer. The first part is worship—"Hallowed be thy name." "Thy kingdom come" is praying for God's will to be done on earth. It involves the putting down of evil and the putting up of good. It means you have a desire for God's will in your life. It is useless to mouth the words of this prayer without meaning them. This prayer is for the believer; it is not for the unsaved. There is a prayer for the unsaved which is, "God be merciful to me a sinner" (Luke 18:13), but it can be even simpler than that. God is merciful and is able to extend mercy to you. You do not have to beg Him to save you; He will save you if you will come to Him.

Part of this prayer is for physical provision, "Give us day by day our daily bread." Then we are told to pray, "And forgive us our sins; for we also forgive every one that is indebted to us." I do not believe that I can measure up to this standard; I hope you can. Do you forgive everyone? Well, my friend, God wants us to forgive others. Our standard is set for us in Ephesians 4:32 which says, "And be ye kind one to another, tenderhearted, forgiving one another, even as God for Christ's sake hath forgiven you."

God help us to be men and women of prayer. We do not need more preachers, churches, or missionaries, but we do need more people who know how to pray.

God is not through with the subject of prayer in this chapter. Only Luke records this next parable, and it sheds a different light upon the subject of prayer. It is a parable of contrast.

And he said unto them, Which of you shall have a friend, and shall go unto him at midnight, and say unto him, Friend, lend me three loaves;

For a friend of mine in his journey is come to me, and I have nothing to set before him?

And he from within shall answer and say, Trouble me not: the door is now shut, and my children are with me in bed; I cannot rise and give thee [Luke 11:5–7].

I want to bring this parable right up to date. Suppose a man and his wife and children live in California. They receive a letter from her mother saying that she is coming for a visit. She says that she will arrive on a certain day in the middle of the afternoon. The family decides that they will take her out to dinner when she comes. The big day arrives and the mother-in-law does not show up. The afternoon passes into evening and finally they receive a telephone call, and the mother-in-law explains that she has been delayed by car trouble. They are sure she will have dinner before she comes. At midnight here she is. The son-in-law casually inquires, "Have you had dinner?" She replies that she has not and is very hungry! Since there is nothing in the house to eat, the son-in-law decides to go next door to his good neighbor and borrow some food. His neighbor says, "Wait until morning. You are not starving. I am in bed and so are my children. Go home."

I say unto you, Though he will not rise and give him, because he is his friend, yet because of his importunity he will rise and give him as many as he needeth [Luke 11:8].

The man says, "Neighbor, you do not know my mother-in-law. Please get up." So he continues to pound on the door, and finally the neighbor gets up and gives him what he is asking for.

Now this is a parable by contrast.

And I say unto you, Ask, and it shall be given you; seek, and ye shall find; knock, and it shall be opened unto you.

For every one that asketh receiveth; and he that seeketh findeth; and to him that knocketh it shall be opened [Luke 11:9–10].

My friend, do you think that God is asleep? Do you feel that He has gone to bed when you pray, and you cannot get Him up? Do you believe that He does not want to answer your prayers? God *does* want to answer your prayers and He will. That is what this parable is saying. It is a parable by contrast and not by comparison. You do not have to storm the gates of heaven or knock down the door of heaven in order to attract God's attention. God is not reluctant to hear and answer you. God tells us in Isaiah 65:24, "And it shall come to pass, that before they call, I will answer; and while they are yet speaking, I will hear." God wants to hear and answer.

Some people think that God does not hear and answer their prayers. Maybe they do not get the message—sometimes God says, "No!" Our problem is that we do not like to take no for an answer. God *always* hears the prayers of His own, and answers them, but when He says no it is because we are not praying for that which is best for us. I have learned over the years that the best answer God has given to some of my requests has been no.

As a young preacher I prayed for God to open up the door to a certain church where I wanted to serve as pastor. I was asked to candidate, which I did. The machinery of the church and the political bigwigs met behind closed doors to decide if I would be pastor. They decided not to accept me because I was not a church politician, and theirs was a strategic church in that day. I went to the Lord and cried about it and told Him how He had let me down. Today I am ashamed of myself, and I have asked Him to forgive me for my attitude. He did not let me down. He knew what was best for me. He had something much better in store for me. Many times since then I have thanked Him for that no. You do not have to storm the gate of heaven to get God to answer your prayer. God has not gone to bed. The door is wide open and He says, "Knock, seek, and ask." Take everything to God in prayer, and He will give you His very best.

> **If a son shall ask bread of any of you that is a father, will he give him a stone? or if he ask a fish, will he for a fish give him a serpent? [Luke 11:11].**

Before you go to God in prayer, make sure He is really your Father. "But as many as received him, to them gave he power to become the sons of God, even to them that believe on his name" (John 1:12). Believing that the Lord Jesus Christ died for you and rose again for your justification makes you a son of God. When you trust Christ as your Savior, you are baptized by the Spirit of God into the body of Christ, and you are a son who can go to God and say, "Father." If you ask your earthly father for bread, will he give you a stone? If you ask him for a fish, will he give you a serpent? Can you imagine a father doing that?

Or if he shall ask an egg, will he offer him a scorpion?

If ye then, being evil, know how to give good gifts unto your children: how much more shall your heavenly Father give the Holy Spirit to them that ask him? [Luke 11:12–13].

At that time He told His disciples to ask for the Holy Spirit. As far as I can tell, they never did ask for the Spirit. Later on Christ said, ". . . Receive ye the Holy Ghost" (John 20:22). They needed the Holy Spirit during those intervening days before Pentecost. Then on the great Day of Pentecost He came and baptized them into the body of believers, which put them in Christ. They were filled on that day with the Holy Spirit. That filling is something all of us need. All believers have been baptized into the body of Christ—"For by one Spirit are we all baptized into one body, whether we be Jews or Gentiles, whether we be bond or free; and have been all made to drink into one Spirit" (1 Cor. 12:13).

JESUS ACCUSED OF CASTING OUT DEMONS · BY BEELZEBUB

This incident is also recorded in Matthew 12:24–30 and Mark 3:22–30. From this account has come the notion of the so-called unpardonable sin.

And he was casting out a devil, and it was dumb. And it came to pass, when the devil was gone out, the dumb spake; and the people wondered.

**But some of them said, He casteth out devils through
Beelzebub the chief of the devils [Luke 11:14–15].**

The convincing nature of Jesus' miracles forced the Pharisees to offer
some explanation for them. They could not deny the existence of miracles when they were happening before their eyes. They resorted to
the basest and most blasphemous explanation for the miracles of
Jesus. They did not deny that they took place but claimed that they
were done by the power of the Devil.

**And others, tempting him, sought of him a sign from
heaven.**

**But he, knowing their thoughts, said unto them, Every
kingdom divided against itself is brought to desolation;
and a house divided against a house falleth.**

**If Satan also be divided against himself how shall his
kingdom stand? because ye say that I cast out devils
through Beelzebub.**

**And if I by Beelzebub cast out devils, by whom do your
sons cast them out? therefore shall they be your judges
[Luke 11:16–19].**

Christ showed them the utter absurdity of their line of reasoning.

**But if I with the finger of God cast out devils, no doubt
the kingdom of God is come upon you [Luke 11:20].**

"The kingdom of God is come upon you" means that it was among
them in the presence of the person of Jesus who had the credentials of
the King.

**When a strong man armed keepeth his palace, his
goods are in peace:**

But when a stronger than he shall come upon him, and overcome him, he taketh from him all his armour wherein he trusted, and divideth his spoils [Luke 11:21–22].

The "strong man armed" is Satan. The demon-possessed man was an evidence of his power. But, you see, Jesus is stronger than Satan, which was the reason He could cast out the demon.

"A strong man armed keepeth his palace" is a verse that has a message for us. There are those who want to disarm us—disarm us as a nation and disarm us in our homes. But "a strong man armed keepeth his palace." There are wicked men abroad. And Satan is abroad. As long as there is a strong enemy, we do well to be armed.

PARABLE OF UNCLEAN SPIRIT LEAVING A MAN

When the unclean spirit is gone out of a man, he walketh through dry places, seeking rest; and finding none, he saith, I will return unto my house whence I came out.

And when he cometh, he findeth it swept and garnished.

Then goeth he, and taketh to him seven other spirits more wicked than himself; and they enter in, and dwell there: and the last state of that man is worse than the first [Luke 11:24–26].

This parable pictures the precarious position of Israel and the Pharisees. The parable speaks of a man with an unclean spirit. The demon leaves the man, and the man feels that he is clean—empty, swept, and garnished. Reformation is no good, friends. If everyone in the world would quit sinning right now, there would not be more Christians. To stop sinning does not make a Christian. Reformation is not what is needed. Regeneration is what is needed. Israel had swept her house clean through the ministries of John the Baptist and Jesus, but she would not invite the Lord Jesus Christ to occupy it. So this wicked generation of Jews would reach an even worse state, as described in the parable.

THE SIGN OF JONAH

And when the people were gathered thick together, he began to say, This is an evil generation: they seek a sign; and there shall no sign be given it, but the sign of Jonas the prophet.

For as Jonas was a sign unto the Ninevites, so shall also the Son of man be to this generation.

The queen of the south shall rise up in the judgment with the men of this generation, and condemn them: for she came from the utmost parts of the earth to hear the wisdom of Solomon; and behold, a greater than Solomon is here.

The men of Nineve shall rise up in the judgment with this generation, and shall condemn it: for they repented at the preaching of Jonas; and, behold, a greater than Jonas is here [Luke 11:29–32].

The "sign" would be His own resurrection, of course. He directs them back to two incidents in the Old Testament. The first is the account of the prophet Jonah. Jonah was apparently raised from the dead when he was in the fish. God brought him out of darkness and death into light and life. Jonah's experience was typical of the coming death and resurrection of Jesus Christ. The Ninevites received Jonah and his preaching after his miraculous deliverance, and they repented. The acts of Israel, as a nation, place her in a much worse position because she did not receive her Messiah and did not repent.

PARABLE OF THE LIGHTED CANDLE

No man, when he hath lighted a candle, putteth it in a secret place, neither under a bushel, but on a candlestick, that they which come in may see the light.

The light of the body is the eye: therefore when thine eye is single, thy whole body also is full of light; but when thine eye is evil, thy body is also full of darkness.

Take heed therefore that the light which is in thee be not darkness.

If thy whole body therefore be full of light, having no part dark, the whole shall be full of light, as when the bright shining of a candle doth give thee light [Luke 11:33–36].

Our Lord gives a simple explanation on the purpose of a candle. It is a light giver; its purpose is to transmit light. The resurrection of Christ is the light. The resurrection of Christ is the one ray of light in this world. You and I are in a world bounded by birth and death—we are boxed in by these two events. The resurrection of Christ is that which brings hope from the outside. What will men do with the light?

To see an object, two things are essential: light to make the object visible, and eyes to behold the object. A light is of no use to the blind. A man who can see but has no light and a blind man with a light are in the same predicament. A light and an eye are essential for sight.

Even in the presence of Christ, men were obviously not seeing Him; they were stumbling over Him. That did not mean that He was not the Light of the World; it meant that men were blind.

DENOUNCES THE PHARISEES

And as he spake, a certain Pharisee besought him to dine with him: and he went in, and sat down to meat.

> And when the Pharisee saw it, he marvelled that he had
> not first washed before dinner [Luke 11:37–38].

He omitted ceremonial cleansing, which was a religious rite.

> And the Lord said unto him, Now do ye Pharisees make
> clean the outside of the cup and the platter; but your
> inward part is full of ravening and wickedness.

> Ye fools, did not he that made that which is without
> make that which is within also? [Luke 11:39–40].

Religion is not a matter of externalities. It is a heart affair. This is a
great principle.

He pronounces three woes which illustrate this principle.

> But rather give alms of such things as ye have; and, be-
> hold, all things are clean unto you.

> But woe unto you, Pharisees! for ye tithe mint and rue
> and all manner of herbs, and pass over judgment and
> the love of God: these ought ye to have done, and not to
> leave the other undone [Luke 11:41–42].

They had false values. He is not saying that it was wrong to tithe, but
their wrong was in what they had left undone. And, friend, giving of
your substance will not make you a Christian. However, if you love
Christ, you *will* give of your substance.

> Woe unto you, Pharisees! for ye love the uppermost seats
> in the synagogues, and greetings in the markets.

> Woe unto you, scribes and Pharisees, hypocrites! for ye
> are as graves which appear not and the men that walk
> over them are not aware of them [Luke 11:43–44].

In other words, they were a bad influence.

Then answered one of the lawyers, and said unto him, Master, thus saying thou reproachest us also [Luke 11:45].

The shoe was beginning to fit. The Pharisees were occupied with externalities. The sin of the scribes was insincerity. They were adding to the Law, making it more difficult, yet not attempting to follow it themselves.

And he said, Woe unto you also, ye lawyers! for ye lade men with burdens grievous to be born, and ye yourselves touch not the burdens with one of your fingers.

Woe unto you! for ye build the sepulchres of the prophets, and your fathers killed them.

Truly ye bear witness that ye allow the deeds of your fathers: for they indeed killed them, and ye build their sepulchres.

Therefore also said the wisdom of God, I will send them prophets and apostles, and some of them they shall slay and persecute:

That the blood of all the prophets, which was shed from the foundation of the world, may be required of this generation;

From the blood of Abel unto the blood of Zacharias, which perished between the altar and the temple: verily I say unto you, It shall be required of this generation.

Woe unto you, lawyers! for ye have taken away the key of knowledge: ye entered not in yourselves, and them that were entering in ye hindered [Luke 11:46–52].

These religious rulers occupied very much the same position that church leaders occupy today. People looked to them for the interpretation of the truth. They placed the emphasis on material things rather than on the spiritual purpose for which those things were to be used. And they themselves were not living according to the Scriptures.

Unfortunately, the greatest hindrance to the cause of Christ today is the professed believer. We need to examine our own lives in the light of this Scripture!

> And as he said these things unto them, the scribes and the Pharisees began to urge him vehemently, and to provoke him to speak of many things:
>
> Laying wait for him, and seeking to catch something out of his mouth, that they might accuse him [Luke 11:53–54].

CHAPTER 12

THEME: Jesus warns of the leaven of the Pharisees; parable of the rich fool; parable of the return from the wedding; the testing of servants in light of the coming of Christ; Jesus states He is a divider of men

JESUS WARNS OF THE LEAVEN OF THE PHARISEES

The twelfth chapter continues to record the tremendous ministry of our Lord. Luke adds some new things which I shall emphasize.

In the mean time, when there were gathered together an innumerable multitude of people, insomuch that they trode one upon another, he began to say unto his disciples first of all, Beware ye of the leaven of the Pharisees, which is hypocrisy [Luke 12:1].

This is the period of time when Christ's ministry peaked. Great crowds of people were following Him. It was at this time that He performed so many miracles. There were literally thousands of blind who had their eyes opened, thousands of lame that were made to walk, and thousands of dumb that were made to speak. Christ healed multitudes. In fact, this crowd was so large it was impossible to number them. The people were pushing against one another, and actually some were being trampled. It was a dangerous place to be.

Christ warns the crowd about the leaven of the Pharisees. If leaven symbolized the gospel, as many people think it does, why would the Lord warn His disciples about the *leaven* of the Pharisees? Leaven is a principle of evil, and the leaven of the Pharisees was hypocrisy. There is a great deal of leaven about today!

For there is nothing covered, that shall not be revealed; neither hid, that shall not be known.

> Therefore whatsoever ye have spoken in darkness shall
> be heard in the light; and that which ye have spoken in
> the ear in closets shall be proclaimed upon the house-
> tops.
>
> And I say unto you my friends, Be not afraid of them
> that kill the body, and after that have no more that they
> can do.
>
> But I will forewarn you whom ye shall fear: Fear him,
> which after he hath killed hath power to cast into hell;
> yea, I say unto you, Fear him [Luke 12:2–5].

It was upon this principle that both Cromwell and, I believe, Martin
Luther based the statement, "Fear God and you will have no one else
to fear." Let me repeat that when Cromwell was asked the basis for his
courage and fearlessness, he replied that he had learned that if he
feared God he would fear no man. That is exactly what our Lord is
saying in this passage.

> Are not five sparrows sold for two farthings, and not one
> of them is forgotten before God?
>
> But even the very hairs of your head are all numbered.
> Fear not therefore: ye are of more value than many spar-
> rows.
>
> Also I say unto you, Whosoever shall confess me before
> men, him shall the Son of man also confess before the
> angels of God:
>
> But he that denieth me before men shall be denied before
> the angels of God [Luke 12:6–9].

Our Lord's public rebuke of the religious leaders would, of course,
bring their wrath down upon His head. And His disciples could expect the same kind of treatment from them. The Lord Jesus gives them
these words of comfort and assurance of God's care for them. Since He

sees the fall of a sparrow, He is fully aware of the needs of those who are teaching and preaching His Word.

And whosoever shall speak a word against the Son of man, it shall be forgiven him: but unto him that blasphemeth against the Holy Ghost it shall not be forgiven [Luke 12:10].

When a man blasphemes with his mouth, that is not the thing that condemns him; it is the attitude of his heart. Blasphemy against the Holy Spirit is to resist His convicting work in the heart and life. This is a permanent condition—unless he stops resisting.

And when they bring you unto the synagogues, and unto magistrates, and powers, take ye no thought how or what thing ye shall answer, or what ye shall say:

For the Holy Ghost shall teach you in the same hour what ye ought to say [Luke 12:11–12].

This is not intended to be an excuse for a lazy preacher or Sunday school teacher failing to make preparation. Rather, it was assurance to His own men that the Holy Spirit, whom He would send, would give them courage and wisdom as they faithfully witnessed for Him. We have many examples of this in the Book of Acts.

And one of the company said unto him, Master, speak to my brother, that he divide the inheritance with me.

And he said unto him, Man, who made me a judge or a divider over you? [Luke 12:13–14].

Our Lord absolutely refused to sit in judgment in a case like this. I wish today those of us who attempt to counsel might take this position. Counselors are so quick to judge and tell folk what they should do. The Lord Jesus would not sit in judgment. Now, of course, when the Lord came to earth the first time, He did not come as a judge but as a Savior. The next time He comes it will be as Judge. The Father has committed all judgment unto His Son (see John 5:22).

Out of this incident our Lord made this statement, then gave a parable of the "rich fool."

And he said unto them, Take heed, and beware of covetousness: for a man's life consisteth not in the abundance of the things which he possesseth [Luke 12:15].

This is certainly a good verse for many Christians in this age of crass materialism, when it seems that "things" are so important and occupy so much of our time. Covetousness is one of the outstanding sins of this hour. This is not a sin that others can see you commit, and at times you may not even be aware you are committing it. St. Francis of Assisi once said, "Men have confessed to me every known sin except the sin of covetousness."

The judgment sometimes made of Americans is quite interesting. Several years ago the *Sunday Pictorial* in London gave an assessment of America in which it said: "You shock us by your belief that the almighty dollar and armed might alone can save the world." I am wondering if America is not in this position today: overcome by covetousness.

PARABLE OF THE RICH FOOL

And he spake a parable unto them, saying, The ground of a certain rich man brought forth plentifully:

And he thought within himself, saying, What shall I do, because I have no room where to bestow my fruits? [Luke 12:16–17].

Notice the emphasis on the word *I* in this passage. This man had a bad case of perpendicular "I-tis"—"What shall *I* do, because *I* have no room where to bestow *my* fruits."

And he said, This will I do: I will pull down my barns, and build greater; and there will I bestow all my fruits and my goods.

And I will say to my soul, Soul, thou hast much goods laid up for many years; take thine ease, eat, drink, and be merry.

But God said unto him, Thou fool, this night thy soul shall be required of thee: then whose shall those things be, which thou hast provided?

So is he that layeth up treasure for himself, and is not rich toward God [Luke 12:18–21].

This man had gathered all of his treasure on earth but had stored none in heaven. The same idea is expressed in this epitaph:

> Here lies John Racket
> In his wooden jacket.
> He kept neither horses nor mules.
> He lived like a hog.
> He died like a dog.
> And left all his money to fools.

Our Lord called the man in this parable a fool, but notice what kind of man he was, apparently. All outward appearances indicate that he was a good man. He was a law-abiding citizen. He was a good neighbor. He was living the good life in suburbia in the best residential area of the city. He was not a wicked man or a member of the Mafia. He was not in crooked politics. He was not engaged in shady business. He was not an alcoholic or keeping a woman on the side. This man seems to be all right; yet our Lord called him a fool. Why? This man gave all of his thought to himself, and he was covetous.

> I had a little tea party
> This afternoon at three.
> 'Twas very small—
> Three guests in all
>
> Just I, Myself, and Me.
> Myself ate all the sandwiches,

While I drank up the tea.
'Twas also I who ate the pie
And passed the cake to Me.

This is the way many people live. The parable of the rich fool is one of the most pungent paragraphs in the Word of God. The philosophy of the world today is "Eat, drink and be merry, for tomorrow we die." Our Lord said, "That's the problem, that's what makes a man a fool." If you live as though this life is all there is, and you live just for self, and as though there is nothing beyond death, you are a fool.

And he said unto his disciples. Therefore I say unto you, Take no thought for your life, what ye shall eat; neither for the body, what ye shall put on.

The life is more than meat, and the body is more than raiment.

Consider the ravens: for they neither sow nor reap; which neither have storehouse nor barn; and God feedeth them: how much more are ye better than the fowls? [Luke 12:22–24].

Now, of course it is not wrong to store up things. The problem with the rich fool was covetousness. He was trying to get more, more, and more. That is the curse of godless capitalism. Have you noticed the strong judgment that is pronounced upon the rich in the last days? James 5:1 describes it: "Go to now, ye rich men, weep and howl for your miseries that shall come upon you." Riches have become a curse.

Our great nation thought that the almighty dollar would solve the problems of the world, and we are in a bigger mess than ever. We are arguing about whether or not "In God we trust" should remain on our money. Let's take it off because it is hypocrisy anyway. We are not trusting in God but in the dollar. To have a slogan on money means nothing at all. America needs to turn back to reality and truth and quit mouthing religion. We should search our hearts and ask ourselves,

"Am I living for this life only?" Our Lord said, "Go look at the birds. Learn something from them."

> **If ye then be not able to do that thing which is least, why take ye thought for the rest?**

> **Consider the lilies how they grow: they toil not, they spin not; and yet I say unto you, that Solomon in all his glory was not arrayed like one of these [Luke 12:26-27].**

When I go to the Hawaiian Islands, I look for the hibiscus. It is one of my favorite flowers. I wonder what God had in mind when He made the hibiscus. It is a careless flower. The rose is a careful flower that holds its petals tightly and opens them up gradually. The hibiscus, however, flings open the door and great big petals wave at you. It is a beautiful and colorful flower.

Our Lord said, "Consider the lilies, how they grow." Flowers are saying a lot to us today: "My, you human beings certainly go to a great deal of trouble to take care of your bodies. You use lotions, sprays, ointments, and perfume, among other things upon your bodies, and then you clothe them. Even after you are all perfumed and dressed up, you cannot compare to the beauty of a flower." What a message, friend. Some of us need to depend upon God a little bit more.

> **If then God so clothe the grass, which is to-day in the field, and to-morrow is cast into the oven; how much more will he clothe you, O ye of little faith? [Luke 12:28].**

This is not to encourage indolence. Birds cannot build barns; flowers cannot spin. But man can. God intends him to use the ability He gave him—but not to live as if the exercise of these abilities is all there is to life.

> **And seek not ye what ye shall eat, or what ye shall drink, neither be ye of doubtful mind.**

> For all these things do the nations of the world seek
> after: and your Father knoweth that ye have need of
> these things.
>
> But rather seek ye the kingdom of God; and all these
> things shall be added unto you [Luke 12:29–31].

Our world is engaged in commerce. Half of the world will spend its heart's blood in building a better mouse trap while the other half will go to the ends of the earth to buy the mouse trap. Both groups are forgetting there is a God in heaven and that all men have an eternal soul.

> Fear not, little flock; for it is your Father's good pleasure
> to give you the kingdom.
>
> Sell that ye have, and give alms; provide yourselves
> bags which wax not old, a treasure in the heavens that
> faileth not, where no thief approacheth, neither moth
> corrupteth.
>
> For where your treasure is, there will your heart be also
> [Luke 12:32–34].

All men will one day stand before the awful presence of God, stripped of the "things" that occupied his life on earth. He will have no treasure up there. He lived without God; he will die without God.

PARABLE OF THE RETURN FROM THE WEDDING

Now we have two parables which Christ gave in connection with His return.

> Let your loins be girded about, and your lights burning;
>
> And ye yourselves like unto men that wait for their lord,
> when he will return from the wedding; that when he

cometh and knocketh, they may open unto him immediately.

Blessed are those servants, whom the lord when he cometh shall find watching: verily I say unto you, that he shall gird himself, and make them to sit down to meat, and will come forth and serve them.

And if he shall come in the second watch, or come in the third watch, and find them so, blessed are those servants.

And this know, that if the goodman of the house had known what hour the thief would come, he would have watched, and not have suffered his house to be broken through.

Be ye therefore ready also: for the Son of man cometh at an hour when ye think not [Luke 12:35–40].

Although this parable primarily applies to Israel and the second coming of Christ to set up His Kingdom on earth, the *principle* applies to the church as we anticipate His coming at the Rapture.

In the Orient a groom had a wedding supper with his friends and then went to claim his bride at her home. The servants of the groom were expected to be dressed for work and have their lamps lighted for the return procession. The attitude of the believer to the return of Christ is to be one of readiness, having "the loins . . . girded"—doing all we can for Him, and living in expectation of His return.

When the figure changes from the "bridegroom" to the "thief," it is to emphasize the element of an unexpected appearance. Paul used the same figure of speech for Christ's second coming in 1 Thessalonians 5:2 which says, "For yourselves know perfectly that the day of the Lord so cometh as a thief in the night." However, the Lord does not come as a *thief* to Rapture the church. Rather, we shall arise to meet Him in the air.

THE TESTING OF SERVANTS IN LIGHT OF THE COMING OF CHRIST

And the Lord said, Who then is that faithful and wise steward, whom his lord shall make ruler over his household, to give them their portion of meat in due season?

Blessed is that servant, whom his lord when he cometh shall find so doing [Luke 12:42–43].

This is one of the outstanding parables that teaches our responsibility in light of our Lord's coming. Again, this parable is primarily for Israel, but the principle applies to us as believers, as we anticipate the Rapture. Many people feel that the Lord is coming soon, so they are waiting instead of working. We should work as though the Lord was not coming for another one thousand years. Let's quit all this business of trying to set a date for His coming and get ready. The blessed hope is the coming of Christ, and we should be filling our "hope chests" with works that we can one day lay at His feet.

Of a truth I say unto you, that he will make him ruler over all that he hath.

But and if that servant say in his heart, My lord delayeth his coming; and shall begin to beat the menservants and maidens, and to eat and drink, and to be drunken;

The lord of that servant will come in a day when he looketh not for him, and at an hour when he is not aware, and will cut him in sunder, and will appoint him his portion with the unbelievers [Luke 12:44–46].

This parable teaches us two important lessons. Skepticism about the Lord's coming again produces (1) the mishandling of authority and (2) laziness in one's conduct. We are to live in the expectancy of His return. Our lives should be lived as if the Lord is going to appear the next moment, and we will have to give an account of ourselves to

Him. In truth, we will have to account for ourselves in that day when He comes.

> And that servant, which knew his lord's will, and prepared not himself, neither did according to his will, shall be beaten with many stripes.

> But he that knew not, and did commit things worthy of stripes, shall be beaten with few stripes. For unto whomsoever much is given, of him shall be much required: and to whom men have committed much, of him, they will ask the more [Luke 12:47–48].

Maybe He will not come today or tomorrow, but He is going to come. Our tendency is to let things slip because He has not yet appeared. We feel like we get by with things, but in reality we get by with nothing. In that day when He comes, we will be judged. "For we must all appear before the judgment seat of Christ; that every one may receive the things done in his body, according to that he hath done, whether it be good or bad" (2 Cor. 5:10). Who is "we"? We Christians are to appear before the judgment seat of Christ. Our judgment will not determine whether or not we will be saved. This will not be a criminal court, but a circuit court where our property will be in danger. He will judge us in order to see if we are worthy or not to receive rewards. There will be degrees of rewards for the believer just as there will be degrees of punishment for the unbeliever.

JESUS STATES HE IS A DIVIDER OF MEN

> I am come to send fire on the earth; and what will I, if it be already kindled? [Luke 12:49].

Even at this hour when the world is experiencing the deepest darkness we've had in nineteen hundred years, the Lord Jesus Christ is being blasphemed! The fire has been thrown out on the earth today!

> But I have a baptism to be baptized with; and how am I straitened till it be accomplished! [Luke 12:50].

This verse is speaking of Christ's death upon the cross.

> **Suppose ye that I am come to give peace on the earth? I tell you, Nay; but rather division:**
>
> **For from henceforth there shall be five in one house divided, three against two, and two against three.**
>
> **The father shall be divided against the son, and the son against the father; the mother against the daughter, and the daughter against the mother; the mother-in-law against her daughter-in-law, and the daughter-in-law against her mother-in-law [Luke 12:51–53].**

When a person receives Jesus Christ as his Savior, he is immediately separated from the unbelievers around him. This will be true whether they be his relatives or his friends.

> **And he said also to the people, When ye see a cloud rise out of the west, straightway ye say, There cometh a shower; and so it is.**
>
> **And when ye see the south wind blow, ye say, There will be heat; and it cometh to pass.**
>
> **Ye hypocrites, ye can discern the face of the sky and of the earth; but how is it that ye do not discern this time? [Luke 12:54–56].**

We need to realize and recognize what kind of world we are living in. Man thinks he is big enough and good enough to bring peace on the earth. This is a fallacy—man is a warmonger. The United Nations was formed to bring peace and to keep peace on earth. May I say, the United Nations is one of the best *fighting* arenas in the world today! We need to realize that until Christ comes there can be no real peace.

CHAPTER 13

THEME: Jesus teaches men not to judge but repent; parable of the fig tree; Jesus heals woman with infirmity; parables of the mustard seed and leaven; continues to teach as He goes toward Jerusalem; Jesus weeps over Jerusalem

JESUS TEACHES MEN NOT TO JUDGE BUT REPENT

There were present at that season some that told him of the Galilaeans, whose blood Pilate had mingled with their sacrifices.

And Jesus answering said unto them, Suppose ye that these Galilaeans were sinners above all the Galilaeans, because they suffered such things?

I tell you, Nay: but, except ye repent, ye shall all likewise perish.

Or those eighteen, upon whom the tower in Siloam fell, and slew them, think ye that they were sinners above all men that dwelt in Jerusalem?

I tell you, Nay: but, except ye repent, ye shall all likewise perish [Luke 13:1–5].

The victims of Pilate and the men who were killed when the tower fell were not judged of God. God does nothing in spite. But Christ was telling the religious crowd of His day that unless they repented, they would also perish.

This passage has several fine lessons for us. The first one teaches us that when some Christian has trouble beyond the average amount (and many do), we are not to interpret it to mean that he is a greater sinner than others. Trouble does not always come to a person because of his sins.

The other side of the coin is that just becoming a Christian does not automatically inoculate you against trouble. You will miss the Great Tribulation, but you will not miss the *little* tribulation if you are a Christian. You are going to have a little of it right down here.

Another thing we should see is that when trouble comes to someone else and not to you, it does not indicate that you are superior to that individual. Perhaps God is permitting you to see the other fellow's trouble in order to bring you to Himself.

PARABLE OF THE FIG TREE

The parable of the fig tree grew out of the previous discussion.

> He spake also this parable; A certain man had a fig tree planted in his vineyard; and he came and sought fruit thereon, and found none.
>
> Then said he unto the dresser of his vineyard, Behold, these three years I come seeking fruit on this fig tree, and find none: cut it down; why cumbereth it the ground?
>
> And he answering said unto him, Lord, let it alone this year also, till I shall dig about it, and dung it:
>
> And if it bear fruit, well: and if not, then after that thou shalt cut it down [Luke 13:6–9].

The fig tree without fruit is symbolic, in my opinion, of the nation Israel. The owner of the fig tree expected it to bear fruit and was disappointed when it was barren. He had the unquestioned right to take the fruit and to act in judgment by cutting down the tree. Israel had been promised blessings if they walked in the light God had given them and curses if they rejected the light. The nation was given special attention—cultivated and fertilized. It should have produced fruit, but it did not. Israel rejected Christ, even saying, ". . . His blood be on us, and on our children" (Matt. 27:25). Israel did experience God's judgment and was scattered among the nations of the world.

It is interesting to note that Israel cannot live in her land today and have peace while she continues to reject God. It is not Russia or the Arabs that are giving Israel so much trouble; it is God. Israel is God's chosen people. He is going to bring them back to their land someday in faith and belief. They are returning to the land today in unbelief, and they do not have peace. This is the evidence of the hand of God in the affairs of the world.

JESUS HEALS THE WOMAN WITH THE INFIRMITY

And he was teaching in one of the synagogues on the sabbath.

And, behold, there was a woman which had a spirit of infirmity eighteen years, and was bowed together, and could in no wise lift up herself.

And when Jesus saw her, he called her to him, and said unto her, Woman, thou art loosed from thine infirmity.

And he laid his hands on her: and immediately she was made straight, and glorified God.

And the ruler of the synagogue answered with indignation, because that Jesus had healed on the sabbath day, and said unto the people, There are six days in which men ought to work: in them therefore come and be healed, and not on the sabbath day [Luke 13:10–14].

This woman had one of the worst cases of illness recorded in the Bible. She had a severe malady. The problem arose not because our Lord healed her, but because He healed her on the Sabbath day. The Lord healing people on the Sabbath day was a recurring source of contention between Himself and the religious rulers.

This woman had a spirit of infirmity that had plagued her for eighteen years. It is difficult to translate into English the terminology that Dr. Luke uses to describe her condition. They are medical terms. Her illness was chronic. Because of it she was bowed down or, as Weymouth translates it, "bent double." This poor woman could not lift herself up. Here was a woman in a desperate condition. She was an unfortunate wretch who was an object of pity. This was probably one of the most terrible cases of physical infirmity that the Lord dealt with on earth.

> **The Lord then answered him, and said, Thou hypocrite, doth not each one of you on the sabbath loose his ox or his ass from the stall, and lead him away to watering?**

> **And ought not this woman, being a daughter of Abraham, whom Satan hath bound, lo, these eighteen years, be loosed from this bond on the sabbath day? [Luke 13:15–16].**

I must confess that I do not understand why this woman had been bound by Satan. She apparently was not an immoral person, as she was a regular attendant at the synagogue even in her condition. It was in the synagogue that the Great Physician said to her, "Be loosed." He laid His hands on her, and immediately she was made straight and glorified God. His touch upon her was not essential but was an aid to her faith. It was personal contact. And personal contact with Him is the important thing for us also.

The ruler of the synagogue rebuked her sharply—yet this woman had not come to the synagogue with any intention of being healed. The reaction of the religious ruler was strange indeed. He was more interested in the rule than he was in the fact that a poor woman, who had been shackled for eighteen years with a grievous infirmity, had been freed. The Sabbath question was the most important issue to these religious rulers. Yet Sabbath prohibitions had become a burden too great to be borne. The Sabbath question is still one of heated debate today. The important thing is not to argue about religion, but to learn to live it.

And when he had said these things, all his adversaries were ashamed: and all the people rejoiced for all the glorious things that were done by him [Luke 13:17].

The people, though they heard Him gladly, seemed to go no farther with Him. It is possible to become so religious and callous that you can exclude Jesus from your life too. You may know all the answers and be an expert in argument, but the real question is, "Have you ever let Christ into your heart?" There is no substitute for that. Are you filled with doubts? Are you puzzled or troubled? Are you bent double with the burdens of life? Then come to the Lord Jesus Christ with your burdens and sins. You can come to Him anytime. He is ready and waiting to meet your need.

PARABLES OF THE MUSTARD SEED AND LEAVEN

Then said he, Unto what is the kingdom of God like? and whereunto shall I resemble it?

It is like a grain of mustard seed, which a man took, and cast into his garden; and it grew, and waxed a great tree; and the fowls of the air lodged in the branches of it.

And again he said, Whereunto shall I liken the kingdom of God?

It is like leaven, which a woman took and hid in three measures of meal, till the whole was leavened [Luke 13:18–21].

The mustard seed is symbolic of the outward aspect of Christendom with its multiplied organizations and denominations. The mustard seed is to become an herb and not a tree. Instead of church organizations lagging behind, there is actually an abnormal growth which has been too fast. They have lost their true character as they have become great. The "birds" are the key of this parable. They represent the Devil who is active in Christendom and in many so-called churches.

Leaven represents not the gospel but a principle of evil. Leaven never represents good as used in the Bible. Leaven occurs about ninety-eight times in the Bible—about seventy-five times in the Old Testament and about twenty-three times in the New Testament. It is always used in a bad sense. Although many sincere folk think of leaven as representing the gospel, which will spread over the entire world and convert the world, they are doomed to disappointment. There will be no kingdom and no peace until Christ returns to establish His Kingdom on this earth. The organized church cannot bring in His Kingdom. In His own good time Christ Himself will come and establish His Kingdom.

JESUS CONTINUES TO TEACH AS HE GOES TOWARD JERUSALEM

And he went through the cities and villages, teaching, and journeying toward Jerusalem [Luke 13:22].

Jesus is continuing to move toward Jerusalem. Luke has already told us, "And it came to pass, when the time was come that he should be received up, he stedfastly set his face to go to Jerusalem" (Luke 9:51). He is on His way there, on His way to die in Jerusalem. This was to be our Savior's last journey.

Then said one unto him, Lord, are there few that be saved? and he said unto them,

Strive to enter in at the strait gate: for many, I say unto you, will seek to enter in, and shall not be able.

When once the master of the house is risen up, and hath shut to the door, and ye begin to stand without, and to knock at the door, saying, Lord, Lord, open unto us; and he shall answer and say unto you, I know you not whence ye are:

Then shall ye begin to say, We have eaten and drunk in thy presence, and thou hast taught in our streets.

But he shall say, I tell you, I know you not whence ye
are; depart from me, all ye workers of iniquity.

There shall be weeping and gnashing of teeth, when ye
shall see Abraham, and Isaac, and Jacob, and all the
prophets, in the kingdom of God, and you yourselves
thrust out.

And they shall come from the east, and from the west,
and from the north, and from the south, and shall sit
down in the kingdom of God.

And, behold, there are last which shall be first, and
there are first which shall be last [Luke 13:23–30].

Why this question was asked is difficult to discern. Perhaps it was
sincere. The charisma of Christ drew the multitudes, but they soon
discovered that it cost to follow Him. There were those coming and
going all the time. As He approached Jerusalem this last time it was
noticeable. There came a day when it was written, "And they all forsook him, and fled" (Mark 14:50). He made it abundantly clear that it
would *cost* to follow Him. That we in our sophisticated and soft af-
fluency think otherwise is heresy!

Since this was a speculative question, Jesus did not answer it directly. He is saying to this man, "Make sure you are saved." In the rest
of this brief discourse, the Lord made it clear that many will be saved
who are not sons of Abraham, Isaac, and Jacob.

The same day there came certain of the Pharisees, saying unto him, Get thee out, and depart hence: for Herod
will kill thee.

And he said unto them, Go ye, and tell that fox, Behold,
I cast out devils, and I do cures to-day and to-morrow,
and the third day I shall be perfected.

Nevertheless I must walk today, and tomorrow, and the
day following: for it cannot be that a prophet perish out
of Jerusalem [Luke 13:31–33].

In this warning from the Pharisees, the Lord Jesus labeled Herod a *fox*. Man has not ascended from the animal; but sometimes he descends to the animal plane in living. Our Lord gives here the veiled program of His redemption and resurrection.

JESUS WEEPS OVER JERUSALEM

O Jerusalem, Jerusalem, which killest the prophets, and stonest them that are sent unto thee; how often would I have gathered thy children together, as a hen doth gather her brood under her wings, and ye would not!

Behold, your house is left unto you desolate: and verily I say unto you, Ye shall not see me, until the time come when ye shall say, Blessed is he that cometh in the name of the Lord [Luke 13:34–35].

Again He expresses His love and concern for Jerusalem, the city where He was to die. He also pronounces judgment upon the ". . . city of the great King" (Matt. 5:35). Also He announces that He is coming again. The next time will be the real Triumphal Entry.

CHAPTER 14

THEME: Jesus goes to dinner at home of Pharisee; parable of the impolite guests; parable of the great supper; parable about building a tower; parable of a king going to war; parable about salt that loses its tang

L uke alone records the delightful occasion of the Lord Jesus going out to dinner at the home of one of the chief Pharisees, and of His giving His host and guests a lesson in etiquette in the devastating parable of the ambitious guest. Also there are two other parables in this chapter that are in no other Gospel—the building of a tower and a king preparing to make war, which both relate to discipleship. He concludes with the parable of the salt that loses its tang.

JESUS GOES TO DINNER AT HOME OF PHARISEE

Jesus is going out to dinner again, and this time we are going to have some fun.

> **And it came to pass, as he went into the house of one of the chief Pharisees to eat bread on the sabbath day, that they watched him [Luke 14:1].**

I must confess that if a Pharisee had asked me to come to dinner for the purpose of spying on me, I would have refused. The Pharisee was watching for something that would discredit our Lord. This first verse provides the atmosphere, tone, and color of the situation. It was the prelude before the dinner that produced the tenseness.

> **And, behold, there was a certain man before him which had the dropsy [Luke 14:2].**

A trap was laid to ensnare the Lord. I believe this man was deliberately planted to motivate our Lord to break the Sabbath by healing

him. Notice what He did. The Lord asked the question first, and they
were afraid to answer Him.

> **And Jesus answering spake unto the lawyers and Phari-
> sees, saying, Is it lawful to heal on the sabbath day?**
>
> **And they held their peace. And he took him, and healed
> him, and let him go;**
>
> **And answered them, saying, Which of you shall have an
> ass or an ox fallen into a pit, and will not straightway
> pull him out on the sabbath day? [Luke 14:3–5].**

If their ox or donkey fell into something, they would rescue it. In other
words, if any of those rascals had had a flat tire on the Sabbath, they
would have fixed it, and the Lord knew it. "That's the reason I'm fix-
ing up this fellow here—he's in trouble."

> **And they could not answer him again to these things
> [Luke 14:6].**

This incident created a rather tense situation for dinner.

PARABLE OF THE IMPOLITE GUESTS

> **And he put forth a parable to those which were bidden,
> when he marked how they chose out the chief rooms;
> saying unto them [Luke 14:7].**

This scene is as rich as it can be. In that day they did not have place
cards at the table. Place cards must have been originated by some
hostess who wanted to preserve her furniture! Without place cards at
the table, there was a mad rush to get to the best seats. At the table in
that day there were four chief places. When the cook said, "Soup's
on," everyone made a beeline for the table. In that day couches rather
than chairs were used so that the guests reclined at the table. There
were three places to recline on each side; the center place was the seat

of honor which made four chief places. At the head table there would be seats one, two and three on one side; seat number two, the center seat, would be the place of honor. Around on the other side would be seats four, five, and six, with number five as the seat of honor. Around on the other side are seats seven, eight, and nine, with seat number eight the seat of honor. On the fourth side of the table number eleven would be the seat of honor.

It is understandable that one of these old Pharisees could not move as fast as some of the younger Pharisees. When the cook called, "Soup's on," the old Pharisee, who had moved as close as possible to the dining area, ran for seat number two. One of the younger Pharisees got there before he did; so he turned the corner fast and tried to reach number five seat. He was too late again because someone was already sitting there. Quickly he tried for seat number eight, but he did not make it to that seat in time either. He turned the corner and made a dive for seat number eleven and made it. It was the lowest seat, but still a seat of honor. He reclined there out of breath.

Can you imagine what a hilarious picture it must have been to see these men running as fast as they could for the seats of honor? Now our Lord will correct their manners.

> **When thou art bidden of any man to a wedding, sit not down in the highest room; lest a more honourable man than thou be bidden of him;**

> **And he that bade thee and him come and say to thee, Give this man place; and thou begin with shame to take the lowest room.**

> **But when thou art bidden, go and sit down in the lowest room; that when he that bade thee cometh, he may say unto thee, Friend, go up higher: then shalt thou have worship in the presence of them that sit at meat with thee [Luke 14:8–10].**

The Lord Jesus said, "When you are invited to dinner, don't rush to get the seat of honor. The host may have someone else in mind for that seat. He would have to come to you and say, 'Move over to the lowest seat so my guest of honor can sit here.'" To get to the lowest seat, all you have to do is move over one seat, but it is embarrassing.

"When you are invited to a dinner, always go to the lowest seat. You will not have any trouble getting it because no one else will be trying for it. Then when the host comes in and sees where you are sitting, he will say, 'You are to be my guest of honor. Please sit in the seat of honor.' Then someone else will have to move." This is good manners and just the opposite of the demonstration this group had just put on.

Our Lord draws a great principle from this incident:

For whosoever exalteth himself shall be abased; and he that humbleth himself shall be exalted [Luke 14:11].

This is an important principle for us as believers.

Next our Lord corrects the host.

Then said he also to him that bade him, When thou makest a dinner or a supper, call not thy friends, nor thy brethren, neither thy kinsmen, nor thy rich neighbours; lest they also bid thee again, and a recompence be made thee.

But when thou makest a feast, call the poor, the maimed, the lame, the blind:

And thou shalt be blessed; for they cannot recompense thee: for thou shalt be recompensed at the resurrection of the just [Luke 14:12–14].

Our Lord is setting forth another great principle. Most of us have the same guests over to dinner one time, and the next time we go to one of their homes, and so it goes week after week. It is sort of a round-robin situation. The Lord is condemning that practice. There is nothing wrong with having your group in once in a while, but have you ever thought about doing something for those who have nothing? They cannot pay you back; they will not be able to invite you to dinner next week. Do a few things where you will be the giver with no thought of ever being paid back.

PARABLE OF THE GREAT SUPPER

Can you imagine the tenseness at this dinner? It started with our Lord healing the man with dropsy—in the face of their disapproval. Then He looked the guests straight in the eyes and corrected their manners. Then He corrected the host. Believe me, the atmosphere was tense. Nobody was saying a word.

> **And when one of them that sat at meat with him heard these things, he said unto him, Blessed is he that shall eat bread in the kingdom of God [Luke 14:15].**

This is, without a doubt, one of the pious platitudes that this man is used to giving. In that awkward moment of silence, when no one was saying anything, one old rascal speaks out and says, Blessed is he that shall eat bread in the kingdom of God." I wish I could have been there. I would have asked him, "What do you mean by that?" I doubt that he could have told me what he really meant. At least I have never found a commentator who could explain what he meant. His statement was nothing more than a pious cliché. You hear a lot of pious platitudes in our conservative circles today. I get so tired of hearing them. One of the most common clichés is, "Praise the Lord." It is a wonderful thing to praise the Lord, but sometimes it becomes a little boring when a person uses that phrase constantly, but does not praise the Lord in his heart. Let us steer clear of pious clichés.

The Lord did not let this rascal get by with his cliché. He turned to him, and I think His eyes flashed with anger as He spoke to him.

> **Then said he unto him, A certain man made a great supper, and bade many:**
>
> **And sent his servant at supper time to say to them that were bidden, Come; for all things are now ready [Luke 14:16–17].**

It was the custom to send out invitations to such a dinner a long time in advance, but as the actual day for the dinner arrived, a personal invitation was extended. God has issued an invitation. What is man going to do with it? God's invitation is for salvation. You cannot buy your way into this feast. You cannot elbow your way in. You come to this dinner by the grace of God. "For by grace are ye saved through faith; and that not of yourselves: it is the gift of God: Not of works, lest any man should boast" (Eph. 2:8–9). You get into this dinner by receiving a gift. The only thing that will exclude any human being from heaven is a refusal to accept the invitation.

The Lord Jesus said, "You say, 'Blessed is he that eateth bread in the kingdom'; that is pious nonsense. Here is what men are doing with God's invitation:"

> **And they all with one consent began to make excuse. The first said unto him, I have bought a piece of ground, and I must needs go and see it: I pray thee have me excused [Luke 14:18].**

This is not an excuse, it is an alibi. Someone has said, "An alibi is a lie stuffed in the skin of an excuse." No one who was invited said, "I will not come to the dinner." They were simply making excuses to cover up the fact that they did not want to come.

The first man to give an excuse was either a liar or a fool. Can you imagine buying property without first looking at it?

> **And another said, I have bought five yoke of oxen, and I go to prove them: I pray thee have me excused [Luke 14:19].**

The first man let possessions keep him away. The second man let business keep him away. Again I have to say of this second man that he is either a liar or a fool. How could this man plow at night? In those days they did not have flood lights. This man was making excuses. "I must make a living," is a phrase I hear often. People are so busy with their business they have no time for God. One day you are going to die, and you will discover that business will go on as usual without you.

And another said, I have married a wife, and therefore I cannot come [Luke 14:20].

There was a law in Israel that excused a man from going to war if he had taken a new wife. This man had the weakest excuse of all. Why didn't he bring his wife with him and come to the dinner? His natural affection kept him away from the dinner. How many times I have heard a man say, "I don't come to church because Sunday is the only day I can spend with my family."

These things keep more people from God than anything else: possessions, business, and natural affection. How many people today are kept from God because of these things? Well, God has an engraved invitation for you. It is written in the blood of Jesus Christ and invites you to the great table of salvation.

So that servant came, and shewed his lord these things. Then the master of the house being angry said to his servant, Go out quickly into the streets and lanes of the city, and bring in hither the poor, and the maimed, and the halt, and the blind.

And the servant said, Lord, it is done as thou hast commanded, and yet there is room.

And the lord said unto the servant, Go out into the highways and hedges, and compel them to come in, that my house may be filled.

For I say unto you, That none of those men which were bidden shall taste of my supper [Luke 14:21–24].

This is a severe statement. If you reject God's invitation, He has to reject you. You are excluded because of your refusal to accept His invitation.

And there went great multitudes with him: and he
turned, and said unto them,

If any man come to me, and hate not his father, and
mother, and wife, and children, and brethren, and sis-
ters, yea, and his own life also, he cannot be my disciple.

And whosoever doth not bear his cross, and come after
me, cannot be my disciple [Luke 14:25–27].

These verses are simply saying that we should put God first. A believer's devotedness to Jesus Christ should be such that, by comparison, it
looks as if everything else is hated. All terms which define affections
are comparative.

PARABLE ABOUT BUILDING A TOWER

For which of you, intending to build a tower, sitteth not
down first, and counteth the cost, whether he have suffi-
cient to finish it?

Lest haply, after he hath laid the foundation, and is not
able to finish it, all that behold it begin to mock him,

Saying, This man began to build, and was not able to
finish [Luke 14:28–30].

It will cost something to make a decision for Christ. It will cost something to be His disciple. Think it over, friend. You should count the
cost before you make the decision.

PARABLE OF A KING GOING TO WAR

Or what king, going to make war against another king,
sitteth not down first, and consulteth whether he be able
with ten thousand to meet him that cometh against him
with twenty thousand?

Or else, while the other is yet a great way off, he sendeth an ambassage, and desireth conditions of peace.

So likewise, whosoever he be of you that forsaketh not all that he hath, he cannot be my disciple [Luke 14:31–33].

A person can be saved by accepting Jesus Christ as Savior, but a person will never follow and serve Him until he is willing to make a sacrifice. That is what this passage is teaching. There is a difference between being a believer and being a disciple. Unfortunately, not all believers are disciples.

PARABLE ABOUT SALT THAT LOSES ITS TANG

Salt is good: but if the salt have lost his savour, wherewith shall it be seasoned?

It is neither fit for the land, nor yet for the dunghill; but men cast it out. He that hath ears to hear, let him hear [Luke 14:34–35].

Nothing is more worthless than salt that has lost its saltiness. May the Lord deliver us from being useless Christians!

CHAPTER 15

THEME: Parable of the lost sheep; parable of the lost coin; parable of two lost sons

Now we come to probably the best-loved parable that our Lord told; we call it the parable of the Prodigal Son.

The background for this parable is that the publicans and sinners came in to hear the Lord Jesus by multitudes. The Pharisees and scribes began to murmur, to criticize Him because of this. They were scandalized that He would receive them and even eat with them.

His answer to the murmuring of the Pharisees and scribes is a parable. Customarily it is called three parables: the parable of the lost sheep, the parable of the lost coin, and the parable of the lost son. Actually, it is three parts of one parable; it is three pictures in a single frame.

When I was a youngster, I used to visit my aunt, and I remember seeing a picture called a triptych, which she kept in the attic—that's where she let me sleep when the house was filled up with relatives. I liked to look at that picture because it was three pictures in one frame. This is what our Lord gives us here, three pictures that belong together. It is a triptych.

Then drew near unto him all the publicans and sinners for to hear him.

And the Pharisees and scribes murmured, saying, This man receiveth sinners, and eateth with them [Luke 15:1–2].

I can't resist telling the story of a little girl who heard this verse read. On a cold London night, she stepped, shivering, into the shelter of a church where a service was in progress. After the service, when the congregation had gone, she approached the rector, "Sir, I never knew my name was in the Bible!" He smiled, "Well, little girl what is your name?" "My name," she answered excitedly, "is *Edith*." "Oh, I'm sorry to disappoint you, but *Edith* does not appear in the Bible." She insisted, "Yes, it does. I heard you read it tonight. It said, 'Jesus receiveth sinners, and *Edith* with them!'"

Certainly our Lord receives Edith—and Mary and John and all the rest of us. Thank God, He does receive sinners!

PARABLE OF THE LOST SHEEP

Now in this wonderful parable we see the first picture, that of a lost sheep.

And he spake this parable unto them, saying,

What man of you, having an hundred sheep, if he lose one of them, doth not leave the ninety and nine in the wilderness, and go after that which is lost, until he find it?

And when he hath found it, he layeth it on his shoulders, rejoicing.

And when he cometh home, he calleth together his friends and neighbours, saying unto them, Rejoice with me; for I have found my sheep which was lost.

I say unto you, that likewise joy shall be in heaven over one sinner that repenteth, more than over ninety and nine just persons, which need no repentance [Luke 15:3–7].

The shepherd in this parable is the Great Shepherd, Jesus Christ. We are the sheep. He had one hundred sheep, and one of them got lost. Frankly, that would be a pretty good percentage, to start out with one hundred sheep and end up with ninety-nine. This Shepherd, however, would not be satisfied with just ninety-nine sheep. When one sheep got lost, He went out and looked for it. When He found it, He put it on His shoulders, the place of strength. He is able to save to the uttermost. The high priest of the children of Israel wore an ephod. On the shoulders of the ephod were two stones. On them were engraved the names of the twelve tribes—six tribes on one stone and six on the other. The high priest carried the children of Israel on his shoulders. Our great High Priest carries us on His shoulders, and we will not become lost. When He starts out with one hundred sheep, He will come through with one hundred sheep—not ninety-nine. This is a picture of the Lord Jesus Christ out looking for those who are His own.

PARABLE OF THE LOST COIN

The second picture in this triptych is that of the lost coin.

> **Either what woman having ten pieces of silver, if she lose one piece, doth not light a candle, and sweep the house, and seek diligently till she find it?**

> **And when she hath found it, she calleth her friends and her neighbours together, saying, Rejoice with me; for I have found the piece which I had lost.**

> **Likewise, I say unto you, there is joy in the presence of the angels of God over one sinner that repenteth [Luke 15:8–10].**

The coin was probably part of the row of coins which formed a head-piece, signifying her married state. To lose a part of it was like losing a stone out of one's wedding ring. The woman depicts the Holy Spirit whose ministry is to make sure that each one who belongs to the Bridegroom will be present for the wedding. Every coin will be in place. Every one is valuable to Him.

PARABLE OF TWO LOST SONS

As I mentioned previously, Dr. Luke, a medical doctor and a scientist, was also an artist. And he is the one who records our Lord's glorious parables which no other Gospel writer gives us.

And he said, A certain man had two sons [Luke 15:11].

Immediately our Lord begins to put the background on the canvas. And I see a lovely home (because this will represent the home of the Father, the heavenly Father) and it's a glorious home. It's a home that has all of the comforts and all of the joys and all of the love that ever went into a home. In that home there's the "certain man," and that is God the Father. And this Father had two sons. He has more sons than that, but these are representative, you see. One of these boys is called the elder and the other is called the younger. We see the lovely home, and out in front there stand the Father and two boys.

Now let's watch our Lord put some more in the picture for us.

> **And the younger of them said to his father, Father, give me the portion of goods that falleth to me. And he divided unto them his living.**
>
> **And not many days after the younger son gathered all together, and took his journey into a far country, and there wasted his substance with riotous living [Luke 15:12-13].**

Here in this lovely home, a home in which there was everything in the world that the heart of man could want—love, joy, fellowship, comforts—this younger boy does a very strange thing. He says, "I'm tired of the discipline. I don't like it here. I'd like to stretch my wings. I've been looking over the pasture, and the grass over in the other field looks to me like it's lots greener." And I do not know why that's true, but to you and me the grass in the next pasture always looks greener. The boy looked out from home and said, "If I could only get away off yonder on my own, it would be wonderful." He didn't like it at home; he fell out with his father and lost fellowship with him. And so the father gave to him his living, and the boy left with his pockets full of money—which he did not earn with work that he'd done himself. Every bit that came to him, his father had given to him. He didn't get it by his ability, he didn't get it because he was clever, and he didn't get it because he had worked hard. The money he had in his pocket was there because he had a very generous father. And so the boy starts out for the far country.

Now our scene shifts, and we've got to put in another picture here, and the picture is the far country; you can paint it any way you want to. May I say to you, you can paint it in lurid colors, and many have attempted to paint it that way. I do not think it's exaggerated to paint it in lurid colors. This boy found out what it was to have what the world calls a good time. He made all of the nightclubs; he knew café society; he had money. And when you have money, you can get fair-weather friends. For a time he lived it up. He enjoyed the pleasures of sin for a season there in the far country. You paint your own picture there. Our Lord didn't put in any details of what the boy did. But we can well imagine some of the things that he did. However, there did come a day when he'd finished living it up; he reached into his pocket and there wasn't anything left.

And when he had spent all, there arose a mighty famine in that land; and he began to be in want [Luke 15:14].

Not only is he in a very bad way financially, but the country is also in a bad way. You see, in that country where he thought the grass was greener, the grass has now dried up. They're having a famine in that land, and this boy does not know what to do. If you want to know the truth, he's afraid to go home. He should not have been afraid, but he was afraid to go home. Now he's desperate. He is so desperate that he's going to do something that no Jew would ever have done unless he'd hit the bottom. This boy has hit the bottom. He can't get a job. He goes around to see some of these fair-weather friends, and he says, "Bill, do you remember how you used to come to the banquets I gave and the dinners, and that I always picked up the check and I paid for the li quor and I paid for the girls? Do you remember that? Now I'm in a bad way. I wonder if you couldn't tide me over or maybe you could give me a job." And the fair-weather friend says, "I'm sorry. You say you've lost all your money? Well, I'm through with you. I'm not interested in you anymore. My secretary will show you to the door." And the boy found, after going from place to place, that he didn't have any real friends in the far country. Finally he ended up by going out to the edge of town where there was a man who was raising pigs, and you could tell it a mile away. And the boy went over to him and said, "I'd like to have a job." The man says, "Well, I can't pay you. You know, we're having a lot of difficulty, but if you can beat the pigs to it, you can eat here at least." That's exactly the point to which he had sunk. And when our Lord said that this man "would fain have filled his belly with the husks that the swine did eat," every Israelite, both Pharisee and publican, who was listening to Him that day, winced because a Hebrew couldn't go any lower than that—he was to have nothing to do with swine (the Mosaic Law had shut him off from them), but to stoop to the place where he'd go down and live with them was horrifying! That's the picture, and it's a black picture. You see, this boy has hit the very bottom.

Somebody is immediately going to say, "Well, this is the fellow who is a sinner, and he is going to get saved." No, I'm sorry to tell you that such is not the picture that's given to us here. This is not the picture of a sinner that gets saved. May I say to you, and say it very carefully, that when this boy was living at home with the father and was in fellowship with him, he was a son, and there was never any question about that. When this boy got to the far country and was out there throwing his money around, he was still a son. That is never questioned. And when this boy went down and hit the bottom and was out there with the pigs (and if you'd been a half-mile away looking over there among the pigs, I don't think you could have told him from a pig), he was not a pig—he was a son. In this story that our Lord told there was never any question as to whether the boy was a son or not. He was a son all the time.

Somebody says, "Then this is not the gospel." Yes, it is the gospel also. And I will hold to that for the very simple reason that an evangelist in southern Oklahoma many years ago used this parable to present the gospel. People said he imitated Billy Sunday, but I had never heard of Billy Sunday; so it didn't make any difference to me whom he imitated. He was a little short fellow, holding services under a brush arbor. And the thing that interested us boys was the fact he could jump as high as the pulpit. He'd just stand flat right there and up he'd go—a little short fellow. And we'd sit out there and watch him, and the next day we'd practice to see if we could jump that high. May I say to you, one night he preached on the Prodigal Son, and that's the night I went forward. Don't tell me the gospel is not there. It is there.

However, let's understand what the parable is primarily about. The parable is not how a sinner gets saved; it reveals the heart of a Father who will not only save a sinner but will also take back a son that sins.

> **And he went and joined himself to a citizen of that country; and he sent him into his fields to feed swine.**
>
> **And he would fain have filled his belly with the husks that the swine did eat: and no man gave unto him [Luke 15:15–16].**

Maybe you thought a moment ago I was exaggerating when I said his fair-weather friends wouldn't help him. Our Lord made it very clear that they wouldn't help him—"no man gave unto him." Why is it today that Christians sometimes get the impression that the man of the world is really his friend when he's trying to lead him away from God? Well, believers do get that impression. This boy got that impression also. He was being led away from home, from his father, farther and farther away. And he thought these folks were his friends.

Now we don't have any letters that he wrote back to some of his friends at home. But if we had one, I think that it would have said, "Say, you ought to come over here. You know, there are some real people over here where I am. I tell you, I'm having a big time. You ought to come over." But, may I say to you, the day came when he found out these were not his friends. "No man gave unto him."

Now that's the black part of the picture, and I think it's about time for us to see some of the bright colors our Lord painted into the picture, for our Lord always, always put down a black background and then put the bright colors in the foreground of the picture. Have you ever noticed that God paints that way? And so, on the black background of this boy's sin—down in the pigpen, out of fellowship with his father, having left home in a huff—our Lord begins to put the bright color.

> **And when he came to himself, he said, How many hired servants of my father's have bread enough and to spare, and I perish with hunger! [Luke 15:17].**

He came to himself. Sin does an awful thing for us. It makes us see the world incorrectly. It makes us see ourselves in the wrong light. It makes us see the pleasures of this world in the wrong perspective, and we just don't see clearly when we're in sin. This boy, when he was at home, looked out yonder at the far country, and it all looked so good— the grass was so green and the fun was so keen; but now he came to himself. And the first thing he did was a little reasoning. He began to use his intelligence. He said, "You know, I'm a son of my father, and here I am in a far country. I'm down here in a pigpen with pigs, and back in my father's home the servants are better off than I am, and I'm his son." When he began to think like that, he began to make sense. And this young man now acts like he's intelligent.

> **I will arise and go to my father, and will say unto him, Father, I have sinned against heaven, and before thee,**
>
> **And am no more worthy to be called thy son: make me as one of thy hired servants [Luke 15:18–19].**

Now we get to a really bright picture. This is the brightest one of all, and it's the picture of that lovely home we were telling you about. Oh, it's a beautiful home. It's the father's house. The Lord Jesus said, "In my Father's house there are many abiding places . . ." (John 14:2, translation mine). This is the house. The house is there in the background, and I see a father looking out the window. He's been looking out the window every day since his bcy left. And do you know why he's been looking out the window? He knew that one day that boy would be trudging down the road coming home.

Somebody asks, "Do you believe that if you're once saved you're always saved?" Yes. Somebody asks, "Do you believe that a Christian can get into sin?" Yes. "Can a Christian stay in sin?" No. Because in the Father's house the Father is watching, and He says, "All my sons are coming home. My sons don't like pigpens because they do not have the nature of a pig. They have the nature of a son. They have My nature, and they won't be happy except in the Father's house. The only place in the world where they will be content is the Father's house. And every one of My sons that goes out to the far country and gets into a pigpen—regardless of how dirty he gets, or how low he sinks—if he's My son, one day he'll say, 'I'll arise, and I'll go to my Father.'" And the reason he'll say, "I'll go to my Father," is because the Man who lives in the big house is his Father. Up until now, after at least 6,000 years of recorded human history, there never yet has been a human pig that has said, "I will arise and go to my Father's house." Never, never. Pigs love it down there. They don't want to go to the Father's house. The only one who wants to go to the Father's house is a son; and one day the son will say, "I will arise and I will go to my Father."

Now the son starts home. Maybe you thought a moment ago that I was exaggerating when I said that this father had been looking out the window every day. But he had, and now he sees him coming. He has compassion, and runs, and says to his servant, "Go down to the tree and cut me about a half a dozen hickory limbs. I'm going to switch this boy within an inch of his life." Is that the way your Bible reads? Well, mine doesn't either. It ought to read that way. Under the Mosaic Law a father had a perfect right to bring a disobedient son before the elders and have him stoned to death. This father had a perfect right to say, "This boy took my name and my money, my substance, and he squandered it. He disgraced my name. I'll whip him within an inch of his life." He had a right to do this. But this father, rather, did something amazing. And when our Lord got to this part of the parable, and when He put this bright color on, it caused all those that were present to blink their eyes. They said, "We can't believe that. It's bad enough to see him hit the bottom and go down yonder with the pigs, but it's worse for the father to take him back home without doing something. He ought to punish him. That's the thing that we don't like. He ought to be punished." Will you notice what the father did? Let me read it accurately now.

> **And he arose, and came to his father. But when he was yet a great way off, his father saw him, and had compassion, and ran, and fell on his neck, and kissed him [Luke 15:20].**

He's in rags, and you can almost smell him—oh, that pig smell! There stands the boy, and the father goes and puts his arms around him and kisses him.

> **And the son said unto him, Father, I have sinned against heaven, and in thy sight, and am no more worthy to be called thy son [Luke 15:21].**

Now he'd memorized a little speech, you see. He's saying the thing he'd planned in the far country. I think he repeated that little speech all the way home. I think every step of the way he said, "When I get home, I'm going to say to him, 'Father, I have sinned against heaven, and before thee, and am no more worthy to be called thy son: make me as one of thy hired servants.'" He started to say this to his father but he didn't get very far. He got as far as, "I am no more worthy to be called thy son" when he was interrupted.

> **But the father said to his servants, Bring forth the best robe, and put it on him; and put a ring on his hand, and shoes on his feet:**
>
> **And bring hither the fatted calf, and kill it; and let us eat, and be merry:**
>
> **For this my son was dead, and is alive again; he was lost, and is found. And they began to be merry [Luke 15:22–24].**

If you really want to have a ball, you can't do it in the far country. If you're God's child, you can't sin and get by with it. You may even go to the pigpen, but, my friend, you can never enjoy it. If you're a son of the Father, there'll come a day when you're going to say, "I will arise and go to my Father," and you will go. And when you go, you will confess to Him. "If we confess our sins, he is faithful and just to forgive us our sins, and to cleanse us from all unrighteousness" (1 John 1:9). That's the way a sinning child gets back into the fellowship of the Father's house. In fact, the only way back is by confession.

Have you ever noticed the things the father says he's going to do for the son? He says, "Get a robe." Now a robe was clean clothing that went on him after he'd been washed. "If we confess our sins, he is faithful and just to forgive us our sins, and to cleanse us from all unrighteousness." Our Lord washes us. The One who girded Himself with a towel is the One who will wash one of His sons who comes back to Him; he has to be cleansed when he's been to the far country. And that robe is the robe of the righteousness of Christ that covers the believer after he is cleansed. The ring is the insignia of the full-grown son, with all rights pertaining thereto. He's brought back into his original position. Nothing is taken from him. He's brought back into his place in the Father's house.

Christ right now is at God's right hand, still girded with the towel of service for one of His who gets soiled feet or soiled hands by being in the far country. When we confess to Him, He is faithful and just to forgive us our sins and to cleanse us from all unrighteousness. We have to come like the Prodigal Son came. "Father, I have sinned, and I'm no longer worthy to be called your son. Make me a hired servant." And the Father will say, "I'd never make you a hired servant. You're my son. I'll cleanse you, I'll forgive you, I'll bring you back into the place of fellowship and usefulness."

A son is a son forever.

There is another Prodigal Son in this parable.

Now his elder son was in the field: and as he came and drew nigh to the house, he heard music and dancing.

And he called one of the servants, and asked what these things meant.

> And he said unto him, Thy brother is come; and thy father hath killed the fatted calf, because he hath received him safe and sound.
>
> And he was angry, and would not go in: therefore came his father out, and entreated him [Luke 15:25–28].

Listen to this boy—what a complainer and a griper he is! This is the *real* Prodigal Son. He was angry when he heard that his brother had returned and a party was being given in his honor. He would not go in and join the others at the feast. His father came out and entreated his son to come to the banquet.

> And he answering said to his father, Lo, these many years do I serve thee, neither transgressed I at any time thy commandment: and yet thou never gavest me a kid, that I might make merry with my friends:
>
> But as soon as this thy son was come, which hath devoured thy living with harlots, thou hast killed for him the fatted calf.
>
> And he said unto him, Son, thou art ever with me, and all that I have is thine.
>
> It was meet that we should make merry, and be glad: for this thy brother was dead, and is alive again; and was lost, and is found [Luke 15:29–32].

There are many Christians who are not living in a far country; they are trying to live for God, but they are as poor as Job's turkey. Why? They are blessed with all spiritual blessings, but they will not lay hold upon them. God says, "It is all yours; everything that I have belongs to you—take it." Our heavenly Father is rich in spiritual blessings and they belong to us, but He will not force them upon us. We must reach out and take them for ourselves. The story closes with the elder son out of fellowship with his Father. The Father, however, left the door to fellowship wide open.

Years ago Dr. Chadwick made the statement that there is a third son in the parable of the Prodigal Son. The younger son broke the Father's heart, the elder son was out of fellowship, and the third Son is the One who uttered the parable. He is Jesus Christ, the Son of God. He is the ideal Son without sin. He came to a far country, not to run away, but to do the will of His Father. He did not spend His life in riotous living but in sacrificial dying. He was not a Prodigal Son but a Prince of Peace who shed His blood for the sins of the world. He was not a wayward son but a willing sacrifice. He says, "But as many as received him, to them gave he power to become the sons of God, even to them that believe on his name" (John 1:12). Salvation comes to those who simply believe on His name.

If you are the son who went away to a far country, you can come back to the Father by confessing your sins to Him. Perhaps you are like the elder son who was out of fellowship. He had no concern or love for his brother. He thought he was serving God; he had never transgressed as his brother had. Yet he had never enjoyed a feast with his friends. The Father says to you, "All that I have is thine." How wonderful to have a Father like this!

Sinner friend, if you have never trusted Jesus Christ as your Savior, you are not the Father's son. You can become a son only by putting your faith and trust in Christ who died for you. If you accept Christ and come to Him, God becomes your Father and He will never throw you overboard. If you leave Him and one day return, He will be waiting to put His arms around you. How wonderful He is!

CHAPTER 16

THEME: Parable of the unjust steward; Jesus answers the covetous Pharisees; Jesus speaks on divorce; Jesus recounts the incident of the rich man and Lazarus (poor man)

PARABLE OF THE UNJUST STEWARD

This parable has been greatly misunderstood, and one of the reasons is because it looks as though our Lord is commending a crook. This steward is an out-and-out crook. Some folk assume that anyone whom the Lord Jesus mentioned in a parable is a hero and an example of the noblest character. If this is your assumption, then prepare to make a change because you will have difficulty with this parable. This man is a scoundrel. When I was a pastor, I attempted one summer to run a series of sermons on rascals of revelation, scoundrels of Scripture, thieves of theology, bad men of the Bible, and crooks of Christianity. It was a long series because there were so many rogues! This steward is one of them.

I have already called attention to the fact that Luke gives parables by contrast. He is the only Gospel writer that does this. Most parables are parables by comparison.

In this parable the Lord uses as an example a man who followed the principles of the world. We are told in the Word of God that the world loves its own but hates those who belong to God. "If the world hate you, ye know that it hated me before it hated you. If ye were of the world, the world would love his own: but because ye are not of the world, but I have chosen you out of the world, therefore the world hateth you" (John 15:18–19). A child of God does not belong to this world and does not live by the principles of this world. In Galatians 1:3–4 Paul says, ". . . our Lord Jesus Christ, Who gave himself for our sins, that he might deliver us from this present evil world, according to the will of God and our Father." Again in Romans 12:2 Paul says, "And be not conformed to this world: but be ye transformed by the renewing of your mind, that ye may prove what is that good, and acceptable, and perfect, will of God." Finally, "Love not the world, neither the things that are in the world . . ." (1 John 2:15). Now, in the world is what we call the "law of life" and the unjust steward is a man who operates by that law.

The first commandment of the world is "self-preservation." A shady business deal is winked at, questionable practices countenanced, and a clever crook is commended by the world. The law is on the side of the crook and the criminal many times. Every man, according to the world's law, is considered innocent until he is proven guilty. The Word of God takes the opposite approach. God says that man is guilty until he is proven innocent. He says, "For all have sinned, and come short of the glory of God" (Rom. 3:23). A man can never be innocent before God, but he certainly can become justified before Him. "There is therefore now no condemnation to them which are in Christ Jesus . . ." (Rom. 8:1). When a man trusts Jesus Christ as his Savior, he is justified by faith. This is the only way a man can be justified.

> **And he said also unto his disciples, There was a certain rich man, which had a steward; and the same was accused unto him that he had wasted his goods [Luke 16:1].**

This is the story of a rich man and his unjust steward. A steward is a man who has charge of another man's goods. Abraham had a steward, you remember, who had charge of all his possessions. It was Abraham's steward who went on a trip to Haran to find a bride for Abraham's son Isaac. David had stewards, mentioned in 1 Chronicles 28:1. David's stewards had charge over all of the king's possessions, including his children. Paul tells us, "Moreover it is required in stewards, that a man be found faithful" (1 Cor. 4:2).

The steward in this parable would correspond to the president of a corporation. He had charge of this rich man's goods. He was guilty of malfeasance in office and misappropriation of funds. He was like the bank president who absconds with bank funds. The unjust steward wasted the goods of his master.

> **And he called him, and said unto him, How is it that I
> hear this of thee? give an account of thy stewardship; for
> thou mayest be no longer steward [Luke 16:2].**

The day of reckoning had come for this man. He had to give an account. Now since he had the signet ring of his master and was the paymaster, instead of drawing up a financial statement, he decided to use the law of the world which is self-preservation.

> **Then the steward said within himself, What shall I do?
> for my lord taketh away from me the stewardship: I can-
> not dig; to beg I am ashamed [Luke 16:3].**

This man had soft hands and felt he could not be a common laborer. And he was ashamed to beg. It makes you smile to read this verse—the man may have been ashamed to beg, but he was not ashamed to steal! Unfortunately, there are a lot of people like that today.

> **I am resolved what to do, that, when I am put out of the
> stewardship, they may receive me into their houses
> [Luke 16:4].**

This man did not repent; he had no regret or remorse for his actions. This man was crooked—called clever by the world's standards. He had no training for other work, and his age was probably against him. He was too proud to beg, but he was not ashamed to be dishonest.

> **So he called every one of his lord's debtors unto him,
> and said unto the first, How much owest thou unto my
> lord?**
>
> **And he said, An hundred measures of oil. And he said
> unto him, Take thy bill, and sit down quickly, and write
> fifty [Luke 16:5–6].**

The steward was asking, "How much do you owe my master?" This man owed his master one hundred barrels of oil. "Well," the steward said, "oil is about one dollar a barrel now. I will tell you what we will do. We will let you have it for fifty cents a barrel." The man only had to pay half of what he owed.

> **Then said he to another, And how much owest thou? And he said, An hundred measures of wheat. And he said unto him, Take thy bill, and write fourscore [Luke 16:7].**

I do not know why he did not give this fellow the same discount that he gave the other fellow, but this man had to pay eighty cents on the dollar. The unjust steward is just as big a crook at the end as he was at the beginning of his career.

He is not being punished.

> **And the lord commended the unjust steward, because he had done wisely: for the children of this world are in their generation wiser than the children of light [Luke 16:8].**

This is a shocking statement. Who made it? The lord of the steward, meaning his employer, the rich man. Apparently this man got rich using the same kind of principles that his unjust steward used. He tells him he has done wisely. In what way? According to the principles of the world. This is the world that hates Christ. It makes its own rules. The law of the world is "dog eat dog." The worldly lord commended his worldly steward for his worldly wisdom according to his worldly dealings.

The Lord Jesus said, "For the children of this world are in their generation wiser than the children of light." That is, the children of this world, of this age, use their money more wisely than do the children of light.

> **And I say unto you, Make to yourselves friends of the mammon of unrighteousness; that, when ye fail, they**

may receive you into everlasting habitations [Luke 16:9].

The most shocking and startling statement of all concerns the relationship of the believer to the "mammon of unrighteousness." What is the "mammon of unrighteousness?" It is riches, money. Money is not evil in itself; money is amoral. It is the *love of money* that is the root of all evil. For believers money is to be spiritual. Our Lord said that we should lay up for ourselves treasures in heaven. We should be wise in the way we use our money. Then when we "fail" or come to the end of life, we will be welcomed into heaven.

He that is faithful in that which is least is faithful also in much: and he that is unjust in the least is unjust also in much.

If therefore ye have not been faithful in the unrighteous mammon, who will commit to your trust the true riches?

And if ye have not been faithful in that which is another man's, who shall give you that which is your own? [Luke 16:10–12].

We are stewards of that which is material. We own nothing as believers. We are responsible to God for how we use His goods. He says that the men of this world are wiser than the children of light in their stewardship. For years I was pastor of a church in downtown Los Angeles which was near the financial district. Through the years I watched many of the men go into a broker's office and watch the fluctuation of the stock market. They would sit down in the morning and figure out what they were going to do. They would not invest in any stock unless they thought it was going to go up in value, or they would play the market. A Christian man once told me that he had made his money by playing the stock market. For this reason he would not accept an office in the church—I do not know how he reconciled to himself the fact that he was a church member. He was clever at making money.

How many Christians today are smart in the use of the mammon of unrighteousness—money? Do they use it to gather spiritual wealth? God will hold you responsible for the misuse of the material wealth He gives you. I personally know of a program that is run just for the self-interest of one individual. In another organization ninety percent of what is given to that program supports a tremendous overhead that keeps men driving Cadillac automobiles. That means you would have to give one hundred dollars to get ten dollars to the poor folk they are telling you about. There is something wrong with the *way* Christians give their money. This would not happen if Christians were as smart as the men of the world. How smart are you, Christian friend, in money matters? Are you using your money to see that the Word of God reaches those who need it?

In the parable of the unjust steward the Lord Jesus is saying, "Do you think God is going to trust you with heavenly riches if you are not using properly that which He has given you on earth?" Money is a spiritual matter. You are responsible not only for giving it, but for investing it where it will yield the highest dividends in folk reached for Christ.

> **No servant can serve two masters: for either he will hate the one, and love the other; or else he will hold to the one, and despise the other. Ye cannot serve God and mammon [Luke 16:13].**

What are you doing with your money? Are you making money? If you are, what are you doing with it? This is a pertinent question. Are you using it for the things of the world? If you are, you are serving mammon; that is your master. Are you serving God or mammon? You cannot serve them both.

JESUS ANSWERS THE COVETOUS PHARISEES

The Pharisees heard Jesus and began to feel convicted.

> **And the Pharisees also, who were covetous, heard all these things: and they derided him.**

And he said unto them, Ye are they which justify yourselves before men; but God knoweth your hearts: for
that which is highly esteemed among men is abomina-
tion in the sight of God.

The law and the prophets were until John: since that
time the kingdom of God is preached, and every man
presseth into it.

And it is easier for heaven and earth to pass, than one
tittle of the law to fail [Luke 16:14–17].

God knew the hearts of the Pharisees. God knows your heart. God
knows my heart. We can put up a front with each other but not with
God. We cannot measure up to God's standard.

JESUS SPEAKS ON DIVORCE

Whosoever putteth away his wife, and marrieth another, committeth adultery: and whosoever marrieth her
that is put away from her husband committeth adultery
[Luke 16:18].

If this were the only verse of Scripture on the subject of divorce, there
would be no divorce for a Christian. This verse should be compared
with Matthew 19 and 1 Corinthians 7. All of Scripture must be considered on a certain subject to ascertain its truth. Our Lord spoke on
this subject, to these men who were under the Law, because they were
making light of the Law of God.

JESUS RECOUNTS THE INCIDENT OF THE RICH
MAN AND LAZARUS (POOR MAN)

Now we come to another great parable that only Luke presents. I do
not believe this is a fictitious story. I believe He drew this story from
real life just as He did His other parables. Jesus used illustrations that
were familiar to His hearers. They knew exactly what He was talking

about. He uses the name of one of the individuals involved in this parable; the Lord would not have given the name of someone who did not exist.

There was a certain rich man, which was clothed in purple and fine linen, and fared sumptuously every day [Luke 16:19].

This is the story of a rich man who lived and died without God. It moves into a realm that we know nothing about. In this parable the Lord passes from this world to the next without making any break at all. Although we cannot penetrate the curtain between this life and the next life, our Lord speaks of the next world as naturally as He speaks of this life.

When man is left to his own imagination, he seeks out many inventions and out of his wildest dreams he makes unlimited speculations. When man uses his imagination, he gets into trouble. In this parable we learn what the Word of God says. There were only four men who ever spoke with authority concerning the other side of death: the Lord Jesus; Lazarus; John, who was given the Revelation; and Paul, who was ". . . caught up to the third heaven" (2 Cor. 12:2).

And there was a certain beggar named Lazarus, which was laid at his gate, full of sores.

And desiring to be fed with the crumbs which fell from the rich man's table: moreover the dogs came and licked his sores [Luke 16:20–21].

Here are two men at the opposite ends of the social and financial ladder—and, I suppose, every other ladder. One man represents the top echelon in riches, and the other man represents the lowest extreme of poverty. No two men could be farther apart in every way. This poor man was dependent upon the crumbs that fell from the rich man's table. He never was invited to sit at the rich man's table; he had to be kept in a menial place. The dogs came and licked his sores. In a few words our Lord pictures the depths of the terrible degradation and despair into which this man had fallen. I am sure had you lived in that town you might have gotten the impression that poor Lazarus, dressed in rags, did not have much in the way of any spiritual discernment or spiritual riches. I am sure all of us would have written him off as a hopeless case. On the other hand, I am sure that the rich man had several buildings named after him—perhaps a church, a school, or a mission enterprise. I am sure he had a wonderful name in the town in which these two men lived. However, all that the people in the town could see were the outward appearances of the rich man and the beggar whose sores were licked by dogs. This is a picture of abject poverty and extreme riches. Two men could not have been farther apart.

And it came to pass, that the beggar died, and was carried by the angels into Abraham's bosom: the rich man also died, and was buried [Luke 16:22].

Our Lord comes right to the door of death and passes through it as if it were nothing unusual. When the beggar died, there was no funeral. They just took his body out and threw it into the Valley of Gehenna where refuse was thrown and burned; this is the place where they threw the bodies of the poor in that day. The minute the beggar stepped through the doorway of death, angels became his pallbearers and he was carried by them into Abraham's Bosom.

The rich man also died and was buried. He had a big funeral, and the preacher pushed him all the way to the top spot in heaven. The only trouble is that the preacher got his directions mixed up; the rich man went the other way.

And in hell he lift up his eyes, being in torments, and seeth Abraham afar off, and Lazarus in his bosom [Luke 16:23].

Notice two things here: The lost go to a place of conscious torment. Also, people know each other after death. We do not lose our identities.

The word *hell* is in the Greek *hadēs*, meaning "the unseen world." Actually, *hell*, as we think of it, is a place that has not yet been opened up for business; we don't read of it until we get to Revelation 20:10, where it tells us that hell's first occupants will be the Antichrist and the false prophet. When they died, Lazarus and the rich man went to the unseen world, the place of the departed dead.

Death is separation; it never means extinction. Adam, in the day that he ate of the forbidden fruit, died. Physically he did not die until about nine hundred years later, but the day that he ate of the fruit he was separated from God. Jesus spoke of it when He said, ". . . I am the resurrection, and the life: he that believeth in me, though he were dead, yet shall he live: And whosoever liveth and believeth in me shall never die . . ." (John 11:25–26). Man is separated from God by sin. People are dead while they live. Paul told the Ephesians, "And you hath he quickened, who were dead in trespasses and sins" (Eph. 2:1).

Certain spots in a big city are really alive and jumping at night. If you want to see a lot of zombies and dead people, look in on one of these nightclubs. That is where you will find them. They are beating the drums, blaring out the music, getting the beat, drinking all they can, and getting high on drugs because they are dead and want to live.

There is a second death, which is spiritual death, and it means eternal separation from God. At physical death the body becomes inert and lifeless because the person's spirit has moved out. The body is put into the grave, and the elements return to the dust: ". . . for dust thou art, and unto dust shalt thou return" (Gen. 3:19). Therefore, death means separation.

It will help us understand this parable if we realize that Sheol or hades (translated hell in the New Testament) is divided into two compartments: paradise (which is called Abraham's Bosom in this parable) and the place of torment. Paradise was emptied when Christ took with Him at His ascension the Old Testament believers (see Eph. 4:8–10). The place of torment will deliver up the lost for judgment at the Great White Throne (see Rev. 20:11–15). All who stand at this judgment are lost, and they will be cast into the lake of fire, which is the second death.

Now when the rich man died, his spirit went to the place of torment, the compartment where the lost go. The beggar went to the compartment called paradise or Abraham's Bosom.

Note that our Lord is not saying that the rich man went to the place of torment because he was rich and that the poor man went to Abraham's Bosom because he was poor. Going through the doorway of death certainly changed their status, but it was due to what was in the hearts of these two men. This is what our Lord has been saying through this entire section—man cannot judge by the outward appearance.

There are some other things revealed in this story that we would not know if our Lord had not revealed them.

> **And he cried and said, Father Abraham, have mercy on me, and send Lazarus, that he may dip the tip of his finger in water, and cool my tongue; for I am tormented in this flame [Luke 16:24].**

The rich man becomes the beggar, while the beggar is now the rich man.

> **But Abraham said, Son, remember that thou in thy lifetime receivedst thy good things, and likewise Lazarus evil things: but now he is comforted, and thou art tormented.**

> **And beside all this, between us and you there is a great gulf fixed: so that they which would pass from hence to you cannot; neither can they pass to us, that would come from thence [Luke 16:25–26].**

The bodies of believers today, since the resurrection of Jesus Christ, go into the grave and return to dust, but their spirits go to be with Christ. "We are confident, I say, and willing rather to be absent from the body, and to be present with the Lord" (2 Cor. 5:8). The lost today still go to the place of torment in hades. Ephesians 4:8–10 gives us the following picture, "Wherefore he saith, When he ascended up on high, he led captivity captive, and gave gifts unto men. (Now that he ascended, what is it but that he also descended first into the lower parts of the earth? He that descended is the same also that ascended up far above all heavens, that he might fill all things.)" In other words, when our Lord descended into hades after His crucifixion on the cross, He entered the paradise section, emptied it, and took everyone into God's presence. No one occupies the paradise section of hades today. The only part of hades still occupied is the place of torment where unbelievers go when they die. The day is coming when hades will be cast into the lake of fire and men will no longer go there at all (see Rev. 20:14).

The body is merely the physical house in which we live. At death we move out of our old homes. You can do anything you want to with the old house after it is deserted, but the important thing is what happens to the spirit after it has left the body. Where is it going?

Heaven is a place, friend, and the moment you die you will either go there to be with Christ, or you will go to the place of torment where you will ultimately be judged and then cast into the lake of fire. The point is that God never intended the latter as an end for anyone of the human family. The lake of fire was made for the Devil and his angels (see Matt. 25:41). You *choose* your final destination.

"There is a great gulf fixed:" our Lord made that clear. You must make the decision in this life where you will go after your death. You do not get a second chance after death.

Then he said, I pray thee therefore, father, that thou wouldest send him to my father's house [Luke 16:27].

Notice his concern for his living brothers. He wanted them to repent, change their minds before it was too late. Friend, if the lost could come back, they would preach the gospel to us.

For I have five brethren; that he may testify unto them, lest they also come into this place of torment.

Abraham saith unto him, They have Moses and the prophets; let them hear them.

And he said, Nay, father Abraham: but if one went unto them from the dead, they will repent.

And he said unto him, If they hear not Moses and the prophets, neither will they be persuaded, though one rose from the dead [Luke 16:28–31].

Many people believe that multitudes would repent if someone returned from the dead to tell them what it was like. Well, Someone *has* come back from the dead. His name is Jesus Christ. They did not believe Him any more than they believed Moses and the prophets. Friend, do not delay in making your choice. There will be no opportunity after death.

CHAPTER 17

THEME: Jesus instructs His disciples on forgiveness; Jesus instructs His disciples on faithful service; Jesus heals ten lepers; Jesus speaks on the spiritual nature of God's kingdom; Jesus speaks of His coming again

JESUS INSTRUCTS HIS DISCIPLES ON FORGIVENESS

Then said he unto the disciples, It is impossible but that offences will come: but woe unto him, through whom they come!

It were better for him that a millstone were hanged about his neck, and he cast into the sea, than that he should offend one of these little ones [Luke 17:1–2].

What the Lord says here is very severe. I will be honest with you; I think I would rather be most any person than the one selling drugs to young people today. I believe that the punishment for one who sells drugs will be greater than for some others. It is serious business to cause someone, especially a youngster, to offend. There is one thing worse than going to hell; it is going to hell and having a son or daughter say to you, "Dad, I am here because I followed you." That is the worst thing that can happen to a person.

Take heed to yourselves: If thy brother trespass against thee, rebuke him; and if he repent, forgive him.

And if he trespass against thee seven times in a day, and seven times in a day turn again to thee, saying, I repent; thou shalt forgive him.

And the apostles said unto the Lord, Increase our faith.

> And the Lord said, If ye had faith as a grain of mustard
> seed, ye might say unto this sycamine tree, Be thou
> plucked up by the root, and be thou planted in the sea;
> and it should obey you [Luke 17:3–6].

In other words, His disciples should be ready always to forgive. He does not say that the one who offends should not be rebuked. He should be made to appreciate his fault, but when he sincerely repents, he should be forgiven—even if he repeats his sin over and over.

JESUS INSTRUCTS HIS DISCIPLES
ON FAITHFUL SERVICE

Once again Jesus is severe. There are those who talk about the gentle Jesus, but if you read some of these passages, you will find that He was not always gentle. He was gentle with children, but not with those who offended them.

> But which of you, having a servant plowing or feeding
> cattle, will say unto him by and by, when he is come
> from the field, Go and sit down to meat?
>
> And will not rather say unto him, Make ready where-
> with I may sup, and gird thyself, and serve me, till I
> have eaten and drunken; and afterward thou shalt eat
> and drink?
>
> Doth he thank that servant because he did the things
> that were commanded him? I trow not [Luke 17:7–9].

Let me make an application of this passage. There are people who believe that because they try to follow the Sermon on the Mount and are good neighbors and try to love people, that someday God is going to pat them on the back and say, "What a fine person you are. You have earned your way to heaven." If you keep the Ten Commandments and the Sermon on the Mount, which you cannot, you are doing only what you are supposed to do. Do you think you would receive salvation for that? My friend, that's what you are supposed to do as one of His creatures. We need to recognize that salvation is a *gift;* you cannot work for it. Keeping God's Law is a duty.

So likewise ye, when ye shall have done all those things which are commanded you, say, We are unprofitable servants: we have done that which was our duty to do [Luke 17:10].

JESUS HEALS TEN LEPERS (ONE SAMARITAN RETURNS TO GIVE THANKS)

And it came to pass, as he went to Jerusalem, that he passed through the midst of Samaria and Galilee [Luke 17:11].

Remember, our Lord is on His way to Jerusalem.

And as he entered into a certain village, there met him ten men that were lepers, which stood afar off:

And they lifted up their voices, and said, Jesus, Master, have mercy on us.

And when he saw them, he said unto them, Go shew yourselves unto the priests. And it came to pass, that, as they went, they were cleansed.

And one of them, when he saw that he was healed, turned back, and with a loud voice glorified God,

And fell down on his face at his feet, giving him thanks: and he was a Samaritan [Luke 17:12–16].

The Pharisees winced at this one!

And Jesus answering said, Were there not ten cleansed? but where are the nine?

There are not found that returned to give glory to God, save this stranger.

And he said unto him, Arise, go thy way: thy faith hath made thee whole [Luke 17:17-19].

Jesus healed ten lepers. Only one of the ten, who was a Samaritan, returned to thank Jesus for what He had done. Jesus then did a second thing for him—He forgave his sins. The other nine lepers were healed but were not saved. Thankfulness should be in the Christian's heart. Why do you go to church on Sunday? Do you go there to worship God and thank Him for all He has done for you? Part of your worship is to thank Him. About the only thing we can give to God is our thanksgiving. How wonderful it is just to thank Him. We are even to make our requests to God *with thanksgiving*. We ought to have a thankful heart toward Him.

JESUS SPEAKS ON THE SPIRITUAL NATURE OF GOD'S KINGDOM

And when he was demanded of the Pharisees, when the kingdom of God should come, he answered them and said, The kingdom of God cometh not with observation:

Neither shall they say, Lo here! or, lo there! for, behold, the kingdom of God is within you [Luke 17:20-21].

Jesus speaks of the fact that the "kingdom of God cometh not with observation." To whom is He talking? He is answering the Pharisees who are demanding that He tell them when the Kingdom will come. He is not saying that the Kingdom of God is inside the hearts of these godless and hostile Pharisees. Rather, the Kingdom of God was in their midst, in the person of the King, the Lord Jesus Christ. He was right *then* standing among them.

JESUS SPEAKS OF HIS COMING AGAIN

One of the greatest delusions of our time is that man is going to improve himself and his world; that he is going to build the Kingdom of God without God. He expects to bring in the Millennium without Christ.

Now the glorious day of the Kingdom was the subject of much of what Christ had to say. In fact, He emphasized the future—the change coming and His return. A liberal theologian of the past, who had been teaching that Jesus was an ethical teacher, got tired of being a parrot, and began to study the words of the Lord Jesus Christ. He made the discovery (and he wrote a book on it) that Christ was an eschatological teacher, that His main subject was the future, His coming to earth again.

In this important section before us, our Lord warns His disciples not to be deceived concerning His return.

Now the return of Christ is in two phases. The first phase is what we call the "Rapture of the church" which is the taking away of true believers (detailed for us in 1 Thess. 4:13–18). But in this passage He is talking about the second phase of His return, which is returning to the earth to establish His Kingdom. This will take place after the Rapture and after the Great Tribulation.

And he said unto the disciples, The days will come, when ye shall desire to see one of the days of the Son of man, and ye shall not see it.

And they shall say to you, See here; or see there: go not after them, nor follow them [Luke 17:22–23].

The first time He came, they failed to recognize Him because they were looking for a conquering Messiah to come and deliver them from Rome. Instead He came as a baby and lived as a peasant. The next time He comes it will not be in an isolated place like Bethlehem, but He will come in glory. Therefore He warns them not to pay any attention to those who say He is here or there—or who say He is coming at a certain time. This is one reason you cannot set the date of the coming of Christ.

> **For as the lightning, that lighteneth out of the one part under heaven, shineth unto the other part under heaven; so shall also the Son of man be in his day [Luke 17:24].**

When He comes to this earth to establish His Kingdom, it will be as public as lightning. Compare this with His extensive discourse in Matthew 24.

> **But first must he suffer many things, and be rejected of this generation [Luke 17:25].**

The Cross was in the program of God. He went by way of the Cross to get you and me. He outlined His program very clearly: He would suffer and be rejected by His people.

> **And as it was in the days of Noe, so shall it be also in the days of the Son of man [Luke 17:26].**

How was it in the days of Noah? What does He have reference to?

> **They did eat, they drank, they married wives, they were given in marriage, until the day that Noe entered into the ark, and the flood came, and destroyed them all [Luke 17:27].**

What is wrong with these things? Marriage is not wrong—it is right. What is wrong with eating and drinking? We must do this to live. Why does Jesus mention these things? Well, the generation of Noah was living as if God did not exist when judgment was imminent. Today men and women are eating and drinking (and not even marrying though living together), and they do not recognize that the judgment of God is out there in the future—when, we do not know.

Likewise also as it was in the days of Lot; they did eat, they drank, they bought, they sold, they planted, they builded;

But the same day that Lot went out of Sodom it rained fire and brimstone from heaven, and destroyed them all [Luke 17:28–29].

This is a tremendous thing our Lord says at this juncture. Lot is altogether different from Noah; yet there are similarities. None in Sodom were panicking, selling out their property and getting out of town. The stock market did not collapse because Lot said that judgment was coming. They simply didn't believe it.

God would not destroy the city until Lot had been taken out of it. Neither will He bring the Great Tribulation upon this earth (which immediately precedes the coming of Christ to the earth) until He takes His own out of the world. It is interesting that He uses Lot as an example here, which He does not do in the Olivet Discourse in Matthew 24. The reason is that in Matthew, He is answering their question about His coming to earth to establish His Kingdom. Here in Luke it is a wider subject. Sodom, because of her sin, stood on the brink of destruction, and the moment Lot left town, judgment fell. I believe that the minute believers leave this earth in the Rapture, the Great Tribulation will begin.

Even thus shall it be in the day when the Son of man is revealed [Luke 17:30].

God has a people in the world today who are just like Lot in many respects. Although they have trusted Christ as Savior, they compromise with the world. Yet as believers they will be taken out of the world before the day of judgment comes. Today the world doesn't listen to the church. As in Lot's day, they think we are mocking.

In that day, he which shall be upon the housetop, and his stuff in the house, let him not come down to take it

away: and he that is in the field, let him likewise not return back [Luke 17:31].

In Matthew's account of the Olivet Discourse, the Lord Jesus labels this period the Great Tribulation.

Remember Lot's wife [Luke 17:32].

She is an example of one who did not believe God. She had daughters and friends in Sodom. Probably they were having a bridge party that afternoon. She kept saying, "Let's go back." Why did she look back? She didn't believe God would destroy that city. Therefore we are to remember Lot's wife. To believe God is the important thing for us.

Whosoever shall seek to save his life shall lose it; and whosoever shall lose his life shall preserve it [Luke 17:33].

This is one of those great paradoxes of Scripture. In that day there will be a great scramble to save their lives, but it will be too late. They are to be willing to lose their lives and just turn them over to Jesus Christ. Any attempt to save life in that day will avoid nothing.

I tell you, in that night there shall be two men in one bed; the one shall be taken, and the other shall be left.

Two women shall be grinding together; the one shall be taken, and the other left.

Two men shall be in the field; the one shall be taken, and the other left [Luke 17:34–36].

In the days of Noah, who was taken out of the world? Who was left in the world? This is not the Rapture He is talking about. This is, as in the Olivet Discourse in Matthew 24:37–41, a direct reference to taking away the ungodly in judgment and leaving on earth those who will enter the millennial kingdom.

Notice that Christ implied that the earth was round—one will be in bed and another working out in the field. There will be night on one side of the earth and day on the other side.

And they answered and said unto him, Where, Lord? And he said unto them, Wheresoever the body is, thither will the eagles be gathered together [Luke 17:37].

Compare this verse with Revelation 19:17. This is what we call the Battle of Armaggedon, which is actually the *war* of Armageddon, and will be ended when Christ comes to establish His Kingdom upon the earth.

CHAPTER 18

THEME: Parable of the unjust judge; parable of the Pharisee and the publican; Jesus blesses the little children; Jesus confronts the rich young ruler with five of the Ten Commandments; Jesus heals the blind man on entering Jericho

Before we begin this chapter, I want to say a word about our Lord personally. I believe that He was God manifest in the flesh. I also believe that He was not any less God because He was man. On the other hand, I believe He was not any more man because He was God. He was a perfect man—a real man. Frankly, if you had been there in that day, you would have enjoyed His company. It would have been a real privilege to be in His company and to hear His laughter. I don't like any picture I see of Him; the artists never picture Him laughing, and I think He laughed many times. Our Lord was so human. In His presence you would have the best time you ever had. You know folk, I am sure, whom you love to be with. I know several preachers whose company I especially enjoy. They sharpen my wits and my mental powers; yet they tell the funniest jokes I've ever heard. I think our Lord was good at that. We are coming to an incident that I am confident made many people smile.

And he spake a parable unto them to this end, that men ought always to pray, and not to faint [Luke 18:1].

He concluded chapter 17 with a discourse on the last days and the fact that He would be coming again. And He likened the last days to the days of Noah, that they would be difficult days—days that would not be conducive to faith. So now He talks to them about a life of faith in days that are devoid of faith. That is the reason it is so pertinent for this hour. We are living in days, as He indicated, when men's hearts are failing them for fear. What we have in this first parable is a perti-

nent paragraph on prayer for the present hour. Notice that He says He
spoke a parable to them to this end; that is, for this *purpose*, that men
should always pray, and not to faint.

He opens two alternatives to any man who is living in difficult
days. You and I will have to do one of the two. You will have to make
up your mind which you are going to do. Men in difficult days will
either faint or they will pray. Either there will be days of fear or days of
faith.

During World War II, when the bombing was so intense on the city
of London, a sign appeared in front of one of the churches in London
that read, "If your knees knock together, kneel on them!" That is practically a restatement of what our Lord has said, "Men ought always to
pray, and not to faint."

It is the same thought that Paul put a little differently, "Pray without ceasing" (1 Thess. 5:17). This does not mean you are to go to an
all-day or all-night prayer meeting. Prayer is an attitude of the life. It is
more an attitude of life than an action of the lips. Remember that Paul
said to the Romans, ". . . the Spirit itself maketh intercession for us
with groanings which cannot be uttered" (Rom. 8:26). That is, they
cannot be put into our *words*. And many times we do not have the
words to pray, but we are praying nonetheless. And it is the entire life
that is behind the words which are spoken that makes prayer effective.

There was a famous preacher, years ago in the state of Georgia,
who had many very unusual expressions. One of them was this,
"When a man prays for a corn crop, God expects him to say Amen
with a hoe." You can't just stay on your knees all the time and pray for
a corn crop. That's pious nonsense. But to pray for the corn crop and
then go to work is the thing our Lord is talking about in days when
men's hearts are failing them. "Men ought always to pray, and not to
faint."

PARABLE OF THE UNJUST JUDGE

When He told this story about the unjust judge and the widow, it
probably was well known to the hearers of that day. They knew exactly
what He was talking about. The story goes like this:

Saying, there was in a city a judge, which feared not God, neither regarded man:

And there was a widow in that city; and she came unto him, saying, Avenge me of mine adversary [Luke 18:2–3].

Now in this city there was a judge who was a godless fellow. He was an unscrupulous politician, scheming, cold, and calculating. Everything he did was for himself, as we shall see. Everything he did had to minister to his own advancement and satisfy his own ambition. He did not fear God. God had no place in this man's thinking. And since he did not fear God, he had no regard for man. He had no respect for this widow at all.

The widow likely was being beaten out of her little home. The mortgage was being foreclosed, and she was being treated unjustly. She went to this prominent judge, took her place in his office, and asked the secretary if she might talk to the judge. The secretary told her, "He's very busy. If you will just tell me the nature of your complaint. . . ."

So the widow told her, "I'm just a poor widow. I live out here at the edge of town, and I'm about to lose my place. It is unfair and unjust, and I want to appeal to the judge."

The secretary went into the judge's office and said, "There is a widow out there. . . ."

"Well, I can get rid of her in three minutes. I'm a politician, I know how to handle her. Let her come in."

She came in. He listened to her for three minutes. Then he said, "I'm sorry, but that's out of my realm. I'd *love* to do something for you, but I am unable to do anything. Good day."

The next day when he came into the office, there was the widow. He hurried into his office, called his secretary in, and asked, "What's that widow doing back?"

"She says she wants to see you."

"You go back and tell her I am busy until lunch time."

"I've already told her that. But she brought her lunch. She says she will stay here as long as necessary."

She stayed all that day and didn't get to see him. He thought he had gotten rid of her. But the next morning when he came in, there she was! She did that for several days, and finally he said, "I'll have to do something about this. I can't go on like this." Notice that our Lord records what he said "within himself."

And he would not for a while: but afterward he said within himself, Though I fear not God, nor regard man;

Yet because this widow troubleth me, I will avenge her, lest by her continual coming she weary me [Luke 18:4–5].

The word *weary* is a very poor translation. I only wish it were translated literally. What he said was this, "I must see her lest she give me a black eye!"

You see, he was thinking of himself. I don't know if he meant a literal black eye—we are not told that the widow had threatened him! But the very fact that a widow is sitting in the judge's office every day doesn't look good. He had gotten into office by saying, "I'm thinking of the poor people," but he wasn't—he was thinking of himself. "And lest she give me a black eye, I'd better hear her." To his secretary he said, "Bring her in." This time he said to the widow, "I'll give you legal protection."

That's the parable.

And the Lord said, Hear what the unjust judge saith.

And shall not God avenge his own elect, which cry day and night unto him, though he bear long with them? [Luke 18:6–7].

Now, I have heard many Bible teachers say that this parable teaches the value of importunate prayer. Although I don't like to disagree with men who are greater than I, that isn't so. This is not a parable on the persistency or the pertinacity of prayer—as though somehow God will hear if you hold on long enough.

This is a parable by *contrast*, not by comparison.

Parables were stories given by our Lord to illustrate truths. The word *parable* comes from two Greek words. *Para* means "beside" and *ballo* is the verb, meaning "to throw"—(we get our word *ball* from it). A parable means something that is thrown beside something else to tell you something about it. For instance, a yardstick placed beside a table is a parable to the table—it tells you how high it is. A parable is a story our Lord told to illustrate divine truth. There are two ways He did this. One is by comparison, but the other is by *contrast*.

Our Lord is saying, "When you come to God in prayer, do you think that God is an *unjust judge*? When you come to Him in prayer, do you think He is a cheap politician? Do you think God is doing things just for political reasons?" My friend, if you think this, you are wrong. God is not an unjust judge.

If this unjust judge would hear a poor widow because she kept coming continually, then why do you get discouraged going to God who is *not* an unjust judge, but who actually *wants* to hear and answer prayer? Why are God's people today so discouraged in their prayer life? Don't you know, my friend, He is not an unjust judge? You don't have to hang on to His coattail and beg Him and plead with Him. God *wants* to act in your behalf! If we had that attitude, it would change our prayer life—to come in to His presence knowing He wants to hear. We act as if He is an unjust judge, and we have to hold on to Him or He will not hear us at all. God is not an unjust judge.

PARABLE OF THE PHARISEE AND THE PUBLICAN

Now our Lord gives another parable on prayer.

And he spake this parable unto certain which trusted in themselves that they were righteous, and despised others:

Two men went up into the temple to pray; the one a Pharisee, and the other a publican [Luke 18:9–10].

This is a parable that is familiar to all of us. Oh, with what trenchant and biting satire He gave them this! But He didn't do it to hurt them; He did it to help them. He said that two men went up to the temple to pray—a Pharisee and a publican. You could not get any two as far apart as those two men were. The Pharisee was at the top of the religious ladder. The publican was at the bottom. His parable wasn't about publicans and sinners—publicans were right down there with the sinners. The Pharisee was at the top, supposedly the most acceptable one to God. He went into the temple to pray, he had access to the temple, he brought the appointed sacrifice. As he stood and prayed, his priest was yonder in the Holy Place putting incense on the altar. This old Pharisee had it made.

> **The Pharisee stood and prayed thus with himself, God, I thank thee, that I am not as other men are, extortioners, unjust, adulterers, or even as this publican [Luke 18:11].**

Isn't that an awful way to begin a prayer! And that is the way many of us do. You say, "I don't do *that*." Yes, you do. I hear prayers like that. Oh, we don't say it exactly that way. We are fundamental—we have learned to say it better than that. We have our own way of putting it, "Lord, I thank You I can give You my time and my service." How I hear that! What a compliment that is for the Lord! Friend, we don't get anywhere in prayer when we pray like that. God doesn't need our service.

The Pharisee said, "I thank thee, that I am not as other men"; then he began to enumerate what he wasn't. "I'm not an extortioner"— evidently there was somebody around who was an extortioner. "I am not unjust. I am not an adulterer." Then he spied that publican way outside, and said, "And believe me, Lord, I'm not like that publican. I'm not like that sinner out there."

Then he began to tell the Lord what he did:

> **I fast twice in the week, I give tithes of all that I possess [Luke 18:12].**

My, isn't he a wonderful fellow! Wouldn't we love to have him in our church!

Our Lord said he "prayed thus *with himself.*" In other words, he was doing a Hamlet soliloquy. Hamlet, you know, goes off and stands talking to himself—and Hamlet is "off," by the way; he is a mental case. Hamlet says, "To be, or not to be, that is the question." And this old Pharisee is out there talking to himself—he thinks he is talking to God, but his prayer never got out of the rafters. All he did was have a pep talk; he patted himself on the back and went out proud as a peacock. God never heard that prayer.

The old publican—oh, he was a rascal. He was a sinner; he was as low as they come. He had sold his nation down the river when he had become a tax collector. When he became a tax gatherer, he denied his nation. When he denied his nation, as a Jew, he denied his religion. He turned his back on God. He took a one-way street, never to come back to God. Why did he do it? It was lucrative. He said, "There's money down this way." He became rich as a publican. But it did not satisfy his heart. Read the story of Levi; read the story of Zacchaeus in Luke 19—a publican's heart was *empty.* This poor publican in his misery and desperation, knowing that he had no access to the mercy seat in the temple, cried out to God.

And the publican, standing afar off, would not lift up so much as his eyes unto heaven, but smote upon his breast, saying, God be merciful to me a sinner [Luke 18:13].

"God be merciful to me a sinner" does not adequately express it. Let me give it to you in the language that he used. He would not so much as lift up his eyes unto heaven, but he smote on his breast, and said, "O God, I'm a poor publican. I have no access to that mercy seat yonder in the Holy of Holies. Oh, if you could only make a mercy seat for me! I want to come."

Our Lord said *that* man was heard. Do you know why he was heard? Because Jesus Christ right there and then was on the way to the cross to make a mercy seat for him. John writes: "And he is the propitiation for our sins: and not for ours only, but also for the sins of the whole world" (1 John 2:2). *Propitiation* means "mercy seat." Christ is the mercy seat for our sins, and not for ours only, but also for the sins of the *whole world*.

The publican's prayer has been answered. Actually, today you don't have to ask God to be merciful. He *is* merciful. Many people say, "We have to beg Him to be merciful." My friend, what do you want Him to do? He gave His Son to die for you. He says to the worst sinner you know, "You can come. There is a mercy seat for you." I have to admit to you that I had to come to that mercy seat. And if you are God's child, you have come to that mercy seat where He died yonder on the cross for your sins and my sins. The penalty has been paid. The holy God is able to hold His arms outstretched. You don't have to beg Him; you don't have to promise Him anything because He knows your weakness; you do not have to join something; you do not even have to be somebody. You can be like a poor publican. You can come and trust Him, and He will save you. God is merciful.

> I tell you, this man went down to his house justified rather than the other: for every one that exalteth himself shall be abased; and he that humbleth himself shall be exalted [Luke 18:14].

JESUS BLESSES THE LITTLE CHILDREN

The little children loved to be with the Lord Jesus.

> And they brought unto him also infants, that he would touch them: but when his disciples saw it, they rebuked them [Luke 18:15].

Even the disciples said, "Do not bring the little children to Him. Do not bother Him."

> But Jesus called them unto him, and said, Suffer little children to come unto me, and forbid them not: for of such is the kingdom of God [Luke 18:16].

The feeling was that small children were not too important. The Lord Jesus felt differently about children. They were not a bother to Him.

Verily I say unto you, Whosoever shall not receive the kingdom of God as a little child shall in no wise enter therein [Luke 18:17].

Children normally and naturally came to the Lord. He did not want the adults to keep them away from Him. God have mercy on any adult who keeps little children away from God. Concerning this subject, Luke has already said, "It were better for him that a millstone were hanged about his neck, and he cast into the sea, than that he should offend one of these little ones" (Luke 17:2). You see, the little ones will follow you. They have complete trust in you. They will do anything you want them to do. God have mercy on you if you don't bring them to God! Children would normally come to Him.

Someone may object, "But children have a fallen nature." Yes, they do. But that little one has not reached the age of accountability; the only decision he can make is the decision that is suggested to him. That's the nature of the little child. Of course, the little one will grow up and develop a will of his own. Then that's when the trouble begins! But while he is still pliable, make sure that he comes to Christ.

JESUS CONFRONTS THE RICH YOUNG RULER WITH FIVE OF THE TEN COMMANDMENTS

The account of the rich young ruler is also given in Matthew 19:16–30 and in Mark 10:17–31. It is a wonderful story. In this account our Lord made inquiry into the conduct of the rich young ruler.

And a certain ruler asked him, saying, Good Master, what shall I do to inherit eternal life?

And Jesus said unto him, Why callest thou me good? none is good, save one, that is, God [Luke 18:18–19].

The Lord Jesus Christ was leading this young man to see that if he recognized goodness in Jesus, it was because He was God. That is the reason Jesus urged him to follow. It would have led him to accept Jesus as the disciples had—". . . the Christ, the Son of the living God" (Matt. 16:16).

> **Thou knowest the commandments, Do not commit adultery, Do not kill, Do not steal, Do not bear false witness, Honour thy father and thy mother.**
>
> **And he said, All these have I kept from my youth up.**
>
> **Now when Jesus heard these things, he said unto him, Yet lackest thou one thing: sell all that thou hast, and distribute unto the poor, and thou shalt have treasure in heaven: and come, follow me [Luke 18:20–22].**

Jesus flashed on the young ruler the second section of the Ten Commandments which is labeled "probitas." This section deals with man's relationship with man. The first section has to do with man's relationship to God and is labeled "pietas." This young man could meet the second section, but not the first. He needed a relationship with God, which he evidently lacked. Riches stood in the way of this. The Law condemned this attractive young man. Riches were the stumbling block for him. For another man it might be something else. It is impossible for any man to get into the Kingdom of Heaven by riches or by any human means. Only God could put a camel through a needle's eye, and only God can *regenerate.*

> **And when he heard this, he was very sorrowful: for he was very rich.**
>
> **And when Jesus saw that he was very sorrowful, he said, How hardly shall they that have riches enter into the kingdom of God!**
>
> **For it is easier for a camel to go through a needle's eye, than for a rich man to enter into the kingdom of God.**

And they that heard it said, Who then can be saved?

And he said, The things which are impossible with men are possible with God.

Then Peter said, Lo, we have left all, and followed thee.

And he said unto them, Verily I say unto you, There is no man that hath left house, or parents, or brethren, or wife, or children, for the kingdom of God's sake,

Who shall not receive manifold more in this present time, and in the world to come life everlasting [Luke 18:23–30].

In spite of the lack and unwillingness in his life, it is said that Jesus loved him. Riches separated this young man from Jesus. Had he followed Jesus, he would have come to the cross for redemption, for Jesus was very close to the cross at this time. Who was this young man? I do not know who he was. You may be like him today, I do not know. Did he follow the Lord later on? We hope so. Will you follow the Lord? He loves you.

JESUS HEALS THE BLIND MAN
ON ENTERING JERICHO

Before we look at this incident, I should mention that critics of the Bible find in this a contradiction, because Matthew speaks of two blind men, while Mark and Luke mention only one. However, if you will read this passage carefully, you will see that Matthew and Mark obviously refer to a work of healing as Jesus *departed* from Jericho. Bartimaeus, the active one of the two, the one who cried, ". . . Jesus, thou son of David. . . ," is specifically mentioned in Mark 10:46. The healing described by Luke, in verses 40–43, occurred before Jesus *entered* Jericho. This man also used the familiar form of address, "son of David."

And it came to pass, that as he was come nigh unto Jericho, a certain blind man sat by the way side begging:

> And hearing the multitude pass by, he asked what it
> meant.
>
> And they told him, that Jesus of Nazareth passeth by
> [Luke 18:35–37].

By addressing Jesus as the "son of David," he acknowledged His king-
ship. He knew Jesus was able to heal him and so it was impossible to
keep him quiet. He knew what he wanted, and he had great faith in
Jesus. Jesus' dealing with this blind man is tender and thrilling.

> And he cried, saying, Jesus, thou son of David, have
> mercy on me.
>
> And they which went before rebuked him, that he
> should hold his peace: but he cried so much the more,
> Thou son of David, have mercy on me.
>
> And Jesus stood, and commanded him to be brought
> unto him: and when he was come near, he asked him,
>
> Saying, What wilt thou that I shall do unto thee? And he
> said, Lord, that I may receive my sight.
>
> And Jesus said unto him, Receive thy sight: thy faith
> hath saved thee.
>
> And immediately he received his sight, and followed
> him, glorifying God: and all the people, when they saw
> it, gave praise unto God [Luke 18:38–43].

After he was healed, he followed Jesus with his eyes open. What will
he see in a few days? He will see Jesus dying on the cross. Multitudes
of people today with 20-20 vision have not yet seen Jesus' death on the
cross related to their lives and the forgiveness of their sins. If you have
not yet done so—look and live!

CHAPTER 19

THEME: Jesus enters Jericho and home of Zacchaeus; the conversion of Zacchaeus; parable of ten pounds; Jesus enters Jerusalem; Jesus weeps over the city; Jesus cleanses the temple

JESUS ENTERS JERICHO AND HOME OF ZACCHAEUS

Remember that at the time of this incident, the Lord Jesus Christ is on His way to Jerusalem to die on the cross. On His way, He goes through Jericho.

And Jesus entered and passed through Jericho [Luke 19:1].

Luke tells us that Jesus had been over in Samaritan country. When He left Samaria, He headed toward Jerusalem. He seems to be off the beaten path—but is He? He goes to Jericho because there is a sinner there. In fact, there are two or three sinners in Jericho. The Lord is going after them. If you miss the movement here, you will miss the entire message of this passage.

Jericho was the city that God had given into the hand of Joshua. A curse was placed on whoever would rebuild it. The man who rebuilt it in the days of Ahab reaped the curse in all its fullness. In Jesus' day it was like a resort area, the Las Vegas of that time. Many people spent their vacations there. Here the publicans lived. The publicans were like the modern Mafia. They were tax gatherers and were despised.

We are told that Jesus "entered and passed through Jericho." He also entered and passed through this world. He did not come to earth to stay but to die. I entered this world to live, and I would like to live a long time. But Jesus' only purpose in coming to earth was to die for the sins of the world. This tremendous movement is mirrored in the fact that He entered and passed through Jericho. Do not miss that.

THE CONVERSION OF ZACCHAEUS

And, behold, there was a man named Zacchaeus, which was the chief among the publicans, and he was rich [Luke 19:2].

Three things are said about this man in verse two. The Spirit of God has a way—with one flourish of the pen—of telling us all we need to know about a person. The first thing we learn about this man is that his name is Zacchaeus. When I found out that his name meant "pure," I began to laugh, and my wife came into my study to find out what was so funny. Imagine a publican who was pure! He was given that name as a baby. His father and mother looked down at him and thought he was the most precious little fellow in the world. When he grew up, I think there was a lot of fun in Jericho when he was called by his name. They would say, "Hello, Pure." What a name for a tax gatherer!

Zacchaeus was a chief among publicans. His parents never dreamed he would turn out this way. One dark night he had to decide whether or not he would sell out to Rome. As a publican he would have to pay Rome a stated amount for a certain territory in which he would gather taxes. Then, of course, he would gather more taxes than he paid Rome, which made him rich. Zacchaeus was the leader among the publicans. He had given up his religion. He had no more access to the temple. He was probably the publican who stood afar off, and smote his breast, as he said, "God be merciful to me a sinner" (Luke 18:13). Zacchaeus wanted a mercy seat to which he could come as a poor sinner. He wanted to come back to God.

Zacchaeus was rich. He made his profession pay. He did not conduct his business halfheartedly. If he went to collect taxes from a widow who would not pay, he would put her out of the house. If a man could not pay enough, he would take out a mortgage on the place. He had robbed many people. Although he had once made a decision to become a publican, he found out that all the wealth in the world would not satisfy his heart. He wished he could go back and start over. He had gone down a one-way street and he knew of no way to get back

to the mercy seat. He wanted mercy, and our Lord knew that. The Lord
went to Jericho for the purpose of helping this man. He wanted to take
Zacchaeus with Him, not to Jerusalem, but to the cross for salvation.

**And he sought to see Jesus who he was; and could not
for the press, because he was little of stature [Luke
19:3].**

A friend of mine who is a seminary professor is puzzled about
whether there was one blind man or two blind men in Jericho. (His
problem is that Matthew tells of two blind men who were healed in
Jericho, while Luke speaks of only one.) I kiddingly told him once that
there were two blind men and I could prove it from the Bible. The
second blind man was Zacchaeus because the Bible says, "He could
not see for the press." He was a small man. He had eyes but they were
too close to the ground. He did what I used to do every New Year's day
at the Rose Parade. I would climb up a ladder and look over the heads
of everyone in front of me at the parade. Zacchaeus was not able to
find a ladder, so he climbed up into a sycamore tree.

**And he ran before, and climbed up into a sycamore tree
to see him: for he was to pass that way [Luke 19:4].**

When I was in Jericho, I took a good look at a sycamore tree. It has a
slick bark, and it is always a long way to the first limb. This is a difficult tree to climb, and I think this little man had a hard time climbing
a tree like this. Zacchaeus sweated it out but finally got up the tree and
settled down on a limb among the leaves. He thought he was secluded
there, and he had a private box for the parade. He waited. Sure
enough, Jesus came by. Our Lord knew he was there. Jesus was passing through Jericho to reach him.

**And when Jesus came to the place, he looked up, and
saw him, and said unto him, Zacchaeus, make haste,
and come down; for today I must abide at thy house
[Luke 19:5].**

When our Lord looked up into that sycamore tree and saw Zacchaeus, I think He laughed. It is true that the text does not say that He did, but it is difficult to read this account without seeing the humor in it. The Lord looked into that tree as if to say, "Well, Zacchaeus, you wanted to see Me. You really worked hard to get up into that tree. Now make haste and come down." Make haste? This poor fellow had spent half a day getting up into the tree! But it did not take long for him to get down. It is always easier to come down than to go up. Our Lord said to him, "I must abide at thy house." Our Lord did not stop at the home of a Pharisee; He did not stop at the home of any prominent person. He was going home with a publican!

> **And he made haste, and came down, and received him joyfully.**
>
> **And when they saw it, they all murmured, saying, That he was gone to be guest with a man that is a sinner [Luke 19:6-7].**

Zacchaeus was having fun now. For him it was a joyful occasion, but "they" murmured. Who are "they"? They are the gossiping crowd. They were saying, "Can you imagine that He is going to dinner at the house of a man who is a sinner?"

There was a lapse of time—how much, we are not told. Jesus had dinner with Zacchaeus, but He did not stay all night. They shut the door and the crowd milled around outside and gossiped, but no one knew what went on inside. Finally the door opened, and there stood Zacchaeus.

> **And Zacchaeus stood, and said unto the Lord; Behold, Lord, the half of my goods I give to the poor; and if I have taken any thing from any man by false accusation, I restore him fourfold [Luke 19:8].**

Something had happened to this man! He admitted that he had been robbing the poor and promised to give half of his goods to the poor and to restore fourfold to those whom he had falsely taxed. He was acting according to the Mosaic Law (see Exod. 22). Something had happened inside Zacchaeus, and he was a new man.

We are not given an account of the conversation between Zacchaeus and our Lord. For some reason the Holy Spirit did not give us an account of what transpired between these two men. However, when our Lord talked to men He usually spoke of two things: (1) man's need and (2) God's ability to meet that need. He did not have to tell Zacchaeus that he was a sinner. Zacchaeus knew he was a sinner, and so did everyone else. The Lord told him there was a remedy for sin. He said, "I am going to Jerusalem to die on the cross so that there will be a mercy seat for you, Zacchaeus."

And Jesus said unto him, This day is salvation come to this house, forsomuch as he also is a son of Abraham [Luke 19:9].

Zacchaeus was shut out from the mercy seat in the temple when he became a publican. That mercy seat pointed to the Lord Jesus Christ and to His blood that He shed for us on the cross. The Lord wanted this hated man to know that He was going to Jerusalem to die, and His death would provide for him a mercy seat. This publican made a decision for Christ and became a new man.

For the Son of man is come to seek and to save that which was lost [Luke 19:10].

Note that Zacchaeus did not come to the door and say, "I want to give my testimony: Jesus saves and keeps and satisfies." Rather he said, "Half my goods I will give to the poor, and I will make right the things that have been wrong." By this I know he has been converted. And, friend, this is the only way the world will know that you are converted. They do not know it by testimony; they know it only by what they see in your life. If it were not for his changed life, I would never know that this old publican got converted.

The experience of Zacchaeus is a good illustration of what James says: "Yea, a man may say, Thou hast faith, and I have works: shew me thy faith without thy works, and I will shew thee my faith by my works" (James 2:18). Zacchaeus showed his faith by his works. He did not talk about his faith; he demonstrated it. The world is not *listening* for something today; it is *looking* for something. Zacchaeus had what the world is looking for. Jesus had dinner with him and his life changed.

Jesus is still entering and passing through your town wherever it is, and He wants to have dinner with those who do not know Him. He wants to talk about your soul and salvation. What about it? Has He passed through your home? Has He knocked on your heart's door? Have you let Him in?

PARABLE OF TEN POUNDS

And as they heard these things, he added and spake a parable, because he was nigh to Jerusalem, and because they thought that the kingdom of God should immediately appear [Luke 19:11].

Jesus now is approaching Jerusalem. Many of His followers, including His apostles, think that He was about to set up His Kingdom on earth. But He is coming to Jerusalem to *die*. He is showing them that the Kingdom is going to be postponed.

He said therefore, A certain nobleman went into a far country to receive for himself a kingdom, and to return [Luke 19:12].

The "certain nobleman" represents the Lord Jesus Christ. He will receive the Kingdom from His Father—not from us. He is not asking anyone to vote for Him the next time He comes. People will either receive Him or they will be destroyed. He came the first time as a Savior. Next time He will come as King.

And he called his ten servants, and delivered them ten pounds, and said unto them, Occupy till I come.

> But his citizens hated him, and sent a message after
> him, saying, We will not have this man to reign over us
> [Luke 19:13–14].

This is the message the world has for the Lord Jesus Christ today. This, however, will not keep God from sending His Son back to earth. They rebelled against God and His Messiah. They did not want Him to rule over them; so they nailed Him to a cross.

> And it came to pass, that when he was returned, having
> received the kingdom, then he commanded these ser-
> vants to be called unto him, to whom he had given the
> money, that he might know how much every man had
> gained by trading.

> Then came the first, saying, Lord, thy pound hath
> gained ten pounds.

> And he said unto him. Well, thou good servant: because
> thou hast been faithful in a very little, have thou author-
> ity over ten cities [Luke 19:15–17].

While He is away, friend, He has given you a pound. He has given every one of His servants an opportunity, and that opportunity is the pound. You are to be faithful to that over which He has made you steward. Your pound may be an entire city, a handful of people, or a home. Whatever it is, you are to be *faithful*. Some may gain five pounds and some may gain ten pounds while the Lord is away but when He comes again, He will reward you according to your faithfulness.

> And the second came, saying, Lord, thy pound hath
> gained five pounds.

> And he said likewise to him, Be thou also over five
> cities.

> And another came, saying, Lord, behold, here is thy
> pound, which I have kept laid up in a napkin:

> For I feared thee, because thou art an austere man: thou takest up that thou layedst not down, and reapest that thou didst not sow.
>
> And he saith unto him, Out of thine own mouth will I judge thee, thou wicked servant. Thou knewest that I was an austere man, taking up that I laid not down, and reaping that I did not sow:
>
> Wherefore then gavest not thou my money into the bank, that at my coming I might have required mine own with usury?
>
> And he said unto them that stood by, Take from him the pound, and give it to him that hath ten pounds.
>
> (And they said unto him, Lord, he hath ten pounds.)
>
> For I say unto you, That unto every one which hath shall be given; and from him that hath not, even that he hath shall be taken away from him.
>
> But those mine enemies, which would not that I should reign over them, bring hither, and slay them before me [Luke 19:18–27].

When He returns, He will reward them according to their faithfulness, you see. The important thing is *faithfulness*.

> And when he had thus spoken, he went before, ascending up to Jerusalem [Luke 19:28].

He continues on His way to Jerusalem to deliver Himself up into the hands of His enemies.

JESUS ENTERS JERUSALEM

The Gospels present a composite picture of the so-called triumphal entry. By piecing the Gospels together, the conclusion is obvious that He entered Jerusalem three times, once a day on three separate days:

First—Saturday (the Sabbath day). There were no money changers on that day, and He looked around and left, "And Jesus entered into Jerusalem, and into the temple: and when he had looked round about upon all things, and now the eventide was come, he went out unto Bethany with the twelve" (Mark 11:11). *He entered as Priest.*

Second—Sunday (first day of week). The money changers were there and He cleansed the temple (see Matt. 21:12–13). *He entered as King.*

Third—Monday (second day of week). He wept over Jerusalem and entered the temple and taught and healed (see vv. 41–44, 47–48). *He entered as Prophet.*

And it came to pass, when he was come nigh to Bethphage and Bethany, at the mount called the mount of Olives, he sent two of his disciples,

Saying, Go ye into the village over against you; in the which at your entering ye shall find a colt tied, whereon yet never man sat: loose him, and bring him hither,

And if any man ask you, Why do ye loose him? thus shall ye say unto him, Because the Lord hath need of him.

And they that were sent went their way, and found even as he had said unto them.

And as they were loosing the colt, the owners thereof said unto them, Why loose ye the colt?

And they said, The Lord hath need of him [Luke 19:29–34].

I see no point in reading a miracle into this incident, although many people do so. I believe this is a normal, natural situation. Probably when our Lord was in Jerusalem previously He made arrangements with some friends to use these animals the next time He came to the city. His friends agreed to let Him use the animals at the time of the

Passover Feast. The owners of these animals were expecting the Lord and had them tied outside for Him. He told His disciples what to say in case anyone asked, so that they would know the Lord had sent them on this errand. The important thing in this passage is that Jesus asserts His authority, "The Lord hath need of him."

> **And they brought him to Jesus: and they cast their garments upon the colt, and they set Jesus thereon.**
>
> **And as he went, they spread their clothes in the way.**
>
> **And when he was come nigh, even now at the descent of the mount of Olives, the whole multitude of the disciples began to rejoice and praise God with a loud voice for all the mighty works that they had seen;**
>
> **Saying, Blessed be the King that cometh in the name of the Lord: peace in heaven, and glory in the highest [Luke 19:35–38].**

The crowd did not know the full significance of this action. A few days later the crowd cried, "Crucify Him!"

Even the disciples did not know the significance until later: "These things understood not his disciples at the first: but when Jesus was glorified, then remembered they that these things were written of him, and that they had done these things unto him" (John 12:16).

> **And some of the Pharisees from among the multitude said unto him, Master, rebuke thy disciples.**
>
> **And he answered and said unto them, I tell you that, if these should hold their peace, the stones would immediately cry out [Luke 19:39–40].**

This episode of coming into Jerusalem as the Lord Jesus Christ did was bound to incite the Roman ruler to act because of two things that He did. First, He accepted the reverence and loyalty of these followers. In the second place, He did not silence them.

The Lord Jesus Christ recognized that eternal and significant issues were at stake and that to rebuke His followers would force the silent stones to cry out. In fact, they were crying out, for when Nehemiah had rebuilt the walls and gates of the city, there was a message in the stones. Those very stones and walls were proclaiming the gospel message, and the gates were fairly shouting, "Lift up your heads, O ye gates; and be ye lift up, ye everlasting doors; and the King of glory shall come in" (Ps. 24:7). (For amplification of this, see the author's booklet, *The Gospel in the Gates of Jerusalem.*)

It should be remembered that the so-called triumphal entry ended at the Cross. Christ will come the second time in triumph. Hebrews 9:28 says, "So Christ was once offered to bear the sins of many; and unto them that look for him shall he appear the second time without sin unto salvation." The second time the Lord will come to this earth, His feet will stand on the Mount of Olives (see Zech. 14:4). Then the Lord will enter Jerusalem. His true Triumphal Entry will be at His second coming. His first entry into Jerusalem took Him to the Cross to die for our sins. By His death and resurrection, salvation is offered unto us.

JESUS WEEPS OVER THE CITY

And when he was come near, he beheld the city, and wept over it,

Saying, If thou hadst known, even thou, at least in this thy day, the things which belong unto thy peace! but now they are hid from thine eyes [Luke 19:41–42].

And, friend, they are still hidden from their eyes. I saw a picture of a convention they were having in Jerusalem some time ago. Stretched across the auditorium was a huge motto which read: "Science Will Give Us Peace In Our Day." Well, science has not brought them peace. It has produced sophisticated weapons and the atom bomb, but it has not brought peace.

> For the days shall come upon thee, that thine enemies shall cast a trench about thee, and compass thee round, and keep thee in on every side,
>
> And shall lay thee even with the ground, and thy children within thee; and they shall not leave in thee one stone upon another; because thou knewest not the time of thy visitation [Luke 19:43–44].

The fulfillment of this prophecy is written in history. In A.D. 70, Titus the Roman leveled Jerusalem and slaughtered the inhabitants without mercy.

JESUS CLEANSES THE TEMPLE

> And he went into the temple, and began to cast out them that sold therein, and them that bought;
>
> Saying unto them, It is written, My house is the house of prayer: but ye have made it a den of thieves.
>
> And he taught daily in the temple. But the chief priests and the scribes and the chief of the people sought to destroy him,
>
> And could not find what they might do: for all the people were very attentive to hear him [Luke 19:45–48].

Our Lord uses very strong language as He cleans up the temple for the second time. This action of Jesus officially closes His ministry to the nation.

CHAPTER 20

THEME: Jesus' authority challenged; parable of the vineyard; Jesus is questioned about paying tribute to Caesar; Jesus silences the Sadducees about resurrection; Jesus questions the scribes

JESUS' AUTHORITY CHALLENGED

And it came to pass, that on one of those days, as he taught the people in the temple, and preached the gospel, the chief priests and the scribes came upon him with the elders,

And spake unto him, saying, Tell us, by what authority doest thou these things? or who is he that gave thee this authority?

And he answered and said unto them, I will also ask you one thing; and answer me [Luke 20:1–3].

Jesus came into the temple every day and taught until He was arrested at the time of the Passover. He used the Socratic method of answering a question with a question. This was His question:

The baptism of John, was it from heaven, or of men? [Luke 20:4].

This was one question the religious rulers could not answer without condemning themselves. They had to go off in a huddle to decide on an answer.

And they reasoned with themselves, saying, If we shall say, From heaven; he will say, Why then believed ye him not?

> But and if we say, Of men; all the people will stone us: for they be persuaded that John was a prophet.
>
> And they answered, that they could not tell whence it was.
>
> And Jesus said unto them, Neither tell I you by what authority I do these things [Luke 20:5-8].

Their question was not honest and sincere. If they had been willing to accept John, they would have been willing to accept the Lord Jesus Christ also. If they had believed John, they would have never questioned the authority of the Lord Jesus.

PARABLE OF THE VINEYARD

The parable of the vineyard is recorded in Matthew and Mark.

> Then began he to speak to the people this parable; A certain man planted a vineyard, and let it forth to husbandmen, and went into a far country for a long time.
>
> And at the season he sent a servant to the husbandmen, that they should give him of the fruit of the vineyard: but the husbandmen beat him, and sent him away empty [Luke 20:9-10].

The owner of the vineyard kept sending servants to the husbandmen to see how things were going. One by one the servants were beaten. God sent prophet after prophet to Israel, and they were absolutely rejected. Many of them were stoned and killed. Finally the Father sent His Son.

Jesus Christ was the Son and He was telling these religious rulers exactly what was in their hearts and minds to do with Him. They were going to crucify Him, and God was going to permit it.

> And he beheld them, and said, What is this then that is written, The stone which the builders rejected, the same is become the head of the corner? [Luke 20:17].

The Lord was telling them they could kill Him but could not destroy the purpose of God. The Stone that they reject will become the head of the corner. This is a clear prediction of the Lord's rejection and subsequent triumph.

Whosoever shall fall upon that stone shall be broken; but on whomsoever it shall fall, it will grind him to powder [Luke 20:18].

Today you and I can fall on that Stone, who is Christ Jesus, and be saved—that is, we have to come to Him as a sinner, broken in spirit, broken in heart. When we do this, we are on the foundation that no man can lay, which is Jesus Christ the Stone. "For other foundation can no man lay than that is laid, which is Jesus Christ" (1 Cor. 3:11). Daniel tells of that Stone which will fall in judgment someday and "grind to powder" the nations that reject Him (see Dan. 2). What the Lord is saying in this parable is as clear as the noonday sun. It could not have been misunderstood.

JESUS IS QUESTIONED ABOUT PAYING TRIBUTE TO CAESAR

And the chief priests and the scribes the same hour sought to lay hands on him; and they feared the people: for they perceived that he had spoken this parable against them [Luke 20:19].

We can see that the religious rulers certainly got the point of His parable. The problem is that too many people in our churches today miss the point.

And they asked him, saying, Master, we know that thou sayest and teachest rightly, neither acceptest thou the person of any, but teachest the way of God truly [Luke 20:21].

This was spoken like the true hypocrites these men were.

**Is it lawful for us to give tribute unto Caesar, or no?
[Luke 20:22].**

The Herodians are the ones who posed this question because they wanted to get rid of Caesar and put the house of Herod over Israel.

But he perceived their craftiness, and said unto them, Why tempt ye me?

Shew me a penny. Whose image and superscription hath it? They answered and said, Caesar's [Luke 20:23–24].

The question of the Herodians was a loaded one designed to trap Jesus. Had He said "Yes"—to pay tribute to Caesar, then He would have put Caesar ahead of Moses and ahead of their Messiah. If He had said "No"—not to pay tribute to Caesar, then He would have been subject to arrest by Rome.

The method Jesus adopted in dealing with this question is a masterpiece. He asked for the Roman denarius. Does this mean that Jesus did not have any money? At least He made them produce the coin.

And he said unto them, Render therefore unto Caesar the things which be Caesar's, and unto God the things which be God's [Luke 20:25].

They were using the legal tender of the Roman Empire. Rome did provide certain advantages and privileges. Rome maintained law and order by her standards and provided protection. Rome made and maintained roads and kept the sea lanes open. She had a universal currency system which was an aid to business. The Jews owed Rome something for the use of coins, roads, and law and order. Caesar had something coming to him.

God had something coming to Him also. He provided all the utilities: lights, air, water, and the elements from which roads and coins are made. There are two areas of life in which we have a responsibility. Man has both an earthly and a heavenly obligation. He has both a physical and a spiritual responsibility. Citizens of heaven pay taxes down here. Pilgrims down here should deposit eternal wealth in heaven.

JESUS SILENCES THE SADDUCEES ABOUT RESURRECTION

Then came to him certain of the Sadducees, which deny that there is any resurrection; and they asked him,

Saying, Master, Moses wrote unto us, If any man's brother die, having a wife, and he die without children, that his brother should take his wife, and raise up seed unto his brother [Luke 20:27-28].

You find this in Deuteronomy 25:5-6. It was an unusual law, but we see it in action in the Book of Ruth.

There were therefore seven brethren: and the first took a wife, and died without children.

And the second took her to wife, and he died childless.

And the third took her; and in like manner the seven also: and they left no children, and died.

Last of all the woman died also.

Therefore in the resurrection whose wife of them is she? for seven had her to wife [Luke 20:29-33].

Of course their question was ridiculous.

And Jesus answering said unto them, The children of this world marry, and are given in marriage:

> But they which shall be accounted worthy to obtain that world, and the resurrection from the dead, neither marry, nor are given in marriage:

> Neither can they die any more: for they are equal unto the angels; and are the children of God, being the children of the resurrection [Luke 20:34–36].

According to both Matthew and Mark, He told them their problem was that they knew neither the Scriptures nor the power of God.

> Now that the dead are raised, even Moses shewed at the bush, when he calleth the Lord the God of Abraham, and the God of Isaac, and the God of Jacob.

> For he is not a God of the dead, but of the living: for all live unto him [Luke 20:37–38].

You see, after Jesus had answered the Herodians and the Pharisees soundly, the Sadducees bring this old cliché to Him with the thought that anyone answering their question would be ridiculous. The Sadducees would correspond to the liberal section of the contemporary church, while the Pharisees could be equated with the conservatives. The Sadducees rejected the supernatural. They, therefore, did not believe in the Resurrection.

Their question grows out of a situation created by the Mosaic system. The Sadducees attempted to make it preposterous by saying that the woman married seven times. That in itself is not likely, but it could happen. In our day there are examples of those who have been married as often, but they are more concerned about the present life than anything beyond.

The Sadducees, as a sect, arose about 300 B.C. Most of the high priests and temple politicians were Sadducees. They were prominent and rich. Isn't it interesting that today most of the church politicians and the rich churches are liberal? That tells us that human nature has not changed down through the centuries.

The Sadducees denied the miraculous. They stripped the Scriptures of the supernatural. (They were in direct conflict with the Pharisees who were supernaturalists.) They never accepted the inerrancy of Scripture. There is a striking similarity between the beliefs of the Sadducees and liberalism today. Liberalism is a departure from historic Christianity. Concerning conservatism and liberalism, Dr. Louis Berkhof said, "The difference is so great between them that one of them will have to surrender the term *Christian*." I have decided that the liberal is not Christian at all. Many churches should call themselves the "Boulevard Religious Club" or the "First" or "Second Religious Club" because they are not Christian.

There was a time when those who were unregenerate were outside the church. They denied the authority of Scripture, the deity of Christ, and the supernatural. They were called infidels and skeptics. When I first came to Southern California, you could see them on soap boxes in front of downtown churches or in the city parks. Now they are in the pulpits of the city. They are still infidels and skeptics; they still deny the deity of Christ and the supernatural. They have crept into the church unawares.

The Sadducees were the greatest enemies which Christ had and were the main instigators of the first persecution of the church. The Pharisees with the Sadduccees were the leaders in the persecution of the Lord Jesus. After the death of the Lord, the Pharisees dropped the entire affair. They were no longer interested in persecuting Him or His followers; in fact, many of them became Christians. The Sadducees, however, went on with the persecution of the church. You can read about it in the third and fourth chapters of Acts.

The Resurrection was the acid test of the Sadducees, and it is the acid test of the liberal. They do not believe in a literal resurrection. It is interesting that there is no account in Scripture of a Sadducee ever coming to Christ for salvation. A Pharisee named Nicodemus was converted, and Acts 6:7 tells us, ". . . a great company of the priests were obedient to the faith." Many priests became believers, but there is no record of a Sadducee being converted.

Every young minister soon discovers that the preaching of the cross is an offense. He will never be voted the most outstanding citizen in his town. He will never find himself in a great political position, nor will he be on television very often. The subtle temptation is to throw overboard the gospel of the Lord Jesus Christ and become a popular preacher. Judas sold out the Lord. Peter denied Him but loved Him and came back to Him. When a man sells Christ for popularity, he will never come back. "Can the Ethiopian change his skin, or the leopard his spots? . . ." (Jer. 13:23). The next time some starry-eyed optimist tells you that the liberals are coming back to Christ, forget it. The Sadducees were the worst enemies that the gospel of Christ ever had—whether in the first or the twentieth centuries.

JESUS QUESTIONS THE SCRIBES

The Lord concludes this question-and-answer period by asking the scribes a question.

Then certain of the scribes answering said, Master, thou hast well said.

And after that they durst not ask him any question at all.

And he said unto them, How say they that Christ is David's son?

And David himself saith in the book of Psalms, The LORD said unto my Lord, Sit thou on my right hand,

Till I make thine enemies thy footstool.

David therefore calleth him Lord, how is he then his son?

Then in the audience of all the people he said unto his disciples,

Beware of the scribes, which desire to walk in long robes, and love greetings in the markets, and the highest seats in the synagogues, and the chief rooms at feasts;

**Which devour widows' houses, and for a shew make
long prayers: the same shall receive greater damnation
[Luke 20:39–47].**

Right here, Jesus is teaching His own virgin birth. How could David,
in Psalm 110 where he is speaking of a future descendant call his own
great-great-great-grandson his Lord? Well, the only way he can call
Him his Lord is for Him to be the The Lord, friend. The only way He
can be The Lord is to be more than David's son. He must be virgin
born to be the Son of God. This is a great thought that our Lord is
teaching here.

Notice also that here Jesus definitely ascribes Psalm 110 to David.
He says that David wrote this Psalm by the Holy Spirit. And Jesus says
that this psalm is speaking concerning Him, the Messiah.

CHAPTER 21

THEME: Jesus notes how people give and commends the widow; Jesus answers question in Olivet Discourse "When shall these things be?"

Now we come to the prophetic section of Luke's Gospel. Although it corresponds to the Olivet Discourse in Matthew and Mark, there is a contrast with the similarity. Matthew's Gospel gives us the three questions which the disciples asked the Lord Jesus: (1) When shall these things be?—that is, one stone not left upon another; (2) What shall be the sign of thy coming? (3) And of the end of the age? (see Matt. 24:3). In the chapter before us He answers the first question. Luke deals with one of the most practical aspects of the prophecy, and there is no mystery or speculation to his meaning, because most of Luke's record is no longer prophecy; it is history. It was fulfilled in A.D. 70. After all, "prophecy is the mold into which history is poured," and there has already been some pouring done here.

JESUS NOTES HOW PEOPLE GIVE AND COMMENDS THE WIDOW

And he looked up, and saw the rich men casting their gifts into the treasury.

And he saw also a certain poor widow casting in thither two mites.

And he said, Of a truth I say unto you, that this poor widow hath cast in more than they all:

For all these have of their abundance cast in unto the offerings of God: but she of her penury hath cast in all the living that she had [Luke 21:1–4].

Compared to the wealth of that temple (and it was a wealthy temple), the widow's gift did not amount to very much. Her two little coppers did not do much to help in the upkeep of the temple. Our Lord, however, does not measure giving that way. He measures it, not by what you give, but by what you keep for yourself. We are not living under the tithe system because that dictates what you must give. What you keep for yourself is "grace" giving. There are many people who should be giving more than one tenth to the Lord because of the way He has blessed them. One man told me, "If I gave only a tenth of my substance to the Lord, I would feel as though I was stealing from Him." God looks at the sacrifice of the giver. Generally it is the one who cannot give much who is making the real sacrifice. God looks at what you keep for yourself.

Next Sunday morning someone may observe what you give, and say, "My, he gives a whole lot to the Lord's work!" But what does *God* say? He is looking at what you are keeping for yourself.

JESUS ANSWERS QUESTION IN OLIVET DISCOURSE "WHEN SHALL THESE THINGS BE?"

And as some spake of the temple, how it was adorned with goodly stones and gifts, he said,

As for these things which ye behold, the days will come, in the which there shall not be left one stone upon another, that shall not be thrown down [Luke 21:5–6].

When the Lord mentioned that the poor widow gave more than all the rich, the disciples said, "Look at this temple, the riches in it, the valuable stones in its construction!" The wealth was impressive. But did they really *see* it? Its magnificence would soon be gone. It would soon lie in rubble, not one stone left upon another. And, friend, that is the way you and I should see the wealth of this world. It won't be here long; it will soon pass away.

And they asked him, saying, Master, but when shall these things be? and what sign will there be when these things shall come to pass? [Luke 21:7].

You will find that in Matthew's and Mark's Gospels the emphasis is put upon the last two questions asked of the Lord Jesus: "What is the sign of Your coming?" and "the end of the age?" The return of Christ is the more important thing in Matthew, and He answers questions that relate to it. Now here in Luke He emphasizes when "there shall not be left one stone upon another"; that is, the destruction of Jerusalem. Although this is part of the Olivet Discourse, our Lord probably answered the first question of the disciples; then later, as they came to the Mount of Olives and asked Him in detail, He gave the more formal and complete statement which we find in Matthew's Gospel. Undoubtedly, our Lord gave His teachings over and over again. After all, repetition is the way we all learn.

And he said, Take heed that ye be not deceived: for many shall come in my name, saying, I am Christ; and the time draweth near: go ye not therefore after them [Luke 21:8].

The characteristic of the times would be that there would be false Christs, which is a feature of the age in which we live, and has been since He was here. There were false messiahs in His day, and today there are those who claim supernatural power. Although they talk a great deal about Jesus, they move themselves into His place and take to themselves the glory that should be His. I think there are quite a few false Christs walking about, and certainly false religions abound.

But when ye shall hear of wars and commotions, be not terrified: for these things must first come to pass; but the end is not by and by.

Then said he unto them, Nation shall rise against nation, and kingdom against kingdom [Luke 21:9–10].

War is another characteristic of the age. War will be intensified toward the end of the age. Although pacifism is growing, the Word of God says, "For when they shall say, Peace and safety; then sudden destruction cometh upon them, as travail upon a woman with child; and they shall not escape" (1 Thess. 5:3). We are right now in that position. Wars identify the entire period until the Lord returns.

> **And great earthquakes shall be in divers places, and famines, and pestilences; and fearful sights and great signs shall there be from heaven [Luke 21:11].**

These are another feature of the age, probably intensified toward the end.

> **But before all these, they shall lay their hands on you, and persecute you, delivering you up to the synagogues, and into prisons, being brought before kings and rulers for my name's sake.**
>
> **And it shall turn to you for a testimony.**
>
> **Settle it therefore in your hearts, not to meditate before what ye shall answer:**
>
> **For I will give you a mouth and wisdom, which all your adversaries shall not be able to gainsay nor resist [Luke 21:12–15].**

The Lord is speaking to the nation Israel in these verses. All of these things apply specifically to the Jews. John 15:18–19 tell us, "If the world hate you, ye know that it hated me before it hated you. If we were of the world, the world would love his own: but because ye are not of the world, but I have chosen you out of the world, therefore the world hateth you." If you are a follower of the Lord Jesus Christ, you are not going to win any popularity contest, I can assure you.

> **And ye shall be betrayed both by parents, and brethren, and kinsfolks, and friends; and some of you shall they cause to be put to death.**
>
> **And ye shall be hated of all men for my name's sake.**
>
> **But there shall not an hair of your head perish.**
>
> **In your patience possess ye your souls [Luke 21:16–19].**

These verses apply directly to the 144,000 Jews who will be indestructible during the time of the Great Tribulation period. The suffering of these Jews will be much greater during the Tribulation than it was under the German persecution with the ovens and concentration camps.

> **And when ye shall see Jerusalem compassed with armies, then know that the desolation thereof is nigh [Luke 21:20].**

Remember they had asked Him, "When shall these things be?" (v. 7)—that is, when one stone would not be left upon another. Well, that took place when Titus the Roman besieged Jerusalem in A.D. 70. I am of the opinion that many of these men, about forty years later, remembered Christ's words when they looked over the battlements of the walls of Jerusalem and saw the banners of Titus' army unfurled, and said, "This is the day the Lord talked about." (This same thing will happen again during the last days.)

> **Then let them which are in Judaea flee to the mountains; and let them which are in the midst of it depart out; and let not them that are in the countries enter thereinto [Luke 21:21].**

They were to do then what they are to do in the Great Tribulation Period. They were to get out of Jerusalem as quickly as possible. The great Jewish historian Josephus tells us about the horrible siege of

Jerusalem. During the extended blockage of the city, mothers ate their own children. People died like flies, and the dead were thrown over the walls. Those who stayed either died of starvation or were sold as slaves. Again the Lord is drawing a miniature picture of what it is going to be like in the last days. There are those who claim that it could never happen a second time. It happened once, friend; that is a matter of history. The Lord said it would happen, and it did. He said it will happen again, and I believe He is right.

> **For these be the days of vengeance, that all things which are written may be fulfilled.**

> **But woe unto them that are with child, and to them that give suck, in those days! for there shall be great distress in the land, and wrath upon this people.**

> **And they shall fall by the edge of the sword, and shall be led away captive into all nations: and Jerusalem shall be trodden down of the Gentiles, until the times of the Gentiles be fulfilled [Luke 21:22–24].**

The Jews were scattered. Titus put them in slavery. They built the great Colosseum in Rome. Great distress and wrath fell upon the nation of Israel. From the day that Titus entered that city, about 1900 years ago, the Jews have never been able to get the Gentiles out of Jerusalem. Gentiles have controlled Jerusalem from the day Titus conquered it until the present day. "Holy places" in Jerusalem are held by Gentiles. And there stands the Mosque of Omar where their temple should stand. Our Lord said Jerusalem would be trodden down of the Gentiles until the time of the Gentiles is fulfilled. I have watched Jerusalem for a long time, and it is still trodden down by the Gentiles. The Gentiles are still in Jerusalem. Isn't it amazing how accurate the Word of God is?

> **And there shall be signs in the sun, and in the moon, and in the stars; and upon the earth distress of nations, with perplexity; the sea and the waves roaring [Luke 21:25].**

I think this has reference to the last days before Christ returns to the earth. This is the way it is going to be in the last days.

> **Men's hearts failing them for fear, and for looking after those things which are coming on the earth: for the powers of heaven shall be shaken [Luke 21:26].**

There are people who quote this verse and say it is a picture of today. My friend, if I may use a common colloquialism of the streets, "You ain't seen nothin' yet." If you think we are seeing a fulfillment of this verse now, you are wrong. Things are bad today, I agree. Political crises and social distress are cause for great concern. Physical disturbances are overwhelming, but they are going to get much worse in the last days.

> **And then shall they see the Son of man coming in a cloud with power and great glory [Luke 21:27].**

Christ could return at any moment. Things are happening so fast today that the church, the body of Christ, could be taken from this earth before you have finished reading this paragraph. If it is, I hope you will be with me in His presence.

> **And when these things begin to come to pass, then look up, and lift up your heads; for your redemption draweth nigh [Luke 21:28].**

Are these things beginning to come to pass? I am not in a position to know. I have no inside information. All I can say is that my salvation and redemption is nearer now than when I first believed. I know that He is coming back and that is what is important to me.

> **And he spake to them a parable; Behold the fig tree, and all the trees;**
>
> **When they now shoot forth, ye see and know of your own selves that summer is now nigh at hand.**

So likewise ye, when ye see these things come to pass, know ye that the kingdom of God is nigh at hand [Luke 21:29–31].

I still consider the fig tree symbolic of the nation Israel. God's timepiece is not Gruen or Bulova, but Israel. The fig tree represents Israel (see Jer. 24:1–5; Hos. 9:10).

Verily I say unto you, This generation shall not pass away, till all be fulfilled [Luke 21:32].

"This generation" could refer to the race of Israel. It would then teach the indestructibility of this people. Or it could refer to a generation of people and their total life span. In that case it would mean that those who saw the beginning of these events would see the conclusion of them also. Because the emphasis appears to be on the rapidity in which these events transpire, rather than upon the permanence of the nation Israel, I favor the second explanation.

Heaven and earth shall pass away: but my words shall not pass away.

And take heed to yourselves, lest at any time your hearts be overcharged with surfeiting, and drunkenness, and cares of this life, and so that day come upon you unawares.

For as a snare shall it come on all them that dwell on the face of the whole earth [Luke 21:33–35].

Don't let down your guard today, friend. Don't give up. These are great days to live for God! I am not called upon to reform the world, or change the world. That is God's business, not my business. He has asked me to live for Him, and He has asked me to get His Word out. That is what I am attempting to do, and I hope you are doing this also. It is very comfortable to be in the will of God.

> Watch ye therefore, and pray always, that ye may be ac-
> counted worthy to escape all these things that shall
> come to pass, and to stand before the Son of man [Luke
> 21:36].

How are you going to be worthy? The only thing that will make me worthy is my position in Christ. Therefore, I have trusted Him as my Savior, and I have committed my way to Him, so that if I am alive at the time of the Rapture, I'll be going to meet Him in the air by the grace of God.

> And in the day time he was teaching in the temple; and
> at night he went out, and abode in the mount that is
> called the mount of Olives.

> And all the people came early in the morning to him in
> the temple, for to hear him [Luke 21:37–38].

Many of us would like to have been with the group to hear Him.

CHAPTER 22

THEME: Judas plots with the chief priests to betray Jesus; Jesus plans for the last Passover and institutes the Lord's Supper; Jesus announces His betrayal; position of the apostles in the future kingdom; Peter's denial; Jesus warns the disciples of the future; Jesus goes to Gethsemane; Jesus betrayed by Judas; Jesus arrested and led to the High Priest's house; Jesus denied by Peter; Jesus is mocked and beaten; Jesus is brought before the Sanhedrin

JUDAS PLOTS WITH THE CHIEF PRIESTS TO BETRAY JESUS

Now the feast of unleavened bread drew nigh, which is called the Passover [Luke 22:1].

Jesus has come to Jerusalem. Six months before, in Caesarea Philippi, He had steadfastly set His face to go to Jerusalem to die. Everything He did from then on was a movement toward Jerusalem. The Mount of Transfiguration and the so-called triumphal entry are behind Him. It is the time of the Passover and He, the Lamb of God which taketh away the sins of the world, is going to die.

And the chief priests and scribes sought how they might kill him; for they feared the people [Luke 22:2].

The religious rulers would have taken Him immediately and slain Him, but they were afraid of the people. It was the Passover, which meant that people from everywhere were in the city; and they were for Him. They were the silent majority.

Then entered Satan into Judas surnamed Iscariot, being of the number of the twelve [Luke 22:3].

Is it possible for a Christian to be demon-possessed? Is it possible for Satan or a demon to enter a Christian? The answer, of course, is no. It is possible, however, for a church member who is not a Christian to be possessed. Some of the meanest people I have met were not in the Mafia or in jail but were members of a church. I have met some people in the church that I am confident were demon-possessed. It would be difficult to explain their conduct on any other basis. My friend, if you are going to stand on the sidelines and listen to the preaching of the gospel and do nothing about it but mix and mingle with God's people, the day will come when Satan will move into the vacant house, as we saw in Luke 11:24–26. One of Satan's demons will take up residence. That is what happened to Judas who had rejected Jesus.

And he went his way, and communed with the chief priests and captains, how he might betray him unto them.

And they were glad, and covenanted to give him money [Luke 22:4–5].

The religious rulers had been wondering how they were going to take Him. Now one of His own men comes along and offers to betray Him.

And he promised, and sought opportunity to betray him unto them in the absence of the multitude [Luke 22:6].

The plot was: Wait until the crowd leaves Jerusalem. Wait until we can get Him alone so people will not know what we are doing. They planned to take Him secretly. Judas was to bide his time and let the religious rulers know when the time was right. Actually that time never came, because Jesus forced them to act immediately. Jesus, as recorded in the Gospel of John, gave Judas that sop in the Upper Room at the Last Supper and told him, "What you do, do quickly. The time has come. You are going to have to move hurriedly." And Judas did just that.

JESUS PLANS FOR THE LAST PASSOVER AND
INSTITUTES THE LORD'S SUPPER

Jesus and His disciples now plan the last Passover.

Then came the day of unleavened bread, when the passover must be killed.

And he sent Peter and John, saying, Go and prepare us the passover, that we may eat.

And they said unto him, Where wilt thou that we prepare?

And he said unto them, Behold, when ye are entered into the city, there shall a man meet you, bearing a pitcher of water; follow him into the house where he entereth in.

And ye shall say unto the goodman of the house, The Master saith unto thee, Where is the guestchamber, where I shall eat the passover with my disciples?

And he shall shew you a large upper room furnished: there make ready.

And they went, and found as he had said unto them: and they made ready the passover [Luke 22:7–13].

I see no reason to read a miracle into this passage. Our Lord had been to Jerusalem many times. He knew the man who had this upper room. I am sure he had said to our Lord, "When you are in Jerusalem, bring your disciples here." Probably the Lord had already made arrangements with him to use the room and was letting him know that He needed it at this time.

And when the hour was come, he sat down, and the twelve apostles with him [Luke 22:14].

This is the time of the Last Supper, and Judas was present.

> **And he said unto them, With desire I have desired to eat this passover with you before I suffer:**
>
> **For I say unto you, I will not any more eat thereof, until it be fulfilled in the kingdom of God.**
>
> **And he took the cup, and gave thanks, and said, Take this, and divide it among yourselves:**
>
> **For I say unto you, I will not drink of the fruit of the vine, until the kingdom of God shall come [Luke 22:15–18].**

At the Passover the cup circulated several times, and I think the Lord participated up to the last cup. That was the cup of joy. He did not drink it. The question arises, "Did He ever drink that cup?" I think He did. On the cross they gave Him vinegar to drink, and in Hebrews it says, ". . . for the joy that was set before him [he] endured the cross . . ." (Heb. 12:2).

On the dying embers of the fading feast of Passover, the Lord Jesus Christ fanned into flame the new feast of the Lord's Supper.

> **And he took bread, and gave thanks, and brake it, and gave unto them, saying, This is my body which is given for you: this do in remembrance of me.**
>
> **Likewise also the cup after supper, saying, This cup is the new testament in my blood, which is shed for you [Luke 22:19–20].**

The Lord took two of the most frail elements in the world as symbols of His body and blood. Bread and wine—both will spoil in a few days. When He raised a monument, it was not made of brass or marble, but of two frail elements that perish. He declared that the bread spoke of His body and the wine spoke of His blood. The bread speaks of His body broken—not a *bone* broken but a broken *body* because He was made sin for us (see 2 Cor. 5:21). I do not believe He even looked human when He was taken down from that cross. Isaiah had said of Him, ". . . his visage was so marred more than any man, and his form more than the sons of men" (Isa. 52:14); and ". . . there is no beauty that we should desire him" (Isa. 53:2).

For centuries the Passover feast had looked forward to the Lord's coming and His death. Now He is in the shadow of the cross, and this is the last Passover. The Passover feast has now been fulfilled. We gather about the Lord's Table and search our hearts. What we do at this Table is in remembrance of Him. We look back to what He did for us on the cross, and we look forward to His coming again. "For as often as ye eat this bread, and drink this cup ye do shew the Lord's death till he come" (1 Cor. 11:26).

JESUS ANNOUNCES HIS BETRAYAL

But, behold, the hand of him that betrayeth me is with me on the table [Luke 22:21].

The one who was going to betray Him was in their midst. There are those who believe that Judas actually left before the institution of the Lord's Supper. I think that is accurate. Luke doesn't give the chronological order; he gives us those facts necessary to the purpose of his commentary. John makes it clear that during the Passover our Lord took the sop, gave it to Judas, and said, "That thou doest, do quickly" (see John 13:26–30). Then Judas left.

And truly the Son of man goeth, as it was determined: but woe unto that man by whom he is betrayed!

And they began to inquire among themselves, which of them it was that should do this thing [Luke 22:22–23].

Every one of the disciples believed he was capable of denying and betraying the Lord. If you are honest, you know that you also could betray Him. If He did not keep His hand on me, I could deny Him in the next five minutes. Thank God, however, He will not take His hand off me, and I rejoice in that.

POSITION OF THE APOSTLES
IN THE FUTURE KINGDOM

And there was also a strife among them, which of them should be accounted the greatest [Luke 22:24].

These men who had recognized how low they could stoop also had ambitions to be the greatest. Can you imagine that? Right in the shadow of the cross these men are grasping for position. We see that in the church today. The saints today are not much of an improvement over the apostles.

And he said unto them, The kings of the Gentiles exercise lordship over them; and they that exercise authority upon them are called benefactors.

But ye shall not be so: but he that is greatest among you, let him be as the younger; and he that is chief, as he that doth serve.

For whether is greater, he that sitteth at meat, or he that serveth? is not he that sitteth at meat? but I am among you as he that serveth [Luke 22:25–27].

The Lord is telling them that He has taken the lower position. That is what He did when He took my place on the cross. It is like a master getting up from the table and telling his servant, "You sit down and eat, and I will serve you." When Jesus Christ came to earth, all mankind should have been His servant! Instead, He served mankind. He set a table of salvation and has invited us to this great feast of salvation.

Ye are they which have continued with me in my temptations [Luke 22:28].

The Lord is gracious to His disciples and commends them for continuing with Him through His testings here on earth.

And I appoint unto you a kingdom, as my Father hath appointed unto me;

That ye may eat and drink at my table in my kingdom, and sit on thrones judging the twelve tribes of Israel [Luke 22:29–30].

I am sure the apostles will have a special place in the kingdom. They bridged the gap between the Old and New Testaments. They came out of the Old Testament economy and moved into the New Testament economy. You and I are not in that position today. None of us fits into that particular place because chronologically they bridged the gap. They will be given a prominent position and will not only eat and drink at the Lord's table but will also sit on thrones and judge the twelve tribes of Israel. That will be their position.

The child of God has some great things in store for the future. The redeemed are going to occupy exalted positions. I wonder if you are working for a place in heaven. I do not mean to say that you should work for your salvation. You do not work for salvation, but you do work for your *place* in heaven. You are going to heaven by the grace of God, but you are going to be judged according to your works to see what position will be yours. Are you interested in your good works? You should be!

Now I believe that the only thing God will judge is the exercise of the gift He gave us. He gives us a gift when we are put into the body of believers at the time of salvation, and there are literally thousands of gifts. The subject of gifts is an interesting one. Do you know what one of the gifts was in the early church? There was a woman named Dorcas who sewed. Sewing was her gift. She made clothes for widows who otherwise would not have had any clothes. You will be rewarded according to your faithfulness in exercising the gift God has given to you. The way you live your Christian life is important before God, my beloved.

PETER'S DENIAL

And the Lord said, Simon, Simon, behold, Satan hath desired to have you, that he may sift you as wheat:

But I have prayed for thee, that thy faith fail not: and when thou art converted, strengthen thy brethren [Luke 22:31–32].

The word *converted* in this passage does not mean conversion as we think of it. The Lord is speaking about the time when Peter will have a change of heart and mind and his faith will be increased. At that time such a tremendous change would be wrought in Peter that he would be able to strengthen his brethren. The Lord knew that Peter would deny Him, and yet He said, "I have prayed for thee, that thy faith fail not."

The Lord today is our intercessor. He knows when you are moving toward the place of failure and stumbling. If you belong to Him, my friend, He has already prayed for you that your faith fail not. You may fail Him, but if you belong to Him, your *faith* will not fail. The reason your faith will not fail is because He has prayed for you. My, what a picture of His love!

In John 17:9 our Lord prayed to the Father, "I pray for them: I pray not for the world, but for them which thou hast given me; for they are thine." The Lord does not pray for the world. He died for the world, and you cannot ask Him to do any more than that. He died for the world, but He prays for His own that they will be kept while they are in the world. The Lord Jesus Christ prayed for you today. It may be that you did not pray for yourself but He has prayed for you.

Peter was later able to strengthen his brethren. The man who has been tested is the man who is really able to help others, even if he has failed and has come back to the Lord. This is the reason I always send a converted drunkard to talk to a drunkard. When I was a young preacher, one drunkard whom I tried to help just patted me on the knee and said, "Vernon, you are a good boy." However, he did not think I could understand his case. He was right; I could not. I found a man who had been an old drunken bum before coming to Christ and asked him to see this man. He went to his home, sat down beside him, and said, "Bill, you know you and I used to drink together. Jesus has saved me, and He can save you too." And He did—He saved Bill too. The man who has been through the experience himself is the one who can help.

And he said unto him, Lord, I am ready to go with thee, both into prison, and to death [Luke 22:33].

Peter meant every word of this, but he did not know himself. Many of us do not really know how weak we are.

And he said, I tell thee, Peter, the cock shall not crow this day, before that thou shalt thrice deny that thou knowest me [Luke 22:34].

Simon Peter simply did not believe that he could deny his Lord, but he did—before that night was over.

JESUS WARNS THE DISCIPLES OF THE FUTURE

And he said unto them, When I sent you without purse, and scrip, and shoes, lacked ye any thing? And they said, Nothing [Luke 22:35].

It is marvelous the way the disciples were provided for during that particular period of time when the Lord sent them to the lost sheep of the house of Israel. He is now going to send them on a new mission with a new message. They will actually have a new audience because they will not be confined to Israel but will carry the message to the world.

Then said he unto them, But now, he that hath a purse, let him take it, and likewise his scrip; and he that hath no sword, let him sell his garment, and buy one [Luke 22:36].

You had better pack your suitcase and get your traveler's checks if you are going out for the Lord today and give out the gospel. You had better be prepared to protect yourself and your loved ones. We are living in difficult days. The Lord said, "He that hath no sword, let him sell his garment, and buy one." Why? For self protection, of course. They were living in days that required a sword. We need to recognize that fact also. If we do not resist evil today, all kinds of evil will befall us. We could end up in the hospital or have some of our loved ones slain.

> **For I say unto you, that this that is written must yet be accomplished in me, And he was reckoned among the transgressors: for the things concerning me have an end [Luke 22:37].**

When the enemies of the Lord Jesus Christ put Him to death on the cross, that ended His payment for the sins of the world.

> **And they said, Lord, behold, here are two swords. And he said unto them, It is enough [Luke 22:38].**

You do not need to overdo this thing and make your home an armed garrison, but you do need to protect yourself.

JESUS GOES TO GETHSEMANE

Gethsemane is holy ground, so I need to remove my spiritual shoes as I stand on this sacred spot, and remove my spiritual hat as I gaze in rapture upon Him. Many people glibly sing, "I'll go with Him through the garden." I cannot go with Him through the garden. The Lord Jesus left His disciples outside the garden. I will stay outside with them and peer over the wall into the darkness and listen to the travail of His soul. If our hearts are sensible, we shall thank God for the One who pressed the cup of our sorrow and suffering to His lips and drank to the very dregs. We cannot penetrate the darkness of the garden, but we can understand more fully the significance of the cup as He gave it to His own in the Upper Room. Everywhere I have tasted the cup, it has been sweet. He drank the bitter cup that my cup might be sweet. There is a mystery and a depth in that garden but not ambiguity or obscurity. We will do well to worship as we behold Him in the garden and catch the note of His voice.

Now we see through a glass darkly. It was Gregory of Nazianzen who years ago wrote: "I love God because I know Him. I adore Him, because I cannot comprehend Him." So I worship at the Garden of Gethsemane, and I do not try to have all the answers.

And he came out, and went, as he was wont, to the mount of Olives; and his disciples also followed him.

And when he was at the place, he said unto them, Pray that ye enter not into temptation [Luke 22:39–40].

There are two expressions in this passage that are quite interesting. The first one is "as he was wont" and the second one is "at the place." Apparently the Lord did not stay in the city of Jerusalem at night. We have seen this to be true in the so-called triumphal entry. He had been rejected by the city, and so He rejected the city. It is thought that He spent every night for the final week of His life either in the garden or in Bethany.

After the Lord's Supper He went to the garden. On that last night an unfamiliar transaction took place there. Although I don't know all about it, it is obvious that He wrestled with an unseen foe. He overcame the enemy there and gained the victory. The victory of Calvary was won in Gethsemane. You see, at the beginning of our Lord's ministry, Satan came and tempted Him. Satan offered our Lord the kingdoms of the world if He would worship him but He would have to miss the cross, of course. Then we are told, by Dr. Luke, that Satan left Him ". . . for a season" (Luke 4:13). When did Satan return? I presume Satan returned many times, but there was a special effort at the beginning of the Lord's ministry to get Him to avoid the cross, and now at the end of the Lord's ministry this is the temptation of Satan again.

You will recall that during His ministry the Lord told His disciples that He would suffer many things and that His enemies would put

Him to death. Peter replied, ". . . Be it far from thee, Lord: this shall
not be unto thee" (Matt. 16:22). Do you remember the Lord's answer
to Peter? The Lord says, ". . . Get thee behind me, Satan: thou art an
offence unto me: for thou savourest not the things that be of God, but
those that be of men" (Matt. 16:23). Satan's theology has no place for
the cross of Christ. It was Satan who came to Him in the garden. It was
at this time that the Lord said to His disciples, "Pray that ye enter not
into temptation."

> **And he was withdrawn from them about a stone's cast,
> and kneeled down, and prayed,**
>
> **Saying, Father, if thou be willing, remove this cup from
> me: nevertheless not my will, but thine, be done [Luke
> 22:41–42].**

How far can you throw a stone? That is how far our Lord went ahead of
His disciples before He kneeled down to pray. He prayed that the cup
might be removed. This is a topic that has caused quite a bit of discussion. There are those who believe that He was afraid He would die
before He got to the cross. I do not wish to be dogmatic, but I do not
see the sense of that theory. There is no merit in a Roman cross. There
is no merit in the wood. The merit is in the One who died. If He had
died on the gallows or in the electric chair, His death would have had
just as much value. If Christ had died in the Garden of Gethsemane, it
still would have been His death that had the merit.

The cup, I think, was the cross, and I do not mean the suffering of
death. The cup was that He was made sin for us. He is the Holy One of
God. When my sin was put upon Him, it was repulsive. I do not know
why we think we are so attractive to God. My sin put upon Christ was
repulsive and awful. It was terrible, and for a moment He rebelled
against it. It was in the Garden of Gethsemane under the shadow of the
cross that the Tempter came to offer the Lord once again the crown
without the cross. The Lord, however, had come to do His Father's will
and so He could say "nevertheless not my will, but thine, be done."
He committed Himself to His Father's will, although bearing your sin
and mine was so repulsive to Him.

And there appeared an angel unto him from heaven, strengthening him [Luke 22:43].

There was an angelic ministry at the time of our Lord's temptation in the desert. Now there is an angelic ministry in the garden when Satan comes to tempt Him again. Luke alone recalls this fact.

And being in an agony he prayed more earnestly: and his sweat was as it were great drops of blood falling down to the ground [Luke 22:44].

Only Dr. Luke tells us that the Lord sweat great drops of blood. The Lord showed a tremendous physical reaction to the agony and conflict that confronted Him. I cannot explain what happened and do not propose to try. I am not, however, impressed by the biological explanations offered today. I realize there are some wonderful Christian doctors that have come up with some interesting explanations, but I still am not impressed. He shed His blood for me and I bow in reverence and worship.

> But none of the ransomed ever knew
> How deep were the waters crossed,
> Nor how dark was the night that the Lord
> passed through,
> Ere He found His sheep that was lost.
> From "The Ninety and Nine"
> —Elizabeth C. Clephane

One of the tragic things of the moment is all of the American boys who have bled and died on various battlefields around the world to keep America free. How many Americans appreciate what they have done? I am not impressed with the crowd that protests war while they are living it up in pleasure-mad America. However, there is a worse tragedy than this. Christ's heart was broken because of our lost condition. He bled and died for our eternal liberty. He said, ". . . I am come that they might have life, and that they might have it more abundantly" (John 10:10). He loved a lost world so much that He went to the very depths of hell itself to offer it salvation. And the world spurns the Holy One of God, the spotless Savior who was made sin for us. Let me ask you a question. Have you rejected Him? Have you spurned Him? Are you ungrateful for what He did for you?

Stand in the hush of Gethsemane and listen. Do you hear the sob of His soul? Do you hear the falling drops of blood? Look yonder in the garden by an olive tree and see, bending low in agonizing prayer, the Savior who took upon Himself your humanity and mine. The next day He went to the cross.

JESUS BETRAYED BY JUDAS

And when he rose up from prayer, and was come to his disciples, he found them sleeping for sorrow,

And said unto them, Why sleep ye? rise and pray, lest ye enter into temptation.

And while he yet spake, behold a multitude, and he that was called Judas, one of the twelve, went before them, and drew near unto Jesus to kiss him.

But Jesus said unto him, Judas, betrayest thou the Son of man with a kiss? [Luke 22:45–48].

This is the basest act of treachery ever recorded. It is foul and loathsome. Judas knew our Lord's accustomed place of retirement, and he led the enemy there. A kiss is a badge of love and affection. Judas used it to betray Christ, which makes his act more dastardly and repugnant. It is well to observe that our Lord in His humanity was not different from other men. He needed to be identified in a crowd. This marks the moment that Jesus was delivered into the hands of sinful men.

When they which were about him saw what would follow, they said unto him, Lord, shall we smite with the sword?

And one of them smote the servant of the high priest, and cut off his right ear.

And Jesus answered and said, Suffer ye thus far. And he touched his ear, and healed him.

Then Jesus said unto the chief priests, and captains of the temple, and the elders, which were come to him, Be ye come out, as against a thief, with swords and staves?

When I was daily with you in the temple, ye stretched forth no hands against me: but this is your hour, and the power of darkness [Luke 22:49–53].

The disciples thought it was time to use that sword. It was not the time to use the sword, however, because Jesus was now on His way to the cross. The sword was for their personal defense after He was gone. Darkness and light met at the cross of Christ.

JESUS ARRESTED AND LED TO THE
HIGH PRIEST'S HOUSE

Then took they him, and led him, and brought him into the high priest's house. And Peter followed afar off [Luke 22:54].

It is a dangerous thing to follow the Lord afar off. This is what Peter did. Jesus is arrested and brought before Caiaphas, the high priest acceptable to Rome. Annas, his father-in-law, was actually the high priest according to the Mosaic Law. Jesus was first brought before Annas which is recorded by John. Some believe Annas was the real rascal in back of the plot to kill Jesus. This was a meeting of the Sanhedrin.

Peter was moving toward his shameful fall as he followed afar off and then sat with the wrong crowd.

JESUS DENIED BY PETER

And when they had kindled a fire in the midst of the hall, and were set down together, Peter sat down among them.

But a certain maid beheld him as he sat by the fire, and earnestly looked upon him, and said, This man was also with him.

And he denied him, saying, Woman, I know him not [Luke 22:55–57].

While the farce of the trial of Jesus was in progress, Simon Peter was in the place of great temptation. A little wisp of a maid caused him to deny His Lord. Peter was ashamed to be known as a follower of Jesus at this time. Have we ever been in a similar position? May God forgive our cowardice and weakness as He did that of Peter.

And after a little while another saw him, and said, Thou art also of them. And Peter said, Man, I am not.

And about the space of one hour after another confidently affirmed, saying, Of a truth this fellow also was with him: for he is a Galilaean [Luke 22:58–59].

Another person pointed him out as a follower of Jesus when he attempted to get in with a different crowd. Again Simon Peter denied it and withdrew to a different spot. This time his weakness in wanting to talk too much got him into trouble. His speech gave him away as a Galilaean.

And Peter said, Man, I know not what thou sayest. And immediately, while he yet spake, the cock crew [Luke 22:60].

Friend, if Peter had left things like this, it would have been his finish. He would have ended like Judas Iscariot, but notice what happened:

And the Lord turned, and looked upon Peter. And Peter remembered the word of the Lord, how he had said unto him, Before the cock crow, thou shalt deny me thrice.

And Peter went out, and wept bitterly [Luke 22:61–62].

Simon Peter loved Jesus, and he was sincere when he promised to be loyal to Him, but he did not know his own weakness. He had not yet come to the place where he saw no good in the flesh at all. Peter wept. These were tears of genuine repentance.

Any child of God can come back to Him. "If we confess our sins, he is faithful and just to forgive us our sins, and to cleanse us from all unrighteousness" (1 John 1:9). Simon Peter was as bad as Judas—he did not sell Him, but he denied Him. The difference between Judas and Peter is that Peter repented. Our Lord prayed that Peter's faith would not fail.

JESUS IS MOCKED AND BEATEN

And the men that held Jesus mocked him, and smote him.

And when they had blindfolded him, they struck him on the face, and asked him, saying, Prophesy, who is it that smote thee?

And many other things blasphemously spake they against him [Luke 22:63–65].

The chief priests and elders took Jesus to the home of Annas. It was illegal to hold Christ without a charge, but they held Him until they could formulate one in a meeting of the Sanhedrin. You see, they arrested Him before they had a plan. The interesting thing is that they did not intend to take Him as quickly as they did. Probably Judas had come to them and said, "You better get Him while you can," thinking He might leave the city. The Lord, of course, had no intention of leaving. Have you ever noticed the many things that were illegal in the trial of Jesus? The religious rulers arrested Him for breaking the Mosaic Law; yet they broke the Law by trying Him at night and by rendering a decision the same day He was tried, which too was illegal. Also the high priest tore his garment, which was specifically prohibited by the Law.

The religious rulers put Jesus into the hands of soldiers until a charge was made against Him. If the death sentence was going to be brought against a prisoner, the soldiers played games with him. The game they played with the Lord was called "hot hand." Each soldier would double up his fist in front of the blindfolded prisoner and hit him. Only one soldier would not hit him. Then the blindfold was removed and the prisoner was to guess which soldier had not hit him. They played the game again and again until I think they beat the face of Christ to a pulp. I doubt that anyone could have recognized Him. There was no form left to His face. ". . . his visage was so marred more than any man, and his form more than the sons of men" (Isa. 52:14). The Lord must have been a frightful sight after they got through with Him. This is one of the reasons He could not carry His cross.

JESUS IS BROUGHT BEFORE THE SANHEDRIN

And as soon as it was day, the elders of the people and the chief priests and the scribes came together, and led him into their council, saying,

Art thou the Christ? tell us. And he said unto them, If I tell you, ye will not believe:

And if I also ask you, ye will not answer me, nor let me go.

Hereafter shall the Son of man sit on the right hand of the power of God [Luke 22:66–69].

The Sanhedrin asked Jesus two questions. The first one was, "Art thou the Christ?" If the Lord had answered yes, He could have been charged with treason because anyone claiming to be a messiah was regarded by Rome as potentially dangerous. In Psalm 110:1 the Father says to the Son, ". . . Sit thou at my right hand, until I make thine enemies thy footstool." He is King of kings and Lord of lords.

> **Then said they all, Art thou then the Son of God? And he said unto them, Ye say that I am [Luke 22:70].**

This is their second charge.

> **And they said, What need we any further witness? for we ourselves have heard of his own mouth [Luke 22:71].**

This is the basis on which they agreed to have Him crucified. Notice, however, it is not the charge they brought before the Roman court. When they moved from the Jewish court to a Roman court they changed the charges.

CHAPTER 23

THEME: Jesus is brought before Pilate; Jesus is brought before Herod and Barabbas is released; Jesus foretells destruction of Jerusalem and prays for His enemies; Jesus is crucified; Jesus mocked by rulers and soldiers; Jesus mocked by one thief—the other thief turns to Jesus and is accepted by Him; Jesus dismisses His spirit; Jesus is placed in the new tomb of Joseph of Arimathaea

JESUS IS BROUGHT BEFORE PILATE

And the whole multitude of them arose, and led him unto Pilate.

And they began to accuse him, saying, We found this fellow perverting the nation, and forbidding to give tribute to Caesar, saying that he himself is Christ a King [Luke 23:1–2].

Pilate was the Roman governor of Palestine. He usually came to Jerusalem during the time of Passover to keep an eye on the crowds that came to celebrate the feast. Since a violation of the Mosaic Law would carry absolutely no weight with a Roman, they accused Him of treason which was utterly absurd.

And Pilate asked him, saying, Art thou the King of the Jews? And he answered him and said, Thou sayest it [Luke 23:3].

Imagine this scene. Here is a carpenter in peasant garment standing before Pilate. The Jewish religious leaders have arrested Him. Pilate asks Him a question that I'm sure seemed preposterous, "Art thou the King of the Jews?" Jesus answered, "Thou sayest it." Or, "It is as you say." It was a clear statement of fact. And Pilate wanted to let Him go.

Then said Pilate to the chief priests and to the people, I find no fault in this man [Luke 23:4].

Pilate is saying that Jesus had committed no crime for which He could be charged.

And they were the more fierce, saying, He stirreth up the people, teaching throughout all Jewry, beginning from Galilee to this place [Luke 23:5].

Now the religious rulers accuse Jesus of leading a revolution. They say that He had rebelled against constituted authority.

JESUS IS BROUGHT BEFORE HEROD AND BARABBAS IS RELEASED

When Pilate heard of Galilee, he asked whether the man were a Galilaean.

And as soon as he knew that he belonged unto Herod's jurisdiction, he sent him to Herod, who himself also was at Jerusalem at that time [Luke 23:6–7].

Pilate wanted to get off the hook. Since Galilee was under Herod's jurisdiction and Herod was also in Jerusalem, Pilate sent Jesus to him. I do not believe it was an accident that Herod was in Jerusalem.

And when Herod saw Jesus, he was exceeding glad: for he was desirous to see him of a long season, because he had heard many things of him; and he hoped to have seen some miracle done by him [Luke 23:8].

Prior to this time Jesus had told the Pharisees to deliver a message to Herod which was, "Go ye, and tell that fox, Behold, I cast out devils [demons], and I do cures today and tomorrow, and the third day I shall be perfected" (Luke 13:32). Herod's curiosity was excited about Jesus and he wanted to see Him.

> Then he questioned with him in many words; but he answered him nothing [Luke 23:9].

Our Lord did not have one word for Herod. He was an old fox. He had gone past the point of no return; he was on his way to a lost eternity. He was a member of the notorious Herod family, and our Lord made no effort to reach him.

> And the chief priests and scribes stood and vehemently accused him.

> And Herod with his men of war set him at nought, and mocked him, and arrayed him in a gorgeous robe, and sent him again to Pilate.

> And the same day Pilate and Herod were made friends together: for before they were at enmity between themselves [Luke 23:10–12].

Can't you see the religious rulers jumping up and down and doing everything they could to see that Jesus was convicted? Herod could see that he was not going to get anywhere with Jesus; so with his men of war he decided to mock Him. The "gorgeous robe" they put upon Him was undoubtedly one of Herod's cast-off robes which they used to mock Jesus' claims of royalty. Since there was nothing else Herod could do, he decided to send Jesus back to Pilate. Here is the beginning of an ecumenical movement! Before this problem of Jesus arose, Herod and Pilate had been enemies. Now they come together because they are both opposed to Jesus.

> And Pilate, when he had called together the chief priests and the rulers and the people,

> Said unto them, Ye have brought this man unto me, as one that perverteth the people: and, behold, I, having examined him before you, have found no fault in this man touching those things whereof ye accuse him:

No, nor yet Herod: for I sent you to him; and, lo, nothing worthy of death is done unto him [Luke 23:13–15].

Pilate felt that there was nothing with which they could accuse Jesus. Herod had done nothing but mock Him, put a robe on Him, and send Him back to Pilate. The charges were not worth considering.

I will therefore chastise him, and release him [Luke 23:16].

Wait a minute! That is wrong. If Jesus is guilty of something, He should be punished. If He is innocent, He should be set free. To chastise Him and let Him go is compromise. I agree with Marlowe, the Englishman, that compromise is the most immoral word in the English language.

(For of necessity he must release one unto them at the feast.)

And they cried out all at once, saying, Away with this man, and release unto us Barabbas:

(Who for a certain sedition made in the city, and for murder, was cast into prison.)

Pilate therefore, willing to release Jesus, spake again to them.

But they cried, saying, Crucify him, crucify him.

And he said unto them the third time, Why, what evil hath he done? I have found no cause of death in him: I will therefore chastise him, and let him go.

And they were instant with loud voices, requiring that he might be crucified. And the voices of them and of the chief priests prevailed.

And Pilate gave sentence that it should be as they required.

And he released unto them him that for sedition and murder was cast into prison, whom they had desired; but he delivered Jesus to their will.

And as they led him away, they laid hold upon one Simon, a Cyrenian, coming out of the country, and on him they laid the cross, that he might bear it after Jesus [Luke 23:17-26].

Pilate is trying to escape making a decision about Jesus, but he cannot. Careful analysis of Pilate's part in the trial will reveal that he is on trial and Jesus is the Judge. Jesus is not trying to escape, but Pilate is. Pilate sought for an easy escape from these astute religious politicians. He hit upon giving them a choice between Barabbas and Jesus. To him the decision was obvious. He detected that they wanted Jesus dead because of envy. Pilate did not reckon with the depth to which religion can sink when it goes wrong. Matthew tells us that the chief priests and elders persuaded the multitude to ask for Barabbas. Pilate was startled when the crowd demanded Barabbas to be released. Imagine a judge asking a crowd for their decision as to what should be done with a man on trial! He decided that Jesus was innocent; yet he handed Jesus over to be crucified. What Roman justice!

Pilate finally had to make a decision, just as every man today has to make a decision relative to Jesus Christ. What have you decided about Him?

JESUS FORETELLS DESTRUCTION OF JERUSALEM AND PRAYS FOR HIS ENEMIES

And there followed him a great company of people, and of women, which also bewailed and lamented him.

But Jesus turning unto them said, Daughters of Jerusalem, weep not for me, but weep for yourselves, and for your children.

For, behold, the days are coming, in the which they shall say, Blessed are the barren, and the wombs that never bare, and the paps which never gave suck.

Then shall they begin to say to the mountains, Fall on us; and to the hills, Cover us [Luke 23:27-30].

On His way to the cross He spoke to women who were crying about Him. He said there was a day coming when it would be better not to bring children into the world, referring to the time of the Great Tribulation. Then He told the women not to weep for Him. He does not want our sympathy; He wants our faith. He did not have to die, and He did not die to gain our sympathy.

JESUS IS CRUCIFIED

And when they were come to the place, which is called Calvary, there they crucified him, and the malefactors, one on the right hand, and the other on the left [Luke 23:33].

Two criminals were crucified with the Lord.

Then said Jesus, Father, forgive them; for they know not what they do. And they parted his raiment, and cast lots [Luke 23:34].

The Lord asked His Father to forgive the crowd for crucifying Him. If He had not done this, the crowd would have been guilty of committing the unpardonable sin of putting to death the Son of God.

JESUS MOCKED BY RULERS AND SOLDIERS

And the people stood beholding. And the rulers also with them derided him, saying, He saved others; let him save himself, if he be Christ, the chosen of God [Luke 23:35].

If Jesus had come down from the cross, He would not have been the Christ. He would not have fulfilled all of Isaiah 53 which speaks of His death. "He was taken from prison and from judgment: and who shall declare his generation? for he was cut off out of the land of the living: for the transgression of my people was he stricken" (Isa. 53:8). Because Jesus Christ stayed on the cross, we can be healed of sin, the awful plague of mankind.

> **And the soldiers also mocked him, coming to him, and offering him vinegar,**
>
> **And saying, If thou be the king of the Jews, save thyself.**
>
> **And a superscription also was written over him in letters of Greek, and Latin, and Hebrew, THIS IS THE KING OF THE JEWS [Luke 23:36–38].**

When Jesus was crucified, they put a superscription over Him in Greek, Latin, and Hebrew. Greek was the language of intelligence, of education, of literature, and of science. Latin was the language of law and order, of the military and of government. Hebrew was the language of religion. When Christ returns to set up His Kingdom, He will be the political ruler, the educational ruler, and the spiritual ruler of this universe. How accurate the superscription was!

By the way, to get the full superscription we have to put together all four Gospel records.

JESUS MOCKED BY ONE THIEF—THE OTHER THIEF TURNS TO JESUS AND IS ACCEPTED BY HIM

> **And one of the malefactors which were hanged railed on him, saying, If thou be Christ, save thyself and us.**
>
> **But the other answering rebuked him, saying, Dost not thou fear God, seeing thou art in the same condemnation?**

And we indeed justly; for we receive the due reward of our deeds: but this man hath done nothing amiss [Luke 23:39–41].

Both Matthew and Mark tell us that in the beginning both thieves ridiculed the Lord Jesus. But during the six hours that they were on the cross, especially the last three hours, one thief saw that something unusual was taking place. He recognized that this One dying on the cross was not dying for Himself but for another. Although he knew Barabbas should be on that cross, he also seemed to realize He was dying for him. He recognized that this was a transaction between God and the Man on the cross, and the Man on the cross was God. Then he turned to Him in faith.

And he said unto Jesus, Lord, remember me when thou comest into thy kingdom.

And Jesus said unto him, Verily I say unto thee, Today shalt thou be with me in paradise [Luke 23:42–43].

That very day this thief who was not fit to live on earth, according to the Roman government, went to be with the Lord. This man was a *bad* thief, not a good one, but because of his faith in the Son of God he became a saved thief. This man had faith to believe that the Lord Jesus was coming into a kingdom, and it would come after His death! Obviously, this thief had come a long way theologically while hanging on that cross.

Our Lord made the remarkable statement that this thief would be in paradise with Him that very day. These two thieves had been arrested for the same crime, tried for the same crime, condemned for the same crime, and were dying for the same crime. What was the difference between them? There wasn't any—both were thieves. The difference lies in the fact that one thief believed in Jesus Christ and one did not.

Many years ago I was playing tennis with a friend of mine who was liberal in his theology. I asked him, "What would you tell the thief on the cross? Would you tell him to run on errands of mercy? Would you tell him to use his hands for deeds of kindness?" He looked at me rather startled. I said, "Well, come on, that's what you tell your people to do." "Yes," he said, "but they can do those things." "But what are you going to tell this poor thief? What could he do? His hands and feet are not coming down from that cross until they come down in death. And, by the way, what church would you ask him to join? What ceremony would you ask him to go through?"

Friend, our Lord said to that thief, "Today you'll be with Me in paradise." He went into the presence of God because of His faith in Christ.

JESUS DISMISSES HIS SPIRIT

And it was about the sixth hour, and there was a darkness over all the earth until the ninth hour.

And the sun was darkened, and the veil of the temple was rent in the midst [Luke 23:44–45].

Christ's life was symbolized by the veil which actually shut out man from God in the Old Testament economy. When Christ died on the cross, the veil was torn in two so that the way to the Father was open!

And when Jesus had cried with a loud voice, he said, Father, into thy hands I commend my spirit: and having said thus, he gave up the ghost [Luke 23:46].

Remember, once again, that this is Dr. Luke speaking from a doctor's viewpoint. He had been in the presence of many people who had died. He knew how they died, and he knew how our Lord died. Our Lord's death was different. It has been my unpleasant duty to be in the presence of folk who are dying. There is what is commonly known as the "death rattle" when one draws his last breath. It is always with a struggle and with great effort. The two thieves on their crosses undoubtedly died that way, but the Lord Jesus did not. He voluntarily died. He dismissed His spirit. Did you notice what He said? "Father, into thy hands I commend my spirit," with a loud voice; it doesn't sound like a man whose life is ebbing away. John adds that His final word was a shout of victory—*"Tetelestai!"* It is finished!

Now when the centurion saw what was done, he glorified God, saying, Certainly this was a righteous man [Luke 23:47].

The centurion, I believe, became a saved man. He had charge of the crucifixion of Christ. At the foot of the cross he looked up and saw that something unusual was taking place, and he could glorify God. He saw that Christ was a righteous man. The other Gospel writers add to Luke's account that the centurion said that He was the Son of God. I realize that the centurion's confession of faith was not enough to join the average Bible church, but let us put him back where he stands. He is at the Crucifixion. He knew nothing about the death and resurrection of Jesus Christ. He had never read any books on theology. This poor fellow was in the dark, but he couldn't have said anything that revealed his faith more than this.

And all the people that came together to that sight, beholding the things which were done, smote their breasts, and returned [Luke 23:48].

There was an ominous and fearful sort of atmosphere about the death of Christ. No Gospel writer describes the death of Christ in detail. It is as if the Spirit of God pulled down the veil because the Crucifixion was too horrible to gaze upon. There is nothing here to satisfy your curiosity. Mankind was shut out from what happened on the cross. Just as we had to stand on the fringe at the Garden of Gethsemane, certainly we have to stand on the fringe of what happened at the cross. We can only look up and trust the One who is dying there for us.

And all his acquaintance, and the women that followed him from Galilee, stood afar off, beholding these things [Luke 23:49].

JESUS IS PLACED IN THE NEW TOMB OF JOSEPH
OF ARIMATHAEA

The final section of this chapter deals with the burial and resurrection of Jesus Christ, which belong together. Paul wrote, "For I delivered unto you first of all that which I also received, how that Christ died for our sins according to the scriptures; And that he was buried, and that he rose again the third day according to the scriptures" (1 Cor. 15:3–4). These are the facts of the gospel. What is your relationship to these facts? Jesus died. He was buried. He rose again from the dead. What does that mean to you? Do you believe He died for you? Do you believe that when He was buried your sins were absolutely buried too, so that the sin question was settled? Do you believe that He rose again, and you rose with Him? To believe this puts us in Christ. God sees us in Christ. His righteousness becomes our righteousness; His standing becomes our standing, which is all that you and I have of which we can boast today.

And, behold, there was a man named Joseph, a counsellor; and he was a good man, and a just [Luke 23:50].

This man Joseph was obviously a very prominent man. He was a member of the Sanhedrin. He apparently exercised a lot of influence. He was, however, a man who stood alone when he took a stand for Christ.

(The same had not consented to the counsel and deed of them;) he was of Arimathaea, a city of the Jews: who also himself waited for the kingdom of God [Luke 23:51].

Although Joseph was a member of the Sanhedrin, he did not agree with the action they took, which tells us that the Sanhedrin did not act unanimously when they put down the edict to have the Lord Jesus Christ crucified. He was what could be called a pious, religious man; then having come face-to-face with Christ, he had taken a stand for

Him. Apparently there were many believers in the Lord who were not open about it like the disciples were. However at the time of the Crucifixion the disciples went underground, and those that had been underground came out in the open. Joseph and Nicodemus were two prominent men who finally openly declared their trust in the Savior. John's gospel tells us that Nicodemus joined with Joseph in burying the Lord Jesus. They were the undertakers who had charge of His burial.

> **This man went unto Pilate, and begged the body of Jesus [Luke 23:52].**

The faith of Joseph is out in the open now. As a man of means and influence he asks for the body of Jesus.

> **And he took it down, and wrapped it in linen, and laid it in a sepulchre that was hewn in stone, wherein never man before was laid [Luke 23:53].**

The question arises, "Where was the tomb in which Jesus was laid?" There are two places today that are said to be that tomb. One place has a Roman Catholic church built over it, and the other one is outside the city wall. I, personally, do not believe that either place is where Jesus was buried. There were several groups that so hated Christ and Christianity that they would have removed every vestige and reminder of Him. The forces of Rome under Titus, in A.D. 70, destroyed and actually plowed the city of Jerusalem. The tomb known as the Garden Tomb, which is shown to tourists, somehow escaped destruction. I am sure it is not the tomb in which the body of Jesus was placed, although His tomb was undoubtedly somewhere in that area. God would not leave anything like the tomb intact, because certain people would make it a fetish rather than making the Lord Jesus the object of worship. When I was in Jerusalem at the Garden Tomb, one lady in our tour got down on her hands and knees and began to kiss the floor of the tomb; then she began to weep and howl! There is no value in that! Even if it were the tomb in which He was buried, the value is not in the tomb but in the One who is at God's right hand today, the living Savior. Let us turn our attention to Him.

> **And that day was the preparation, and the sabbath drew on.**
>
> **And the women also, which came with him from Galilee, followed after, and beheld the sepulchre, and how his body was laid [Luke 23:54–55].**

This little group of loyal women, who probably performed the menial tasks for our Lord and His disciples, were with Him to the very end.

As to the actual day of His death, the Bible does not say that He died for our sins on Wednesday, Thursday, or Friday. The Bible simply says that Jesus died for our sins. We should not waste time arguing about which day it was. I do think, however, that since it says the Sabbath drew on, it was Friday.

The women saw how the body of Jesus was laid. In other words, it was not a finished burial. Later Nicodemus and Joseph wrapped the linen around the body in mummy fashion. John's Gospel adds that they wound it in linen clothes with the spices (about one hundred pounds of myrrh and aloes), as ". . . the manner of the Jews is to bury" (John 19:40).

> **And they returned, and prepared spices and ointments; and rested the sabbath day according to the commandment [Luke 23:56].**

Because the Sabbath day was a day of rest, they did not come to the tomb. They prepared the spices to put on the Lord's body, but they wasted their spices because by the time they came to do it, His body was no longer in the tomb. Mary of Bethany, you recall, had anointed His body while He was alive and was criticized for wasting the precious ointment. But hers was not wasted.

CHAPTER 24

THEME: Jesus is raised from the dead—leaves Joseph's tomb; Jesus goes down the road to Emmaus—reveals Himself to two disciples; Jesus goes to the assembled disciples—reveals Himself to the Eleven; Jesus gives commission to go; Jesus promises to send the Holy Spirit; Jesus ascends to heaven in the attitude of blessing His own

JESUS IS RAISED FROM THE DEAD—LEAVES JOSEPH'S TOMB

Now upon the first day of the week, very early in the morning, they came unto the sepulchre, bringing the spices which they had prepared, and certain others with them [Luke 24:1].

The women came bringing their spices. I have always wanted to ask those women what they did with those spices. Mary was rebuked when she anointed the living Lord, "Why are you wasting this expensive ointment?" (see John 12:5). But her ointment was not wasted. The spices of these women were not used, and I think they went to waste. The women were probably so excited that they just left the spices at the tomb.

And they found the stone rolled away from the sepulchre [Luke 24:2].

The stone was not rolled away to let the Lord Jesus out but to let them in.

And they entered in, and found not the body of the Lord Jesus [Luke 24:3].

He had already left.

> **And it came to pass, as they were much perplexed thereabout, behold, two men stood by them in shining garments:**
>
> **And as they were afraid, and bowed down their faces to the earth, they said unto them, Why seek ye the living among the dead?**
>
> **He is not here, but is risen: remember how he spake unto you when he was yet in Galilee,**
>
> **Saying, The Son of man must be delivered into the hands of sinful men, and be crucified, and the third day rise again.**
>
> **And they remembered his words [Luke 24:4–8].**

The question, "Why do you seek the living among the dead?" was a good one. Why did the women come, and why did Peter (and John) come running to the tomb? They were seeking the dead among the dead; they were not seeking the living. They did not believe that the Lord Jesus Christ would come back from the dead.

Some people feel there is conflict among the Gospels concerning the morning of the Resurrection and the events which took place. A thorough study of the Gospels will reveal that there is no conflict at all. Each writer is presenting a different facet of the Resurrection. Luke tells us about the coming of the women to the tomb and dwells on that. The women remembered these words of Jesus when the angels reminded them. Sometimes you can hear something—and almost know it is true—but do not believe it. That is the way a lot of people treat the Word of God today. All of the Gospel writers make it abundantly clear that the Lord Jesus told His disciples again and again that He was going to Jerusalem to die, and be raised again on the third day. They heard what He said but somehow they really did not believe it.

And returned from the sepulchre, and told all these things unto the eleven, and to all the rest.

It was Mary Magdalene, and Joanna, and Mary the mother of James, and other women that were with them, which told these things unto the apostles [Luke 24:9–10].

You would think the apostles would be greatly impressed by what the women told them, but notice their reaction:

And their words seemed to them as idle tales, and they believed them not [Luke 24:11].

You would have thought that these women would have been considered credible witnesses and their testimony would have been accepted. The first disbelievers of the Resurrection were the apostles themselves. Yet our Lord had told them over and over what was going to happen concerning His death and resurrection.

Then arose Peter, and ran unto the sepulchre; and stooping down, he beheld the linen clothes laid by themselves, and departed, wondering in himself at that which was come to pass [Luke 24:12].

Simon Peter had to turn over in his mind all the evidence before he came to a decision about what had happened. I do not think he was quite as alert mentally as was John the apostle. John tells us in his Gospel that when he went to the tomb and looked in, he believed. John was convinced about the Lord's resurrection immediately, but Simon Peter had to think about it for awhile.

JESUS GOES DOWN THE ROAD TO EMMAUS— REVEALS HIMSELF TO TWO DISCIPLES

Now we come to the road to Emmaus. The Emmaus road is an interesting one to be on. We hear a lot today about being on the Jericho road—but that's where you fall among thieves. I would much rather take the Emmaus road where we meet our resurrected Lord.

> **And, behold, two of them went that same day to a village called Emmaus, which was from Jerusalem about three-score furlongs [Luke 24:13].**

There is some question as to the distance of Emmaus from Jerusalem. It was probably about seven miles.

> **And they talked together of all these things which had happened.**
>
> **And it came to pass, that, while they communed together and reasoned, Jesus himself drew near, and went with them.**
>
> **But their eyes were holden that they should not know him [Luke 24:14–16].**

On the road to Emmaus the Lord joined two disciples who were talking about Him. They had not seen the Lord, and candidly, they did not believe that He had risen from the dead. They did not believe that the One who had joined them on the road was the resurrected Christ. To begin with, they were not looking for Him at all.

> **And he said unto them, What manner of communications are these that ye have one to another, as ye walk, and are sad? [Luke 24:17].**

Jesus raised the question.

> **And the one of them, whose name was Cleopas, answering said unto him, Art thou only a stranger in Jerusalem, and hast not known the things which are come to pass there in these days? [Luke 24:18].**

This question, raised by Cleopas, reveals a sidelight not given by anyone but Dr. Luke. The arrest, Crucifixion, and purported Resurrection from the dead had stirred Jerusalem. These two men could not believe that there was anyone in the area that did not know about it. It would be like walking down the street in your hometown with a friend and discussing the trip to the moon. A stranger joins you and says, "You mean someone has been to the moon?" You would naturally react. It would be difficult for someone to live in this day and age and not know that someone has been to the moon and back to earth. It was just as incredible to these disciples that someone had not heard about the events of the past few days. Paul, in his defense before King Agrippa, said that he was persuaded that none of these things were hidden from him ". . . for this thing was not done in a corner" (Acts 26:26). It was public news, and everyone in the area was talking about it.

And he said unto them, What things? And they said unto him, Concerning Jesus of Nazareth, which was a prophet mighty in deed and word before God and all the people [Luke 24:19].

Did you notice what they said? They said that He "*was* a prophet." They thought He was dead. They did not believe that He had come back from the dead.

And how the chief priests and our rulers delivered him to be condemned to death, and have crucified him [Luke 24:20].

Now they gave a witness to the death of Christ.

But we trusted that it had been he which should have redeemed Israel: and beside all this, today is the third day since these things were done [Luke 24:21].

These men were saying that they had hoped Jesus Christ was the Prophet that would redeem Israel, but now it was too late. He had been crucified. He was dead. They did not have much faith in what this Prophet had said, you can be sure of that.

> Yea, and certain women also of our company made us astonished, which were early at the sepulchre;
>
> And when they found not his body, they came, saying, that they had also seen a vision of angels, which said that he was alive [Luke 24:22–23].

These men did not believe the report of the women. They did not believe the tomb was empty. You can see how much unbelief there was in the Resurrection at this time. But there is a little hope and a little light that breaks upon the thinking of these two men.

> And certain of them which were with us went to the sepulchre, and found it even so as the women had said: but him they saw not [Luke 24:24].

Just as it seemed their faith ballooned up, they put a pin in it—"but him they saw not." They did not know what had happened, but somehow the body had been taken away. They were not prepared to explain what had taken place, but the fact remained that no one had seen the Lord.

> Then he said unto them, O fools, and slow of heart to believe all that the prophets have spoken [Luke 24:25].

This is a very important section, friend. The Lord, in speaking about His resurrection, did not show them the prints of the nails in His hands to prove it. He referred them to the Scriptures rather than to the nail prints. He told them, "You should have believed what the prophets said." It is well to note the Lord's attitude toward the Bible.

The day in which we live is a day of doubt. There are people who are actually saying that you cannot be intelligent and believe the Bible. Many people are afraid that they will not be considered intelligent; so they don't come out flat-footed and say whether they believe the Bible or not. I suppose it is the most subtle and satanic trap of our day to discount the inerrancy and integrity of the Word of God. Christ says a man is a *fool* not to believe it. He gave a unanimous and whole-hearted acceptance of the Bible's statements, with no ifs, ands, or buts.

The other day I picked up a seminary professor and took him to a filling station, because he had car trouble. As we rode along, I asked him about his school's viewpoint of the inerrancy of Scripture. "Well," he said, "you mean the infallibility of the Bible?" I replied "Wait a minute, you are arguing semantics. You know what I mean, and I know what you mean. Do you or do you not believe in the inerrancy of Scripture?" Well, he wouldn't make a forthright declaration whether or not he believed it. He wanted to appear intelligent. Frankly, a lot of these men do not have the intestinal fortitude to stand for the Word of God. I think their problem is more intestinal than intellectual!

Now notice that the Lord puts the emphasis upon the Word of God.

Ought not Christ to have suffered these things, and to enter into his glory?

And beginning at Moses and all the prophets, he expounded unto them in all the scriptures the things concerning himself [Luke 24:26–27].

He began with Moses and the prophets. Moses and the prophets had spoken of Him. His death and resurrection had fulfilled their prophecies. I'd love to have been there that evening, listening to Him, wouldn't you? Christ says that there are two things which are essential to the understanding of the Word of God. They are simple but important. First, as verse 25 indicates, we must have faith in the

Bible. Christ said, "O fools, and slow of heart to believe all that the prophets have spoken." Pascal said, "Human knowledge must be understood to be believed, but divine knowledge must be believed to be understood." I think the Bible is a closed book to the critic and the infidel. He can learn a few facts, but he misses the message. On the other hand, some simple soul whose heart is turned in humble faith to God will be enlightened by the Holy Spirit of God. The eyes of his understanding will be opened. Great men of the past have come to the pages of Scripture for light and life in the hours of darkness or crisis. It is not smart to ridicule the Bible. The Lord said, "You are a *fool* not to believe it." I would rather lack sophistication and subtlety than to be a fool.

Then the Lord says that the Bible can only be divinely understood. Human intellect is simply not enough to comprehend its truths. Verse 45 tells us: "Then opened he their understanding, that they might understand the scriptures." Then in 1 Corinthians 2:14 Paul declares, "But the natural man receiveth not the things of the Spirit of God: for they are foolishness unto him: neither can he know them, because they are spiritually discerned." There are things that are above and beyond human comprehension, and only the Holy Spirit of God can make them real to us. Our prayer ought to be, "Open Thou mine eyes that I may behold wondrous things out of Thy Word." We should come with a humble attitude to the Word of God. Just because you read the Bible does not mean that you know it. The Holy Spirit of God will have to make it real to you.

And they drew nigh unto the village, whither they went: and he made as though he would have gone further.

But they constrained him, saying, Abide with us: for it is toward evening, and the day is far spent. And he went in to tarry with them.

And it came to pass, as he sat at meat with them, he took bread, and blessed it, and brake, and gave to them.

And their eyes were opened, and they knew him; and he vanished out of their sight [Luke 24:28–31].

The resurrected, glorified Christ wants to fellowship with those who are His own. He only fellowships with those who believe in Him. They wanted Him to stay with them, and He was known to them at the table in the breaking of the bread.

Eating around a table is a wonderful time to share the things of Christ. There is nothing wrong with a church banquet, provided it is not all given over to hearing some soloist, or watching a magician, or some type of entertainment. We have too many church programs that leave Jesus Christ out. To have true fellowship and blessing, He must be in the midst breaking the bread.

> **And they said one to another, Did not our heart burn within us, while he talked with us by the way, and while he opened to us the scriptures?**
>
> **And they rose up the same hour, and returned to Jerusalem, and found the eleven gathered together, and them that were with them [Luke 24:32–33].**

Late as it is, they hurry back over the miles with the wonderful news.

> **Saying, The Lord is risen indeed, and hath appeared to Simon [Luke 24:34].**

The Lord Jesus Christ appeared to Simon Peter privately because there was something that needed to be straightened out. Remember that Peter had denied Him. The restoration to fellowship was a personal and private transaction between Peter and his Lord.

JESUS GOES TO THE ASSEMBLED DISCIPLES— REVEALS HIMSELF TO THE ELEVEN

> **And they told what things were done in the way, and how he was known of them in breaking of bread.**
>
> **And as they thus spake, Jesus himself stood in the midst of them, and saith unto them, Peace be unto you.**

> But they were terrified and affrighted, and supposed
> that they had seen a spirit [Luke 24:35–37].

I am sure our reaction would have been the same if we had been there.

> And he said unto them, Why are ye troubled? and why
> do thoughts arise in your hearts?
>
> Behold my hands and my feet, that it is I myself: handle
> me, and see; for a spirit hath not flesh and bones, as ye
> see me have [Luke 24:38–39].

I do not want to labor this point, but the glorified body of our Lord
was flesh and *bones* and not flesh and blood. His blood had been shed
on the cross.

> And when he had thus spoken, he shewed them his
> hands and his feet.
>
> And while they yet believed not for joy, and wondered,
> he said unto them, Have ye here any meat?
>
> And they gave him a piece of a broiled fish, and of an
> honeycomb.
>
> And he took it, and did eat before them [Luke
> 24:40–43].

This is a master stroke and Dr. Luke shares it with us. The proof that
He, our Lord and Savior, is a human being is that He could eat food.

> And he said unto them, These are the words which I
> spake unto you, while I was yet with you, that all things
> must be fulfilled, which were written in the law of
> Moses, and in the prophets, and in the psalms, concern-
> ing me.

Then opened he their understanding, that they might understand the scriptures [Luke 24:44–45].

They simply had not believed His Word. In order to understand the Bible you have to have the Spirit of God open your mind and heart. Only the Spirit can make Bible study real to you.

JESUS GIVES COMMISSION TO GO

And said unto them, Thus it is written, and thus it behoved Christ to suffer, and to rise from the dead the third day:

And that repentance and remission of sins should be preached in his name among all nations, beginning at Jerusalem [Luke 24:46–47].

Notice the global outlook of these verses. The viewpoint here is worldwide. This gospel is to go to the ends of the earth.

JESUS PROMISES TO SEND THE HOLY SPIRIT

And ye are witnesses of these things.

And, behold, I send the promise of my Father upon you: but tarry ye in the city of Jerusalem, until ye be endued with power from on high [Luke 24:48–49].

Men witnessing to the world was His method. And the message was that He died and rose again from the dead, and that, by trusting Him, sinners could be saved. The power to carry the witness to the world is the Holy Spirit.

JESUS ASCENDS TO HEAVEN IN THE ATTITUDE OF BLESSING HIS OWN

And he led them out as far as to Bethany, and he lifted up his hands, and blessed them.

And it came to pass, while he blessed them, he was parted from them, and carried up into heaven [Luke 24:50-51].

The last time the disciples saw the Lord He was in the attitude of blessing. When He comes the next time He will come in judgment upon the world. He will not come in judgment for the church; He will come in blessing. We are to look with great joy and anticipation for His coming.

And they worshipped him, and returned to Jerusalem with great joy:

And were continually in the temple, praising and blessing God. Amen [Luke 24:52-53].

This is the testimony of the Gospel of Luke. I trust that it has been a blessing to you. My own heart has been blessed, my mind enriched, and my will strengthened. Because I have studied again this marvelous Gospel of Luke, I want to know Him better. I hope you do too.

BIBLIOGRAPHY

(Recommended for Further Study)

Geldenhuys, Norval. *Commentary on the Gospel of Luke*. Grand Rapids, Michigan: Wm. B. Eerdmans Publishing Co., 1951.

Hendriksen, William. *Exposition of the Gospel of Luke*. Grand Rapids, Michigan: Baker Book House, 1978. (Very comprehensive.)

Ironside, H. A. *Addresses on the Gospel of Luke*. Neptune, New Jersey: Loizeaux Brothers, 1947.

Kelly, William. *An Exposition of the Gospel of Luke*. Addison, Illinois: Bible Truth Publishers, n.d.

Luck, G. Coleman. *Luke*. Chicago, Illinois: Moody Press, n.d. (Concise survey.)

Morgan, G. Campbell. *The Gospel According to Luke*. Old Tappan, New Jersey: Fleming H. Revell Company, n.d.

Morris, Leon. *The Gospel According to St. Luke*. Grand Rapids, Michigan: Wm. B. Eerdmans Publishing Co., 1975.

Pentecost, J. Dwight. *The Words and Works of Jesus Christ*. Chicago, Illinois: Moody Press, 1981.

Thomas, W. H. Griffith. *Outline Studies in the Gospel of St. Luke*. Grand Rapids, Michigan: Wm. B. Eerdmans Publishing Co., 1950.

Van Ryn, August. *Meditations in Luke*. Neptune, New Jersey: Loizeaux Brothers. n.d.

Vos, Howard F. *Beginnings in the Life of Christ*. Chicago, Illinois: Moody Press, 1975.